GRANTSMANSHIP AND FUND RAISING

To Baila, a mother in Israel

GRANTSMANSHIP
AND
FUND RAISING

ARMAND
LAUFFER

 SAGE PUBLICATIONS Beverly Hills London New Delhi

For information address:

SAGE Publications, Inc.
275 South Beverly Drive
Beverly Hills, California 90212

SAGE Publications India Pvt. Ltd.
C-236 Defence Colony
New Delhi 110 024, India

SAGE Publications Ltd
28 Banner Street
London EC1Y 8QE, England

Printed in the United States of America

Library of Congress Cataloging in Publication Data

Lauffer, Armand.
  Grantsmanship and fund raising.

  Expanded ed. of: Grantsmanship. 2nd ed. c1983.
  Bibliography: p.
  1. Fund raising. 2. Proposal writing in the social sciences. I. Lauffer, Armand. Grantsmanship. 2nd ed. II. Title.
HG177.L375   1984   361.7   84-8220
ISBN 0-8039-2234-5

FIRST PRINTING

Contents

Acknowledgments

I learned about grantsmanship and fund raising the way most people do—the hard way, by doing it. But it was not without support, first and foremost from four deans at the University of Michigan School of Social Work. Fedele Fauri, whose spirit continues to infuse the school with social commitment and intellectual honesty, told me when I first arrived at Michigan to "take a few months, get to know the state, and then start building a program." He knew well that professional and career interests, when supportive of institutional interests, are a strong combination. "To win at horse racing," he would say, "you not only have to have horses that can, but will run." The proper motivation is central to any successful fund raising effort.

But so are knowledge and technical competence. I gained a good deal of both from Bob Vinter, who taught me to be rigorous in program design and meticulous in budgeting. Phil Fellin continued in the traditions of his predecessors, knowing when to reign in a feisty colt, and when to let him have his head. And I owe a special thanks to Harold Johnson, who permitted me the freedom to work on this and other volumes, when he might have preferred to have me out there hustling, practicing what I teach.

These acknowledgments would not be complete without referring to Bill Lawrence, Eloise Snyder, and Milan Dluhy, whose contributions to an earlier Sage volume (*Grantsmanship,* first edition) generated sufficient demand to warrant a new, much expanded, and updated book.

Finally, as in most of what I commit to paper, I want to express genuine gratitude to the dozens of human service practitioners whose words and experiences are related in these pages. I am referring to government and foundation officials, agency planners and administrators, community activists, direct service practitioners, professional fund raisers, and others from whom

7

I have learned a great deal and whose knowledge and skill I have tried to share with you. Some of these people have written other useful books on program and resource development, grantsmanship, and fund raising. I refer you to them in suggested reading sections throughout the book, and in Appendix B. You will find their thoughts as useful as I have.

Preface

The mid-1980s have not been encouraging for many practitioners and administrators in the human services. Some have lost their positions through cutbacks, while others have found themselves carrying especially heavy loads in an effort to maintain the quality of services against a background of shrinking resources. The picture has been especially bleak in certain service sectors, and the situation has had a disproportionate impact on different client populations: ethnic and racial minorities, the disabled, those who are among the structurally unemployed, and those who have been defined by society as deviants rather than as the victims of circumstances. The largesse of the 1960s and early 1970s seems to have been replaced by a niggardliness of spirit and resource.

Perhaps—perhaps not. Certainly the distribution of resources has changed considerably over the past decade or two. And this redistribution has caused strains virtually everywhere in the human services. But while strains are perhaps inevitable, they need not be fatal. Individual agencies, even consortia of agencies, may not be able to do much to affect the larger societal forces that have caused this redistribution. But they can do more to assure that they and their clients get their proper share of the resource pie.

It is not an unlimited pie. Nor is it finite. It is probably a good deal larger than it seems (or at least the pie dish can be replenished), even though it is not as large as many of us would like it to be. Unfortunately, we don't all have equal or adequate access to it. That is what this book is all about—increasing our access and increasing the likelihood that we can replenish our resources as new needs are uncovered.

The present volume is an expanded version of the second edition of *Grantsmanship*, published only a year ago. Three new chapters have been added and others have been expanded or rewritten to deal with a wider variety of fund raising strategies. Some of you may recognize in these pages vestiges of the first edition of *Grantsmanship* (published in 1977), but more than 95 percent of this volume reflects changes that have taken place since 1977.

The 1980s are not the same as the 1970s. We have learned much since then. We have come to understand that living in an affluent society is no guarantee that affluence will be shared equitably. And we have learned that not only must resources be secured, but they must be carefully harnessed to do the most good. I have personally learned a great deal from the dozens of successful fund raisers interviewed for this book and whose experiences are reflected in its pages. The vignettes are all taken from practice, although most are heavily disguised in order to maintain confidentiality. I am sure you will agree that we owe a vote of thanks to all those who contributed their stories.

Why a single volume on general fund raising strategies, grantsmanship, program design, and resource development? Could not these topics be treated separately in different volumes? Certainly, and, as the many references at the end of each chapter suggest, they have been. I have chosen to treat them together because, in other efforts to treat these issues independently so as to better understand them, we have lost sight of their interrelationships, and so have sometimes understood them less well. By juxtaposing these concerns, I am making a number of assumptions about you, the reader. I am assuming that your interests are broad, whatever your occupation. Some of you may be direct service practitioners—caseworkers, vocational rehabilitation counselors, teachers, medical practitioners, probation officers, family therapists, community organizers. Others may be supervisors or administrators. Many of you may be active volunteers in the human services, or perhaps members of boards of directors, advisory councils, or public commissions. Still others may be professional fund raisers, proposal writers, or public relations personnel. A number of you may be students in schools of social work or in one of the many occupations that make up the human services.

Whatever your connection to the human services, and whatever use you may want to put this book to, I am also assuming that you wish to understand more fully how grantsmanship, fund raising, and program and resource development are connected. For some, the chapters on program design and proposal writing may be of focal concern. All else will be contextual. For others, finding out where the money is (as described in the chapters on public, foundation, and private sector funding) will be of focal concern. For still others, the design and conduct of campaigns and other direct-appeal fund raising efforts will be central. That is as it should be.

None of us is equally interested in everything at any particular point in our careers. What I have attempted to do is to provide you with an opportunity to concentrate on those issues that are currently of focal interest, while also providing you with sufficient information on other issues so that you may better comprehend that which interests you most. I have done this by including case illustrations and exercises liberally throughout the text. You might chose to do some exercises and look for parallels in those cases that relate to your interests, while putting others aside for future consideration.

Look over the table of contents. Check out some of the exercises in each chapter. Look over the glossary (Appendix A). This will give you a better idea of what is to be covered. Plunge in, splash around a bit, then take off in the direction you have chosen.

—*Armand Lauffer*
Jerusalem, 1984

CHAPTER 1

The Business of Grantseeking and Fund Raising

Let's talk business—the business of raising money and putting it to good use. You may not generally think of yourself as being in the fund raising business; I don't often think of myself that way, either. As an academic, I generally consider myself in the business of knowledge development and dissemination. And I sometimes find myself in the counseling, consulting, and community organizing business. Some of you may identify yourselves primarily as trainers, therapists, managers, supervisors, and planners. You may do your business in the child welfare field, in mental health, in substance abuse services, in public education, or in any of the dozens of fields that make up the human services.

Your business is your rightful work, your personal and occupational concern. It is your justification for meddling in the affairs of others. You make their business yours in order to provide human services to people in need. To support that work, you may have found yourself increasingly involved in seeking funds to support or expand current services, or to start up new programs.

There once was a time when most human service workers needed to concern themselves only with the distribution of money, with what it was spent on and how. Someone else—a public body, an administrator, a professional fund raiser—worried about where the money would come from. Some of you may even remember when that was not much of a worry in certain service sectors. Today, it is a major concern in virtually every community and in every agency. Our jobs may depend on our understanding of and skill in fund raising. In some cases, the lack of funds may create problems that are even more serious than the possibility that an agency may have to lay off staff or even close its doors. The problems are those for which we presumably provide services—the problems faced by agency consumers, by people in desperate need—those for whom we and our agencies are presumably in business.

If you ask, "What are our chances of getting the support we need to do *our* business?" the reply throughout the 1980s is likely to be, "Not very good." Now let us try another question: "What are our chances of getting the support needed to do business?" The answer is, "Not bad." In fact, the chances are probably pretty good, if you are clear about "whose business" you are doing.

Human service and other nonprofit organizations are in the business of doing the public's business. The support you are going to be able to muster will depend on the extent to which its various publics perceive the organization's activities as being in their interests. Successful fund raisers have always known that. Unsuccessful fund raisers are more likely to relate stories such as the following:

> Nothing happened, absolutely nothing. We sent our grant application to the foundation, got a postcard saying it was of interest and that it would be reviewed within three months. When we got no further word at the end of six months, I wrote a letter inquiring as to the status of our proposal. It was a year before we finally got our reply. We were turned down. Luckily, we were no longer dependent on the foundation. By then we had decided to let the whole idea die a natural death.

That may not be the most encouraging way of being introduced to grantsmanship. Unfortunately, it is an experience shared by all too many of us who begin with good intentions, and perhaps with the conviction that what we are doing is important and deserving of support. That is not a bad way to begin. But it must be supported with skill and hard work. Will all the results be worth the effort? The answer to this can be yes, even if you do not get funded. Unlike the person quoted above, fund raisers and grantseekers are not resigned to letting projects die a natural death. It is rarely sufficient to send a proposal off and then wait to see what the potential funding source does with it. When it comes to grants—pardon the pun—take nothing for granted. Prepare for both acceptance and rejection. Prepare the funding source to deal with your proposal or ideas, and prepare other key publics.

In the narrow sense, this is a book about fund raising. In a broader sense, it is about program and resource development, and about articulating your organization's interests with those of suppliers, consumers, and other publics. Without them your organization would have no resources and no business.

THE RESOURCEFUL WAY TO RAISE MONEY

In everyday language, the term "resources" is usually understood to mean "money." It can refer to money, of course, but the term is not limited to that usage. Resources are all those means and commodities needed to achieve an objective, produce a service, or distribute a product. Some resources—such as facilities, equipment, and supplies—may be purchased with money or can be used in lieu of cash. Other resources—such as legitimacy, expertise, and commitment—may or may not be related to money. They are, nevertheless, indispensable to the conduct of organizational affairs. Without them, fund raising and grantsmanship are hardly likely to be successful.

Close attention to resource development and orchestration, and a concern with programs and the various publics they serve distinguish this book from a number of others that deal with grantsmanship, fund raising, or both. Don't get me wrong—many of these other books are excellent, and I recommend a number to you throughout the text. Their step-by-step directions for proposal writing or for organizing campaigns, and their myriad tips on where to look for potential sources of support, will themselves become an important resource for you. But in this book the approach will be a bit different. The process of fund raising and grantseeking within the context of an organization's fiscal policy will be the focus, and that fiscal policy will be discussed within the context of its program and administrative policies.

Administrative policy is rarely set by the agency alone. Agencies are responsible to and must be responsive to the interests of many publics. These include what will be referred to here as "input," "throughput," and "output" publics; these will be described more fully in Chapter 2. Briefly, *input* publics are the suppliers of needed resources and of auspice or legitimacy. *Throughput* publics are the staff, volunteers, and others who transform inputs into outputs—the programs and services that an agency provides to its consumers. Those consumers and the general public who benefit in some way from the agency's programs are its *output* publics. Just as these three types of publics affect an agency's service programs, they are also likely to affect its fund raising programs.

You've probably heard the expression, "It takes money to make money." Just so, it takes various kinds of resources to generate other resources. The availability of some resources may reduce the need for others. For example, the availability of knowledge and skill (or of people with knowledge and skill) in fund raising may reduce the amount of time or money that must be invested in a campaign. Expertise in grant writing, good relationships with potential funding sources, and a reputation for effective work may increase the likelihood of a proposal's success. If these resources are not available, a great deal of time (and perhaps money to purchase the services of an outside consultant) may be required as an up-front investment.

You've also heard the expression, "Bad money drives out good money." Badly written proposals may drive out good ideas, and poorly conceived campaigns or other fund raising events may yield negative assessments of agencies and programs that otherwise are worthy of respect and support.

"Money," as another expression goes, "is the root of all evil."
Not true. First of all, that is a misquote. The proper quote is
"The *love* of money is the root of all evil," and by that is meant
its worship, its elevation to idolatrous proportions. Money is
a commodity, a means to achieve objectives that are important
and meaningful. You and your organization will have to decide
what is important and meaningful, and for whom.

You will also have to decide on the sources of supply you
wish to tap—the government, the voluntary sector, the private
sector, individual donors, or the persons who pay a fee for
service. The wider the net you cast and the more varied the
waters in which to troll, the less dependent you will be on a
single source, and the greater the likelihood that when one
source dries up others will be available from which to draw.

But do not think of fund raising in the same way we usually
think of a "fishing expedition." The objective is not to drop a
line in the water to see what you can hook—the objective is
to get the resources you need and to put them to effective use.
A better analogy might be the marketplace, where people buy
and sell and engage in other forms of bartering, and where
values are set by supply and demand.

Values set by supply and demand? Isn't that a strange notion
for the human services? Not at all. The more scarce the resources we need to provide services, the more likely it is that
those services will be costly in fiscal or other terms and the less
likely it is that they will be available to all who *need* them. In
the not-for-profit sector of our economy, *need* and *demand* are
not identical. The needs of certain populations for family planning, for job training and placement, for expanded health services are not directly translatable into demand because the
publics who are the direct recipients of those services are not
necessarily identical to those who pay for them. The paying
publics include the voluntary giver to the United Way, the
sponsor for a "walkathon" participant, and the taxpayer whose
representative votes an appropriations bill into effect. The willingness of these people to pay in dollars for services that may
be available to all or to targeted populations in need is the
equivalent of "demand" in the more traditional marketplace.

Thus many publics are involved in both the demand side and the supply side of the equation, and sometimes these publics are identical. Those who do the paying may or may not be the recipients of a service. Nevertheless, the approaches used in business marketing are applicable, with some modifications, to the human services.

THE MARKETING APPROACH
TO FUND RAISING AND GRANTSEEKING

"Marketing" refers to the development of relationships with various publics that provide an organization with the resources it needs and/or that consume its products. Within the context of the human services, marketing can be strategic when it is aimed at increasing demand for an agency's products among both consumers and suppliers. Successful strategic marketing requires that an organization have the capacity to deliver what is promised. So far, we have explored one of the "P"s of the marketing process—publics. There are four other "P"s: products, price, place, and promotions. These will be discussed in turn below.

Products are the organization's services and the outcomes of those services. For example, a hospice's services might include counseling, nursing care, medical treatment, and so on. The intended outcome for patients is a more humane way to die; for their families, a reduction in guilt and associated trauma. People may be willing to "buy" an agency's services because they anticipate the outcome to be worth the investment cost. The same would hold true for voluntary recipients of any agency service, such as adoption and foster care, job training and placement, family treatment, and compensatory education. Even involuntary recipients may be willing to pay because the cost of *not* receiving services may be greater than the cost of receiving them. In the case of a court referral, for example, refusing services may result in a jail sentence or a fine.

Other publics may be willing to pay for all or part of the product, even though they will not be direct recipients of the organization's services. These are the supplier publics mentioned earlier, who may be mandated by law to fund certain programs through contracts and grants, and who may see it as advantageous to have someone else perform tasks they are not capable of assuming directly. Some have altruistic, religious, and ideological commitments to certain services for populations in need. Remember that the resources supplied need not be money alone. Other resources include facilities, equipment, energy, technical expertise, and political influence.

Your organization's products will be shaped by the willingness of some publics to consume them, others to supply the necessary resources, and still others to turn those resources into products.

Price is the amount each of these publics is willing to pay. The price may be in dollars: awarded in grants, allocated in yearly appropriations, raised in a "bricks and mortar" drive, paid in fees for services received, donated in response to a telephone campaign. Payment can be made "in kind" through the donation or allocation of facilities or supplies, allocation of volunteer time, or performance of tasks that might otherwise cost your organization money.

There are more than dollar costs to be concerned about, however. There are also *social* costs, *psychological* costs, and *opportunity* costs. When volunteers contribute two evenings a week to a hospice, they may be giving up customary bridge games, family time, or other opportunities to socialize. When a funding agency commits itself to your organization, it may be making a social commitment by identifying itself as your organization's sponsor. When local leaders agree to serve on your organization's board or capital campaign cabinet, they are committing not only their time but their prestige to your organization.

"Psychological costs" refers to what one may have to give up in terms of personal image and sense of self, or the stresses one must endure in order to gain other anticipated benefits. Working with dying patients is painful for both staff and volunteers. Making a commitment to a neighborhood association may require one to take emotional risks. Applying to a family agency for services may require admitting that one is not capable, at least for the moment, of dealing with one's problems without outside help—and it may require at least a partial dependence on the helper or helping system. Working on a demonstration project may require agency staff to work long hours and to undergo stressful periods of uncertainty as a new program is put into practice.

"Opportunity costs" refers not to what is paid out in money, time and energy, supplies, psychological commitment, and so on, but to what might have been gained from making those commitments elsewhere. Thus when the United Way allocates $250,000 to your organization, it has a quarter of a million dollars less to allocate elsewhere. When a client enters a job training program under Goodwill Industries' auspices, he or she may have to give up the opportunity of seeking training or employment elsewhere.

Dollar costs are only a part of what suppliers and consumers may be asked to pay. Other costs may be much more significant. Once having committed themselves to support (or pay) your organization in one way, various publics may be more easily induced to support the organization in other ways as well. Thus if the Area Agency on Aging or the United Way planning staff have been involved in helping to design a particular program or service and are satisfied that your organization can be held accountable for that service, they may be willing to allocate the necessary funds.

In most of the marketing literature, the term "place" refers to the distribution of goods and services. The hospice example discussed in Chapter 2 provides an interesting illustration of how services can be transformed, reduced to cost, and made more effective by being relocated from one facility to another. In this case, however, relocation also required a new auspice, in fact the establishment of a new organization with both the commitments and the technology to provide the service. Neither funding nor legitimacy were at first available. These had to be developed through a promotional campaign. Before we move on to promotions, it may be helpful to examine some other connotations of *place*.

The word "place" can refer to the importance of a particular funder in an agency's support system or the place that the organization plays in the funder's output system. For example, if there are many group home facilities available, and a relatively modest supply of youngsters in need of protective care in a community setting, then the "place" of a particular group home in the array of potential contractors for the state welfare department may not be very secure. But if there is a great need for group homes and no others are available in a particular community, the group home may be in a very secure financial position. It may be able to *place* demands on the state agency for special consideration and for the resources needed to expand its facilities and services.

"Place" can also refer to an organization's development: the organization's readiness to take on a new service program, to modify existing practices, to seek new sources of funding and other support.

"Place" can refer to a position in a person's "life space"— the importance a particular service or activity may have to the person at a specific time in his or her life or career. For example, an outreach worker may not be ready to take on a fund raising task until she has developed confidence in her competence and knowledge of the substantive area for which funds are being sought. Likewise, the lay leadership of the campaign may have had to achieve a certain place, a level of success in business or professional life, prior to being ready to take on responsibility for fund raising. A client may not be willing to pay heavily in fees or in commitment until he or she has come to understand the severity of a problem or the promise of a cure. A childless couple, for example, may feel real pressure to seek medical help or adoption services when they reach their mid- or late thirties.

What place does the service program for which you have responsibility hold in the life or organization space of its various external publics (such as funders, potentially collaborating service organizations, and consumers) and its internal publics (such as staff and volunteers)? That place can be made more visible and more secure through effective *promotions*. Promotional activity can be aimed at selling a particular product, raising public consciousness, or properly positioning your organization and its products for new or expanded relationships with targeted publics. Selling a product, in human service terms, requires informing targeted publics that the product is available, where, and at what cost. It also requires informing the public of the benefits of using a particular product.

At first blush this may seem overly commercial, not the kind of thing that a human service organization does or ought to do. But we do it all the time. Libraries advertise the availability of their bookmobiles or special reading services to the disabled. Museums inform the public of special shows or of the benefits of membership. Agencies interested in reaching new publics may dispatch staff to speaking engagements and outstationed positions in other host organizations. Press releases or feature stories on special services or seasonal programs (such as summer camps) are not uncommon. Some agencies even advertise clients, as in the case of those seeking to find adoptive families for hard-to-place children. What kind of selling activities did the promoters of BAT engage in? What publics did they target?

Consciousness raising is of a slightly different order. It is not aimed at increasing demand for a particular program or product, but at increasing the likelihood that there will be support for the program or demand for it when such support or demand is needed. The general population is likely to be indifferent about the things that concern your organization: a service it provides, a population in need, or a problem to be addressed. Most people do not become interested in hospice services or adoptions until they become aware of a personal need or until they become conscious of the needs and concerns of others.

When agencies seek to promote services for unwed mothers, teenage substance abusers, or the victims of domestic violence, they often find that public awareness or receptivity is so minimal as to preclude any possibility of adequate support. Because these issues often offend the public and challenge our images of ourselves as a society, there is often resistance to dealing with these problems. For this reason, consciousness raising, the building of awareness and concern, may have to precede efforts to promote a particular product.

Consciousness-raising activities can be directed at particular publics: a foundation from whom support may be sought now or in the future; the Area Agency on Aging, from which technical assistance may be solicited first, and funding at a future date; teens who may need family planning services now or in the near future; members of a religious community who may not only need hospice services for themselves, but may be in the position of referring others, raising money, or donating time.

Promotional activities can take many forms. Partners in the process may include the local press, television and radio stations, and the many social agencies, civic associations, and professional groups found in any community. The press features news articles, regular columns, and advertisements. Similar content may be carried in agency newsletters, in corporate house organs, church or civic group newsletters, and so on. Television and radio might also be used for news releases. Public service announcements are another possibility. So are interviews and participation in talk and phone-in shows. Public appearances and community education programs also promote program and services, as do one-on-one personal contacts and relationships. Which of these approaches does your organization use on a regular basis? To what extent do they increase its ability to generate needed fiscal and other supports from those publics upon which it is dependent and for which it is responsible?

FUND RAISING WITHIN OR OUTSIDE THE AGENCY'S PROGRAM PRIORITIES

An effective fund raising and grantseeking strategy should fit within your organization's programs and priorities. One can easily be tempted into new activities or services when new funds become available, and some of these may be out of sync with the agency's primary mission. Taking on a new program may divert attention from existing commitments and may require considerable change in agency structure, staffing, and program patterns. The same may be true when funds are cut—it may be easier to drop costly services that are central to the agency's mission than it is to drop less expensive services. I don't mean to suggest that an organization should not strike out in new directions when an opportunity presents itself or that it should respond unrealistically to a predicament not of its own making. I am suggesting that any changes in basic directions should be thought through carefully. An organization's basic mission is no more sacrosanct than its administrative or managerial structure. Both should be changed in response to new perceptions of what is needed. If the mission is to be changed, a properly designed fund raising strategy should be put into effect, and not vice versa. Fund raising concerns should not preempt concerns about missions and directions. The two vignettes that follow will illustrate this point.

VIGNETTE 1:
OUTREACH TO LOWER-INCOME YOUTH

A community center serving teams from a predominantly middle-class neighborhood received a grant to provide outreach services to lower-income and minority youth. In the four months it received the grant, the new client population seemed to take over the dances, the lounge programs, and other social activities. Drugs were passed frequently within the center building. Fights were almost a nightly occurrence. Many of the kids formerly served stopped coming. Several board members, including the president, threatened to resign unless something was done.

VIGNETTE 2:
NEW POPULATIONS, NEW PROGRAMS,
AND INCREASED SIZE

A communitywide family and children's service agency designed a three-year project to extend its services to the aging. Using a combination of Title IV and Title VII grants from the Administration on Aging, it established a home care service and a nutrition program.

The combined budgets of both projects equaled that of the agency's previous annual budget.

This required doubling the staff. It also required adding a nutritionist and community organizers as well as a large number of volunteers to what had been a staff of highly trained caseworkers and psychologists with clinical orientations. The problems of integrating the new staff and the new projects into the overall agency program soon became apparent. The resulting tensions were only beginning to be resolved when the three-year funding period ended.

Because of cuts in federal programs and shifts in priorities, no new funds from the Administration on Aging were forthcoming. Nor had the agency made arrangements to secure other sources for project continuation. As quickly as they came, the new services had to be dropped. The resultant backlash from the community and from client groups and the drop in staff morale nearly destroyed the agency. Most of the project staff were let go. Some of the old-timers were more than ever convinced that they were right in resisting the project from the start.

For human service agencies in which the primary mission is that of providing social services or instructional programs, the design of a new project for the submission of a grant application should be considered against the context of the populations to be served, the types of services to be offered, and the size of the agency, as well as the types of staff employed. A research organization would be concerned with the issues examined and the methodologies used, as well as the number and types of researchers and support staff currently employed.

Can the new project be absorbed within the existing staff? Will it support, complement, or compete with existing programs or technologies? Is the new project necessary in order to maintain the continuous support of staff currently on salary? Will it require retraining staff or otherwise retooling the agency? Will it require the addition of new personnel? At what level? For how long? At what cost? Will the addition of new personnel or the assignment of new tasks to people currently on staff necessitate the upgrading of job classifications? How disruptive might it be to the organization or to those employed on the project if no new funding is available at the close of the grant period?

FUND RAISING WITHIN THE AGENCY'S OVERALL PROGRAM AND FISCAL STRATEGY

In many human service organizations, grant funds are a small and sometimes insignificant element in the organization's overall income picture. Other sources of financial support include (1) general fund allocations, (2) fees or tuition, (3) sales and royalties, (4) gifts, (5) investments, (6) reserve funds, and (7) in-kind services.

General fund allocations are generally made from the group or organization that sponsors your organization. A state department of public health, for example, will get its general fund allocation from the governor's office, as appropriated by a legislative committee. A school of social work will receive its general fund allocations from the university of which it is a part. A voluntary welfare agency may get its general fund support from the United Way or its own board of directors. A research organization may get its support from a federal agency or through contributions from several local government units.

General funds are usually allocated on an annual basis. Until recently, an organization could assume that the funds allocated each year would be based on the total amount allocated the previous year with inflation and rising costs taken into effect. This may no longer be the case. The partial use of sunset legislation and zero-based budgeting by the federal government and by many state and local authorities has changed the picture considerably.

Sunset legislation puts a time limit on a program's or organization's mandate. At the end of that period, the organization has to rejustify itself by stating the case for its services in relation to needs and priorities. In effect, where the sunset legislation approach has taken root, budget requests have had to be justified in much the way one might justify a request for a project grant or award.

Zero-based budgeting complements sunset legislation. It is a procedure whereby the total budget has to be rejustified each year, unlike than the earlier practice, in which one year's budget was accepted as the basis against which allocations were made for the following year.

This suggests that general fund support should no longer be considered a firm base against which to seek other financial support. Many organizations, in fact, have little if any general fund support and may depend much more extensively on contracts and grants and on some of the other sources of fiscal support discussed in this chapter. Among them are fees and tuition payments.

Fees may be paid by individuals who seek services or by organizations that contract for services with your organization. Purchase of service contracts, for example, is increasingly common in the public sector. Rather than conducting all needed services, a public agency (such as a department of social services) will contract out with local providers using a set fee schedule.

Tuition payments are generally made by individuals who enroll in instructional programs, although in some cases employing organizations may cover the tuition for their staff members. Unlike general fund support and contracts or grants, the income from individual fees or from tuition need not be expended within a given fiscal year. Your organization's bylaws or regulations may permit banking any net gain over your expenses toward some future program or service.

The same is true of sales and royalties. Many research organizations sell their reports or collect royalties on their sales through commercial firms. The same may be true of educational institutions and, to a lesser extent, service agencies. The resulting income may also be used for investing in the development of other publications.

Many human service organizations, especially those in the voluntary field, subsist partially on gifts or the income generated from gifts. Educational institutions may solicit gifts from alumni or from civic groups and from industry within their communities. Social agencies often solicit gifts from local benefactors and from community foundations. Gifts are sometimes earmarked for specific purposes. At other times, they are given for one-time-only expenditures. Alternatively, they may be earmarked for investment, with only the earnings being used for the support of ongoing programs and services.

Investments are of many types. Universities, for example, regularly invest in land and in stock portfolios. Several manage major businesses. While this is less often true of social agencies, the use of stock portfolios and trust funds is taking on increasing importance.

Where permitted, reserve funds are generated through the accumulation of income from investments and from particular activities. They may be drawn on only for specified activities or may be used generally for deficits when and where they occur. In fat years, the reserves may bulge considerably. In lean years, they may be quickly depleted.

Although not often considered as an element of the funding strategy, in-kind services can provide a substantial underpinning for your program. If your organization is a subunit of a larger organization, in-kind services are provided in lieu of general fund support. For example, a large organization may handle all accounting and outreach services for you. The source of in-kind services, however, is not limited to other units within your own organization. In-kind services may be provided in lieu of general funds as an effort to fund community services more efficiently and effectively. For example, the United Way agency may operate an areawide information and referral service, may conduct surveys and needs assessments, and may do budget audits for all the human service agencies in its area. These services are perceived by the United Way as in lieu of fiscal allocations to each of the agencies for which it is responsible.

In a number of instances, your agency's contribution of in-kind services may net or generate other fiscal support. Grant sources often require matching funds by the recipient of an award. You may be permitted to match such an award with in-kind services such as the allocation of space, furniture, clerical assistance, and instructional materials.

ASSESSING THE "CONSENSUS" ENVIRONMENT

Fund raising efforts may be aimed at increasing support for your organization or for a specific program. The "pitch" used may be aimed at convincing some relevant public of the worth of your agency; the importance of a program, service, or project; or the needs of a particular population who are victims of problems not of their own making. There may be a good deal of consensus that the agency, the consumer population, or the project is worthy, and that the problem to be addressed with the funds donated or allocated is appropriate. There may also be total indifferences. Assume, for example, that your fund raising effort is aimed at dealing with a particular problem. Some forces in the community may not want the problem examined at all. For example, many middle-class suburban residents in the early 1970s were shocked to discover that drug abuse problems existed in their senior and junior high schools. Efforts to deal with the problem or to redirect funds toward its solution were rebuffed by efforts to define the problem as nonexistent or as a temporary aberration.

In some cases, there may be agreement that an issue does exist, but total disagreement over the methods proposed to deal with that problem. In designing a project proposal, you should be clear on the extent to which there is consensus, indifference, or disagreement on the issue itself and on the actions proposed to deal with that problem.

When there is consensus that a problem exists, there may also be a better likelihood of agreement on the means toward resolving that problem. Differences, if any, may be based on misinformation, lack of information, or poor communication. If that is the case, get the facts before engaging in efforts to reconcile viewpoints. This will increase the likelihood of arriving at some agreement within the community that the project is worthwhile. Agreement can be promoted through involvement of other agencies and organizations, potential consumers, and potential funders directly concerned with the issue.

Your role in promoting consensus and support for the project may be a facilitative one. You may serve as a guide, a catalyst, a mediator, or a consultant. The inducement you use to support your project or proposal may be the good will and concern of other individuals and organizations.

You will have to pursue a different approach when there is disagreement on the nature of the problem or on whether or not a problem exists. When there is little congruence of values or interests, recognition of the issue may be resisted. The proposed resolution may be strongly opposed. If you do not expect agreement, it makes little sense to use rational persuasion or to marshal the facts in an attempt to move others.

It makes more sense to recognize the opposition and seek the funding sources that would tend to agree with your viewpoint. The idea is to involve as many others with like opinions as possible. Recognize that you may have to play a protagonist, advocate, or adversary role. In this situation, you will be a contestant for support rather than an enabler of those who already agree with the need for the project.

A different strategy is called for when there is indifference to the project. There may be no agreement at all on its substance or on the means of resolving the problem that you have identified. But there may be no disagreement on the objectives of the project. Agreement on means is possible, but more than discussion and marshaling of the facts will be necessary.

Consider a campaign strategy. This is a planned effort to convert apathy to interest and opposition to agreement, or at least to support. Your role will be that of persuader and promoter. You may have to use the media, small meetings, or even small action groups to raise the level of awareness before the project can be designed.

STAFFING THE FUND RAISING EFFORT

You are not alone in these concerns, nor should you act alone. An individual can often initiate a major program development activity or fund raising campaign, but neither are likely to be successful unless others are involved in the process. A major factor in the success of any program development or fund raising effort is the structure of relationships that are built and managed throughout the process. Some agencies delegate this responsibility to one or a few individuals: an executive director, an associate director for planning, a board committee. Others establish special departments to deal with resource development. Too often, persons who could contribute to the process are left out, for many reasons. Bureaucratization leads to a division of responsibilities that limits what staff members and others can or are expected to do. Professionalization also leads to specialization. Caseworkers, teachers, nurses, and other "direct service" practitioners often are all too happy to leave fund raising and grantsmanship to "the experts."

Certainly there are people with expertise in these areas, and that expertise should be tapped whenever appropriate. But the relegation of responsibility to these experts must be done within the context of responsibilities allocated broadly within the organization. The more involved staff members, board and committee people, and other volunteers, the more resources you will have working for you in the recruitment and development of still more resources.

This is a *how-to* book, loaded with tips and tools that can be used by fund raisers and others concerned with program and resource development. Almost every chapter includes exercises and recommended activities for staff and others. You can do the exercises alone, although it might serve your purposes better if you were to complete all or some of them with colleagues from your own organization or from other organizations with which your agency is involved in service delivery. As you work together on the tasks suggested in the chapters that follow, you will find that you establish relationships based on the design and conduct of fund raising and related activities. Some of these working relationships may be temporary, ad hoc, and even one-shot affairs. Others may become more permanent, as you form proposal-writing task forces, campaign cabinets, resource development committees, and perhaps even new departments within your organization. Suggestions for collaborative planning and implementation are made throughout the book.

HOW THE BOOK IS ORGANIZED

Each of the following chapters begins with a description of
a program development, fund raising, or grantsmanship approach. Frequently the person responsible is quoted directly.
In the next chapter, for example, a medical social worker describes how a personal tragedy led to his involvement in the
creation of a hospice, despite opposition within his own employing organization and initial apathy in the general community. His experience and those of others quoted throughout
may serve as guides to your own actions. But don't accept what
they, or I, suggest uncritically. Look for the principles that may
apply to your own situation.

Chapter 2 zeros in on the various publics upon which your
program and resource development efforts will be dependent,
and for whom you may be engaged in those efforts. None of
us operates as an independent agent, nor are the successes of
our efforts independent of the concerns of others. The place
that your agency and its programs occupy will be examined
further in Chapter 2. In particular, the range of exchanges
possible between your agency or a program within it that you
are concerned about and the programs of other organizations
will be addressed. At first glance, this may seem a bit out of
place in a book about fund raising, but it is not. The success
of any fund raising effort will frequently depend on the exchanges you maintain with key publics. Moreover, some of
these exchanges will net you additional resources that may
reduce the need to raise funds independently.

Program development and design is the subject of Chapter
3. It begins with the assessment process that leads to problem
definition and works its way through goal development, the
specification of performance objectives, and the exploration of
alternative interventions. For two reasons, I have chosen in
Chapter 3 to use the development of direct service programs
as the examples around which the discussion and the exercises
are built. First, I suspect that most readers will be more familiar
with services than with fund raising, and the approach I have
chosen may be relatively familiar. Second, any effort to write

a proposal for grantseeking purposes will require competence in program design. You will find that the approach described is as applicable to designing a fund raising program as it is to the design of a direct service program.

Chapters 5 through 8 focus on grantseeking approaches aimed at specific publics: government funders, private foundations, the business and professional communities (the private sector), and voluntary organizations (such as the United Way and civic associations). Chapters 9 and 10 deal with fund raising efforts aimed at unorganized publics through such activities as sales, special events, endowments, and campaigns.

Step-by-step guidelines on proposal writing are provided in Chapter 11. Chapter 12 follows with instructions on the design of line-item and functional budgets and their use for accounting and programming purposes. Chapter 13 explores what you might do if you don't get the funds you aimed for, or what to do if you are successful. A colleague suggest I drop the number 13 as unlucky, much as they eliminate the thirteenth floor in Chicago high-rise buildings (elevators go right from the twelfth to the fourteenth floor). But I don't think of fund raising or grantsmanship as based on luck. Certainly, some organizations are more fortunately placed than others. Whatever circumstances we find ourselves in, there is work to be done. Doing that work well can improve our chances of getting the resources we need to provide the services our consumers need.

Throughout the text, I will be using terms that may be new to you. I suggest you take a moment to examine the glossary provided (Appendix A); become familiar with the terms we will be using. Initially, they may provoke more questions than they answer. Keep those questions in mind as you read on. You will find the answers in the text and in the experiences of others with whom you interact at work.

Appendix B provides a limited number of suggestions about where you can go for additional information. Although the appendix is limited, the book is not. You will find additional resources discussed in the text of each chapter and in the suggestions for further reading that follow each summary statement.

Appendix C includes an example of a project proposal that

was never funded. Look it over. By the time you get to it, you may be able to be more critical of it than I was when I submitted it to a federal agency. There are a number of problems in it, as well as some good points. See if you can spot them.

REVIEW

The business of fund raising is an integral part of *the business of* program development and delivery. Dollars are a major resource for any agency, but the term "resources" should not be limited to money. It also includes facilities, equipment, expertise, commitment, energy, and all the other means and commodities needed to achieve an objective, produce a service, or distribute a product.

Your access to these resources and your ability to transform them into products will depend on the relationships established with key publics: those who supply your organization with resources and legitimacy; those (such as staff and volunteers) who transform resources into services; and those who are the consumers or beneficiaries of those services.

Relationships to these publics can be described in marketing terms. Marketing includes consideration of the products to be developed and delivered (interventions and their outcomes), the place (distribution) of those products in the individual and organizational life space of key publics, the price attached to those products (and who will pay it), and the promotional efforts required to gain necessary support and to stimulate demand.

When viewed this way, fund raising and other forms of resource development can be seen as integral to an organization's program and fiscal policies rather than as separate and detached functions. This viewpont increases the likelihood that many members of the organization—its paid staff, its board and committee members, its volunteers—and representatives of other organizations with which it interacts will all be involved in the process.

CHAPTER *2*

Identifying the Publics
Your Program Serves

VIGNETTE 3:
GOING TO BAT FOR THE DYING

Marylou was 39 when she died. Our children were 16 and 14. It took her six months to die; two in the hospital, but the last, at our insistence, at home. Her death wasn't an easy one; cancer patients don't generally have an easy time of it. It wasn't made any easier by the disapproval we had to deal with for bringing her home.

It happens that I am a medical social worker and that I am employed by the hospital in which she was being treated. I have had a lot of experience working with dying patients and their families. I had always thought that the saddest part of dying was dying alone. As caring as the nursing staff at the hospital might be, a hospital is still a hospital. Dying may be toughest on family members. They seem never to get the chance of "finishing their business" with a loved one, of saying all the things that need saying. Hospitals just aren't the right environment for it.

That's why Marylou came home. She had business of her own to finish and she wanted the kids to come to terms and to understand, and to do and say what they had to, no holds barred, and no guilt later on.

One of the hardest parts of it for me was dealing with some of my colleagues and especially the medical staff at the hospital. It wasn't just suspicion; it was outright hostility. I was accused of being over-emotional and not accepting reality, even of being unprofessional. There were a number of subtle hints suggesting that I might not be fit for hospital work any more. It made me angry. You get that way when you are about to lose someone you love and when someone else tells you how you should deal with that loss. So I decided to fight back.

When one of our local newspaper reporters asked if they could interview us, Marylou and I decided it would be a good idea. The kids agreed. We told our story and why we had decided that home was the best place to die. The paper printed it. The amount of response from people we had never heard of, and from some of my former clients, and even from some of our friends who had not understood before, well, it was overwhelming. "Do something with it," Marylou told me a few days before she died. "Use our experience to help other people take charge of their own dying."

Trying to change things at the hospital, considering the attitudes there, didn't seem like the place to start. I've always believed in building on strength, and the strength seemed to be in the sentiments of all those who had given us encouragement. For several months after Marylou died, the kids and I spoke to any group that invited us: churches, the local PTA at the high school the girls attended, a chapter of the AARP [American Association of Retired Persons], even people in their own homes who invited friends and relatives to attend.

I had by this time read of Dr. Cicely Saunders's experiment at St. Christopher's in London. It was the beginning of what has since come to be known as the hospice movement. Dr. Saunders was on a speaking tour in this country. By now we had organized a committee for Being At Home, and a number of influential people were willing to "go to BAT" for the right of a patient to spend his or her last days at home or in a homelike environment.

More than two hundred people came to hear Dr. Saunders at the Presbyterian church. The press was there, and we arranged to have TV coverage and two radio interviews for her while she was in town. We recorded the talk and made it available to the community college radio station for airing sometime in the future.

That was the start of it. Public opinion was strongly behind us and BAT established several task groups. This was in 1973 and the Connecticut Hospice at Yale was by then a year or two old. We delegated some people to visit and learn about their operation. We organized a health professional's task force, small at first, to look for support in the medical community. An ecumenical group orga-nized to explore the possibilities of a general fund raising campaign. They decided to begin by working with their own congregants and parishioners on fund raising within the churches and synagogues. They also recruited volunteers and so did the AARP and a fledgling Grey Panther group.

Several social workers, nurses, and I set up a training program for volunteers and for anyone who wanted to care for a dying patient at home. We involved others who had had experiences like mine. A small grant from a local pharmaceutical manufacturer helped with mailing. We used an empty office in one of the churches. But we didn't have the kinds of funds we would really need nor a real orga-nization yet.

When contributions began coming in from the churches and syn-agogues and from private, unsolicited donations, we decided to in-corporate BAT. One of the social workers on the board worked for the public welfare department and laid out the range of possibilities for support through Medicare, Medicaid, Title XX of the Social Se-curity Act, which is administered by the State Department of Public Welfare, and Title III of the Older Americans Act of 1973 (it had just been passed).

The chair of the new Area Agency on Aging Advisory Council was also on our board. She pushed for putting BAT on the list of poten-tial recipients for Title III funds. Our fund raisers were also on the lookout for a facility we might use for those people who could not return home but wished to die in a homelike environment. An estate attorney active in one of the churches came through for us. We had a house, if we could bring it up to code and staff it. It took another year to be able to do that.

BAT became a fully operational hospice in 1975. We help about 800 people a year, work with more than 150 volunteers, have a profes-sional staff of 60. Our funds come from the state and federal gov-ernments, the United Fund, and our own endowment program as well as several fund raising events each year. We also charge our consumers on the basis of their ability to pay. One day of hospice care runs about $40. Compare that to $400 or more for a hospital room.

*Our board is made up of lay people, health care, and other profes-
sional people. And while money is always an issue, today, 10 years
after we incorporated, public support no longer is. We are affiliated
with the National Hospice Organization in Vienna, Virginia, and
through that with over 400 hospices throughout the country.*

*We now operate a 37-bed facility, although many patients are helped
to stay at home or to live with relatives and friends. Treatment begins with a home visit or a visit in the hospital if that is when we are
first approached. A hospice team made up of nurses, doctors, social
workers, and volunteers then provides service on a 24-hour basis.
The team is usually coordinated by a nurse. But we don't stop there.*

*We also do follow-up with members of the family after a patient has
died and may refer them to other agencies, attorneys, and so on. We
also do a lot of public education. Our staff and volunteers make frequent addresses to church and synagogue groups, to civic and
professional associations. And we do a lot of consciousness raising
and training with the staffs of hospitals and other health and social
agency personnel.*

GETTING IN POSITION

Those of you who may have been involved in efforts to
establish a local hospice program or, for that matter, any service
alternative or any kind of service expansion will find familiar
elements in the BAT example. It took several years before a
hospice could be established. Many elements had to be in position first. "Positioning" required getting the support of various
publics, including potential consumers and funders. And it required both public *recognition of a need* and *acceptance of the
approach* to be used to meet that need.

In general, positioning requires being in the right place at
the right time and having the capacity to respond to opportunities when they present themselves. It may also require cre-
ating the opportunities when they do not. A good idea will not
get very far if no one is ready to listen to it, if there are no
resources to put it into effect, or if no one is willing to support
it. Finally, getting into position requires access to the right
publics.

All organizations must be able to manage relationships to three kinds of publics: those that provide inputs, those that transform inputs into products or services, and those that consume those outputs. Let us examine each of these publics one at a time.

INPUT PUBLICS AND
THE RESOURCES THEY SUPPLY

Input publics include all those that supply an organization with needed resources and with the legitimacy to do something with those resources. Resources include concrete items such as money, facilities, and equipment and such ephemerals as expertise, political influence, and energy.

Money is supplied by government agencies, voluntary organizations such as the United Way, philanthropic foundations, business organizations, and corporate givers and by individual donors who contribute to campaigns and special fund raising events. Finally, it is supplied by consumers who pay fees to cover part or all of the cost of service.

Facilities and equipment can be purchased with money, but they can also be contributed by other organizations, as in the example of the church that donated office space to BAT in its early days. Individuals might also contribute facilities and equipment in the form of private contributions.

Expertise is found in public or voluntary sector organizations such as universities, libraries, and professional journals or books published by the public, private, and voluntary sectors. It is also found in an organization's staff, in the volunteers who work with the organization or for it, and among consultants who may be available to the organization on a time-limited basis. Sometimes the same organization that provides financial support through grants, contracts, or purchase-of-service agreements also contributes expertise through technical assistance.

Political influence may be generated through association with powerful publics and through their involvement in program development and design. *Energy* also comes from all these publics. It requires a commitment and a willingness to invest time and creativity in the program and resource development processes. Finally, *legitimacy* refers to the consensus that what the organization has set out to do—and how it does it and for whom—is considered appropriate. Agencies are dependent for their legitimacy on a variety of sources.

It is not enough, for example, that an organization be legitimated by a board of directors or a citizen's advisory committee if funding sources do not consider the service to be legitimate. Nor is legitimacy provided by the suppliers of resources sufficient if consumers do not perceive the organization to be legitimate. Well-meaning agencies have all too frequently attempted to provide services to ethnic minorities who see the organization as presenting a hostile and controlling society.

Exercise 2.1 will provide you with an opportunity to inventory the suppliers of an organization with which you are familiar. Take a few moments to complete it before going on to an examination of the agency's throughput and output publics. Complete it by yourself or with colleagues in the organization you are assessing. You may find their input necessary to get accurate information. You may also find that doing it with others stimulates new ideas on where to go for additional resources.

OUTPUT PUBLICS

Let us turn our attention now to the organization's output publics; those that make up the consumers of its products or services. This is what is often referred to as the organization's *market.* In the example of the BAT hospice, individuals and families who use the hospice for residence, counseling, or instruction are clearly consumers. But what of the members of churches and synagogues, or the hospital's medical personnel, who also receive training or new insights from the hospice staff?

Output publics may also include other organizations: those that receive direct services from the first organization and those that may receive referrals of clients. Who are your organization's output publics? Are some more central to the organi-

---

EXERCISE 2.1
INVENTORY OF INPUT PUBLICS

(1) Look over the Input Publics Matrix. Think of an organization with which you are familiar: a social agency, a school, a hospital, or the like. Begin by identifying all the suppliers of financial resources and list these next to the appropriate row in the first column. For the hospice example described in the vignette, you might list Medicare, Medicaid, the Area Agency on Aging, and the Department of Public Welfare next to Government Agencies. Next to Voluntary Associations, you would list the various churches and synagogues and the United Way. The pharmaceutical company would be identified next to Private Sector Organizations. The publics solicited for individual funds and categories of consumers from whom donations and fees were collected would be listed next. Now complete the matrix for each of the other resource categories: facilities and equipment, expertise, political influence, energy, and legitimacy.

You may find that some organizations or groups appear more than once, under several headings or in several rows. What does this suggest to you?

Be as complete as you can. Check with others if your information is limited.

(2) Now go back to each supplier you identified. If you think that it could be tapped for a significant increase in allocations, circle it using a different color pen or pencil.

(3) Finally, go back to the matrix again. In the second color, add new supplier publics that the organization is not currently tapping but that are potentially significant contributors.

(4) What might be done to increase contributions of needed resources from those suppliers identified in the Input Publics Worksheet? Jot down some preliminary ideas on a separate sheet of paper.

You will have occasion to refer back to both worksheets in completing exercises in subsequent chapters.

---

zation's missions than others? Are some targeted for special attention? For example, let us assume that you are employed by a community mental health center. Does the center provide services to everyone in the community, or are the center's services targeted to specific populations? If so, it may have planned to engage in a process of "market segmentation."

Exercise 2.1
INPUT PUBLICS MATRIX

Publics	Resources					
	Money	Equipment/ Facilities	Expertise	Political Influence	Time/ Energy	Legitimacy
Government Agencies						
Voluntary Organizations						
Foundations						
Private Sector Organizations						
Individual Donors						
Consumers						

RESOURCE DEVELOPMENT WORKSHEET
FOR EXERCISE 2.1

Jot down some preliminary ideas on how the organization might increase allocations of resources from those suppliers identified on the Input Publics Worksheet. Use additional sheets of paper if necessary.

Market segmentation refers to a process whereby the market is divided into fairly homogeneous parts such that one or more can be targeted for recruitment or specialized services. The market can be segmented geographically, functionally, demographically, or psychographically. *Geographic* segmentation refers to the locale(s) in which service takes place. It can be drawn up on the basis of size, density, or both. In my home state of Michigan, for example, some community mental health centers serve multiple-county rural areas covering thousands of square miles. Others serve densely populated neighborhoods or clusters of neighborhoods in the Detroit area. The term "catchment area" generally refers to geographic segmentation.

Functional segmentation refers to the way in which services are clustered around given problems: housing, job counseling, protective services, family treatment, and the like. *Demographic* segmentation may be used to target populations by age, race or ethnic identity, religion, national origin, gender, income, education, position in the life cycle, type of employment, and so on. *Psychographic* characteristics are somewhat more subtle. They include such variables as personality, lifestyle, commitment to the organization, and even readiness to use a service.

In the case of the mental health center we have been considering, the market may have been segmented to serve a particular neighborhood. Services may be aimed primarily at teenagers and their parents, particularly if the teens are actual or potential substance abusers. Separate programs may be set up for males and for females. A decision may have been made to work with Black youngsters first because there is a readiness among members of the community to take responsibility for both treatment and prevention (psychographic characteristic = readiness).

In the case of the hospice described earlier, can you identify its market segment from the information provided? What else would you need to know? Now it is your turn to do a market segmentation analysis on an organization with which you are familiar, or a particular work unit within it.

INTERNAL PUBLICS

Input and output publics are external to the organization. Throughput publics are *internal;* they transform resources into products (outcomes and services) that are consumed by output publics. These persons include paid and volunteer staff, members of advisory committees, task groups, and boards. Throughput publics may also be consumers involved in the provision of their own services. Some consumer/providers may be organized, as in the case of unions or other collective bargaining units, professional associations, and self-help groups.

The extent to which your organization will be able to *attract resources* from its input publics is likely to be influenced by the reputation, the competence, and the energy of these internal publics. The extent to which they will be able to turn *resources into products* will depend on how they are organized, the kinds

---

EXERCISE 2.2
MARKET SEGMENTATION ANALYSIS

(1) Start by describing the general geographic area that your organization serves. Now pinpoint it more precisely. For example, the general area may be the northwest suburbs, but you may attempt to recruit most heavily from a particular subarea, or perhaps residents of one or more areas have come to see your organization as the place to go for service, even if you would like to draw from a larger area. Use the Market Segmentation Matrix for recording purposes.

(2) Now do the same for each of the other variables: functional, demographic, and psychographic.

(3) Go over your categories in a second color of ink or pencil, circling those items that require modification.

(4) Now add the segmentation characteristics of populations your organization is not serving, is underserving but *should* be serving, in the second color.

(5) What should be done to increase the likelihood that the organization will be able to serve those populations it should be serving? Record your preliminary ideas on a separate sheet of paper.

You will have opportunities to refer back to this exercise as you progress through the book.

Exercise 2.2
MARKET SEGMENTATION MATRIX

Method of Segmentation	General Population	Specific Segment Within It
Geographic		
Functional		
Demographic		
Psychographic		

MARKET SEGMENTATION WORKSHEET
FOR EXERCISE 2.2

Jot down some of your ideas about how to refine your organization's market segmentation processes. How will you reach the populations you hope to reach? How can you penetrate those markets and perhaps even develop an exclusive or at least commanding attraction for them? How can you discourage market segments currently using those services that should not be?

of knowledge and skill they possess, and their perspectives of
what should be done as well as their commitments to doing it.
The extent to which they will be able to *attract consumers* will
be based on the same variables. Are there other characteristics
that are equally important?

Should internal publics reflect the demographics of the consumer population (perhaps in such characteristics as gender,
marital status, and ethnicity)? Should their skills be general,
as in counseling, or should they be specific to the functions that
they perform in the organization (e.g., substance abuse counseling or counseling battered wives)? Should they reflect certain
desirable psychographic characteristics such as commitment to
the organization or to its consumers, a shared ideological or
ethical perspective, or an ability to be flexible in the way in
which they organize their work hours or apply intervention
techniques? Does the organization require that staff and board
members live in the same geographic area as do consumers?

Time for another exercise.

SUPPORT FROM KEY PUBLICS

Whatever the mix of paid staff, board members, and other
volunteers, you may find that there is little support for starting
up a new service program, for reorganizing so as to become
more effective in fund raising, or for other changes in the ways
in which resources are recruited and transformed into services.
The reasons for resistance to change are many.

A central fact of organizational life is that many find it easier
to keep busy with routine tasks than to take on new functions
or to change accustomed modes of behavior. Program initiators
are often dismayed when some service agency personnel show
a calculated opposition to change. As in the case of the medical
social worker who organized BAT, opposition may even result
in accusations of unprofessionalism. While staff may not always
verbalize their true feelings, their actions may suggest that they
generally prefer to maintain their current structures or modes

EXERCISE 2.3
INTERNAL PUBLICS IDENTIFICATION

(1) Look over the matrix. You will have to do a bit more on this one than on the matrixes for Exercises 2.1 and 2.2. This matrix is only partly constructed. You will have to fill in the numbers under each of the four categories. For example, if there are geographic restrictions on the employment of staff or the involvement of volunteers who perform any numbers of tasks from direct service to fund raising to policymaking, jot down these instructions or requirements next to the numbers in the space to the left.

Do the same for demographic characteristics such as age, gender, and so on. Then do it for functional requirements. These might be defined in terms of knowledge (e.g., *knowledge* about the community, or *knowledge* about child placement practice); skill (for example, skill in behavior modification or in proposal writing or campaign management); and degree or certification requirements, if any (MSW or ACSW or state license). If you do not have enough space, make yourself a larger matrix.

Now do the same for psychographic characteristics such as commitment to the organization, identity with a particular ethnic or cultural community, willingness to assume responsibility for others, and so forth.

You may find it easier to complete this column after you have identified the staff and volunteers in the uppermost row. Staff might include direct service workers, managers, specialists, and consultants. Volunteers may include those who provide direct services, who train or supervise others, who raise funds, who perform specialized tasks such as accounting or legal advice, and who are involved in program development and decision making (such as members of committees, task forces, and boards).

Once you have identified all the paid and volunteer publics, indicate which of the required characteristics are needed by checking the appropriate space in the columns to the right of each characteristic.

(2) Now, using a second color, circle those characteristics in the column under each of the identified publics that require some modification.

(3) If new categories of volunteers or paid staff should be added, add them in your second color on the uppermost row and fill in the required characteristics in the second color.

(4) Jot down notes on a separate piece of paper on how you or the organization might achieve a more desirable mix of paid and volunteer staff.

Keep your notes. We'll be referring to them again shortly.

Exercise 2.3
INTERNAL PUBLICS MATRIX

	Paid Staff						Volunteers				
Characteristics											
Geographic Requirements: 1. 2. 3. 4. 5. 6.											
Demographic Requirements: 1. 2. 3. 4. 5. 6.											
Functional Requirements: 1. 2. 3. 4. 5. 6.											
Psychographic Requirements: 1. 2. 3. 4. 5. 6.											

INTERNAL PUBLICS WORKSHEET
FOR EXERCISE 2.3

Jot down some of your ideas on how you might affect a more appropriate mix of paid and volunteer personnel, and how their functions might be made complementary. What are the desired characteristics of each? How could you move from where you are to where you think you or the organization should be?

of operation even when a change will obviously enhance the accomplishment of the organization's stated goals or mission.

Even getting a grant may not be enough. Being pressured into change by outsiders may result in some loss of face. Under such circumstances, financial incentives to individuals and to agencies may be insufficient inducements, particularly if a change once adopted might result in embarrassment or loss of stature in the event of failure.

Agency administrators may perceive change as an imposition on their personnel and thus disruptive to the management process. Agency personnel may be intent on protecting the advantages they receive from keeping things as they are. Change may require learning new skills and modifying accustomed ways of behaving. Some professional staff members may fear that change will result in an erosion of standards, or will require them to perform tasks that could be performed better by others. Frequently, defenders of the status quo take that stand in what they perceive to be the public interest. Distinguishing between self-interest and public interest is sometimes extremely difficult.

There are significant psychic costs to change. For some personnel, changing established patterns of practice or adding new functions may mean becoming novices again. It takes a long time to master a given craft. Most changes require immediate risks. While not changing may result in eventual erosion of influence or service efficiency and effectiveness, at least that erosion is gradual.

For many professionals and allied staff, precedent is a valuable guide because it defines a safe, if narrow, path. Planners would do well to cite precedent and previous experience in their efforts to induce change. In many agencies, following well-established procedures is more important then accomplishing the stated aims of the agency. This insularity reinforces inflexibility and sometimes results in a ritualism imbued with an almost fundamentalist quality.

Newer organizations are sometimes more apt to take risks. Frequently, as agencies grow older, they institutionalize their early innovations. They establish procedures and formalize rules to ensure predictable behavior and to consolidate whatever gains they may have made. Staff become increasingly concerned with the survival and growth of the organization rather than with finding new, more effective means to reach goals. While new staff people, like some organizations, tend to be more innovative than those with established positions, this is not always the case. Many well-established agencies continue to innovate and seek creative solutions to emerging problems. Unfortunately, this is more the exception than the rule.

There are, of course, other obstacles to change, some of them inherent in the system and rather insidious. An agency may agree to the need for change, but be unable to mobilize necessary resources. At times, resources are rendered inadequate by overly rapid expansion, or by an agency's assumption of commitments beyond its capacity to fulfill. Some agencies are limited by lack of access to new ideas and new technologies.

In addition to resource limitations, there sometimes are sunken costs that limit an agency's ability to move from the status quo. Investment in equipment as in a medical clinic, or in certain kinds of staffs, such as those with specialized training who have become tenured employees, represents commitment to previous conceptions of mission. This investment makes adaptation to new circumstances almost impossible.

Agencies may also accumulate obligations and commitments that constrain their behavior. Over the years, they may have made promises to other service agencies, to consumers, and to providers. The expectations of others may make it extraordinarily difficult for agencies to change their procedures, their programs, or their services without endangering existing relationships. Needless to say, when such relationships are endangered, an organization is less likely to achieve its goals, and its very existence may be threatened.

Since changing too many things at once may destroy a working system, it is important to be clear about those issues that are most important and those practices, procedures, or policies that are in greatest need of changes. Even those who advocate drastic and sweeping changes must tolerate continuation of many established practices. In every organization there must be an accommodation between the proponents of change and the guardians of tradition. What may seem a massive and sudden change to one may seem minor and insignificant to the other.

MATCHING PUBLICS

If this is true within the organization, it may be even more true in the relationships between internal and external publics. The pressure to innovate may come from an organized consumer effort, from a small group within the staff, or from a funding agency. Because any new service program or resource development effort is likely to require some collaboration among elements in each of the organization's publics, careful matching in terms of functional, psychographic, demographic, and geographic characteristics may be necessary. The Pittsburgh Community Fund is hardly likely to finance a program in Cleveland (geographic). An Area Agency on Aging is not likely to fund a pregnancy prevention center for young teens (demographic). A tutorial service for developmentally disabled children is not likely to seek funds from the municipal housing authorities (functional). These examples may seem so obvious as to be hardly worth mentioning. What may not be so obvious is the importance of properly matching psychographic characteristics. For example, consider how important it might be to present your case for program expansion to a funding source on the basis of the characteristics of your staff and the extensiveness of volunteer involvement. What must you say about personnel that will be most appealing to a potential funder? To potential clients?

Will volunteers with certain psychographic characteristics be induced to work on behalf of an agency perceived to serve clients with different characteristics? Middle-income volunteers might be induced to raise funds on behalf of the deserving poor, for example, those who have been victimized by the economy; they may not be willing to work as hard for consum-

ers who are perceived as shiftless, unmotivated, or unresponsive. They might be even less motivated to work on behalf of
persons who are geographically distant, although this is not
necessarily the case. Geographic distance and the mystique
attached to it may be a factor in generating large contributions—witness the various Vietnam relief efforts of the late
1970s and the ongoing support for Israel by American Jews.

Paid staff, too, will require certain characteristics to work
with volunteers, with funders, and with consumer groups. The
characteristics required to work with one set of publics may
not be adequate to work with another. For example, in the
hospice case, physicians were found more effective than others
in negotiating support and referrals from hospitals. Influential
older persons were effective in generating grants from the area
agency, particularly when they could back up the request with
evidence of competent professional personnel at the hospice.
Persons who had themselves made use of the hospice were
among the most effective solicitors in a communitywide telephone campaign.

Just as some publics will be drawn to each other—for example, a government funding source may be drawn to an agency
that has demonstrated extensive local support from the voluntary and private sectors—others may be turned off by the
presence of certain characteristics or by their absence. "You've
got only two Hispanics on your staff of 33, and not a single
resident from the barrio on your board. How can you expect
to understand us? Why should we come to you for service?"
"We cannot approve your request for funding. Although we
appreciate the desirability of community involvement in the
self-help process, the regulations governing allocation of funds
through grants and contracts require evidence of professional
competence in the delivery of services. Should you decide to
reapply in the future, you might consider . . ."

Your organization and your programs, it seems, have no
place in the concerns of these publics. But don't be discouraged.
In the next chapter, we'll explore ways of increasing the interdependence between your organization and its key publics.

REVIEW

To be marketable, your organization and its programs must be properly positioned. Positioning requires being in the right place at the right time and having the capacity to respond to opportunities when they present themselves, or to make those opportunities. Opportunities for program development and expansion depend on relationships with various publics. Input publics provide the organization with the resources it needs to survive and to develop and deliver its products. An effective resource strategy requires development and orchestration of many resources and from many suppliers.

Output publics include the direct and indirect consumers of an organization's products. These may be individual clients, other organizations that receive intelligence or referrals from your organization, and others who transform your outputs into their inputs. Unlike input and output publics that are external to the organization, throughput publics are internal. They include the staff, volunteers, and others who are involved in the transformation of resources into outputs through the agency's various services and programs.

Together, these publics make up the organization's markets. Markets can be segmented such that particular elements within it can be targeted for recruitment, change, service, and so on. Segmentation can be based on geographic, functional, demographic, or psychographic distinctions. The ability of an organization to reach out to consumer publics may have considerable impact on its effectiveness in reaching supplier publics and vice versa. Frequently, its capacity is based on the skill, commitment, and knowledge of its staff and volunteers.

Any of these publics are potential partners of your agency. To the extent that these partners see advantages to themselves of being linked to your organization, they are likely to invest in those relationships.

Unfortunately, the interests of these partners are not always clear to those publics on which your program or organization may be dependent. The price that people may be required to pay may seem greater than the potential benefits. This is as true for agency staff, who may perceive change as psychologically, socially, and professionally not worth the risk, as it is of funders and potential consumers.

SUGGESTIONS FOR FURTHER READING

Kotler, Philip (1982). *Marketing for nonprofit organizations* (2nd ed.). Englewood Cliffs, NJ: Prentice-Hall.
   Clear and straightforward discussion of marketing methods, market analysis, product decisions, and the establishment of a marketing organization within a nonprofit organization.
Lauffer, Armand (1982). *Assessment tools.* Beverly Hills, CA: Sage.
   Seven assessment tools are discussed: ecomaping; force-field analysis, the nominal group technique, Delphi, photography, gaming, and task analysis. Instructions are given for their use in here-and-now, anticipatory, and normative assessment.
Lauffer, Armand (1982). *Getting the resources you need.* Beverly Hills, CA: Sage.
   Focuses on getting the right mix of people, program, and strategic resources, including extensive treatment of interorganizational relationships.
Lauffer, Armand (1984). *Strategic marketing.* New York: Free Press.
   An introduction to the procedures used in making your agency and its products more marketable. Includes chapters on working with each of the organization's publics; on price, place, promotions, and product design strategies; and on the conduct of marketing audits.

CHAPTER 3

Being in the Right Place at the Right Time

VIGNETTE 3:
OUR PLACE IS THE NEIGHBORHOOD

Our business is making others successful. In a way, that's what we've always done. When we started off back in the early 50s, we were a group work agency, had street-corner workers spread out in every neighborhood in the inner city. Times change, and so have we.

By the mid-60s we were actively involved in organizing neighborhood block clubs and civil rights groups. Our base in the neighborhoods made us the natural agency to come to when the feds wanted to test out a model community mental health center. We established the first one in the state, even though we had no experience in the mental health field. But we did have dozens of links with other social and health agencies in the catchment area. We built on those.

In the Model Cities era, the mayor contracted with us to manage all the social service programs in the city's public housing projects. The neighborhood links stood us in good stead again. When revenue sharing was instituted in Nixon's time, we got our share; and so did the clients we represented. Later we ran a neighborhood-based CETA training program.

Now that the Community Development Block Grant programs are in operation, we provide the technical assistance for the CDBG to neighborhood groups who need planning assistance, help with the development of proposals, and so on.

For the past couple of years, we've been organizing group homes and halfway houses for former prisoners, mental patients, and the developmentally disabled. It's no easy task, but we're trusted in many neighborhoods. We can build on previous relationships as well as on our mental health experiences.

Believe it or not, even though at some times almost 95 percent of our funds come from government sources, we still operate as a voluntary agency; still get a regular budget from the United Way. And we get other contributions from churches and service clubs who see us as a first line of defense wherever a neighborhood finds itself under attack.

We've changed plenty over the years, but we never left our neighborhood roots. Our base is in the neighborhoods and we never turned our backs on people in need or on the agencies that can help them and upon whom we depend. So when a number of gangs started organizing around the school yards last year, we were there. And so were several funding sources, ready to help us do the job.

The experience described above is unusual. It should not be. Too many social agencies find themselves poorly positioned to take advantage of new opportunities or to shift gears when one or another source of support disappears. Being in the right place at the right time requires knowing where your organization fits into the scheme of things. "They destroyed us," the director of a legal aid clinic for the poor told me. "We were just too successful for them, so they cut our funds once, twice, and the third time we were out." He and his agency did strike out, but not because the pitches were not coming where they should. They struck out because they were too far off base.

Knowing the scheme of things does not mean accepting things as they are, but it does require an understanding of what is possible and a good handle on what is desirable. And what is desirable, as we discovered in Chapter 2, may be quite different for different publics.

FINDING YOUR PLACE AMONG VARIOUS PUBLICS

The legal aid clinic mentioned above struck out because its staff was not able to respond properly to changes in the funding environment and in public perceptions of what services should be provided to what populations. Moreover, its sources of funding were limited to a single government agency, with only a trickle of support from individuals. The neighborhood agency, on the other hand, had over the years established relationships with many funding sources and had shifted its programs into new areas as needs emerged and sources of support became available.

When we look a bit closer, we also discover that the neighborhood agency had established a wide variety of linkages with other agencies in the community. These included referrals, case-management arrangements, joint projects, and others. The agency saw itself as an integral part of the community. The staff of the legal aid clinic, on the other hand, saw itself in an adversary role. "We were riding high," the director confided, "as long as the bucks were coming in. We had a good service going. And we had good relationships with people in the community; the disadvantaged people who needed our help. Sure, we antagonized some folks; took on the public welfare system and some of the big law firms; even took on the mayor's office. But that was our job. We had clients to serve and we served them well." Perhaps. There is clearly a need for legal aid for the poor. And adversary tactics are frequently appropriate and necessary. But an organization is not going to be in business for long unless it has enough support for its activities to overcome whatever opposition or apathy it may encounter from other sources.

It is not sufficient to decide who your consumers will be, who will supply the necessary resources, or who will cooperate with your organization in providing the planned-for services. Unless others agree that your organization has a legitimate claim over a particular domain, the organization is not likely to be successful in carving out a particular niche of its own. There will need to be agreement that your organization has the capacity to provide needed services, that those services are in fact needed and are likely to produce desired results, that the consumers you intend to serve are deserving and in need, and that your organization is a worthy and dependable partner in the delivery of services. Incidentally, the same considerations apply when you try to carve out a niche for your program or project in your own organization.

INTERAGENCY EXCHANGES

The kind of commitment you can expect from various publics will depend on the stake they have in your organization's success. And that stake is likely to be increased by the extent to which that success is translated into their own success. Let me explain. In order to discharge its mandate, a federal agency may be as interested in finding the right local service organization to fund as your organization is in getting the cash it needs to operate. A corporation is likely to see its contribution to your organization as effective public relations and perhaps as a way of maximizing profits. As we will see in Chapter 8, some insurance companies have funded local neighborhood organizations in hopes of stabilizing those neighborhoods, and in so doing have reduced the numbers of claims for thefts, accidents, or health benefits.

Other social agencies, too, may perceive your organization as central to its ability to perform essential tasks. For example, when hospitals or private physicians refer patients to a hospice, they may view the hospice as an output public, whereas the hospice may view the referral organizations as input publics. Each party to the exchange may perceive the relationship as a way of better serving a mutual client. A referring physician may see the hospice as a resource to be used in his or her practice, a resource that enhances that practice and with it his or her professional reputation and repertoire. The hospice may perceive the physician as an important source of information and legitimacy; its staff and volunteers may invest in that relationship accordingly.

One form of exchange, such as referrals, may lead to a variety of others. The neighborhood service agency discussed earlier built its programs around this notion:

We've been able to stay in business this long not just because people who live in the neighborhoods trust us. It's because the other agencies trust us. We do more than exchange clients. We work together to solve neighborhood problems. The schools know who we are because we helped them set up a tutorial program. So do the police. Our work with the kids in gangs takes the pressure off them. And so has our work in the housing projects, and with ex-offenders, and with people on drugs. In the past, if we knew funds were available from some source that we felt others could do better with than us, we sat down with them and helped work out a proposal. We've done a lot of joint promotional stuff and politicked together at city hall. The result is that hardly anything happens in the inner city that we are not somehow connected with. And if we are involved, others feel the project has a better chance of success.

Some years ago, I was engaged in an evaluation of this agency's programs. I found that its staff members were involved in at least 25 different kinds of exchanges with other service agencies. These are described briefly below. Let's call the agency the All Neighborhood Center, referred to as ANC in the descriptions. Look them over. Think about which of these "linking mechanisms" are currently used by your organization, and which ones might help to secure its place among other service providers in your community.

Case conference: Staff from ANC and other agencies discuss the needs of clients they have in common, informally and as needed.

Case consultation: Staff at other agencies ask advice from staff at ANC regarding the needs of particular clients.

Case management: Staff at ANC are given responsibility for coordinating the services provided by several agencies to meet the needs of particular clients.

Client team: Staff from ANC and two or more agencies coordinate services to meet the needs of mutual clients through continuous and systematic interaction.

Co-location: ANC and other agencies place staff in a given location—coordination of activities is optional.

Cross-referrals: ANC and other local agencies regularly refer clients back and forth, keeping track of their capabilities for providing services and monitoring the effectiveness of the referral process in meeting client needs.

Information clearinghouse: ANC staff at one location have responsibility for collection, classification, and distribution of information to several agencies (on labor market conditions, job openings, client services available, and so on).

Interorganizational consultation and technical assistance: Experts from ANC provide consultation or technical assistance to other organizations in return for similar or other benefit.

Joint budgeting: Programs sponsored by ANC coordinate the development of their annual budgets with other agencies so as to take into account how each agency's budgetary decisions affect the budgets of the others.

Joint community needs assessment or special studies: Services cooperate on the gathering and analysis of information on community needs under ANC coordination.

Joint data gathering or management information system: Collaborative efforts are made to gather data on client populations, resource capacities, or other areas of concern (can be manual or computer based); data are accessible to those designated.

Joint fund raising: ANC and other organizations cooperate in funding drives, in establishing of endowment funds, and in securing grants or contracts.

Joint funding (allocation): Together with several organizations, ANC contributes dollars or in-kind resources for the funding of a collaborative project or for the setting up of an independent program.

Joint intake, screening, diagnosis: Together with other agencies, ANC develops a common system of processing new clients and diagnosing their needs.

Joint program design: Several agencies unite their efforts to plan a new program.

Joint program evaluation: Several agencies unite their efforts with ANC to evaluate the effectiveness of an effort, particularly when the accomplishment of one agency's program goals is dependent on what another organization does.

Joint program operation: Several agencies unite their efforts in the implementation of a program under ANC's leadership.

Joint public relations, news releases, and community education: ANC and other organizations join efforts, on behalf of a client population or their own resource needs, in educating the public or raising critical consciousness.

Joint standards and guidelines: Jointly arrived at or agreed-upon practice standards, personnel standards, or action guidelines are used by ANC and other mental health service agencies.

Joint training and staff development: ANC and other local agencies cooperate in training and development by cosponsoring events, sharing successful programs, or trading expertise.

Loaner staff: Staff from ANC are assigned to work (temporarily) under the direct supervision of another agency to carry out activities for that agency.

Purchase of services: Another agency pays for specific services from ANC (such as outreach, intake, transportation, diagnostic services).

Sharing facilities or equipment: Permanent or ad hoc exchange is arranged for facilities such as meeting rooms, offices, and libraries) and equipment (such as word processors, microcomputers, printing equipment, and audiovisual equipment).

Staff outstationing: Staff from ANC are assigned to do their work in the facilities of another agency—coordination is necessary.

Standardizing procedures: Several agencies use the same procedures as ANC to respond to particular client needs.

In Exercise 3.1, I have regrouped these "linking mechanisms" into four categories; (A) those that are aimed primarily at meeting immediate client needs; (B) those that deal with agency personnel issues; (C) those that deal with the gathering, exchange, and dissemination of information; and (D) those that integrate the programs and administration of several agencies. Look it over, read the instructions, and complete the exercise.

EXERCISES 3.1 AND 3.2
INVENTORY OF POTENTIALLY USEFUL
LINKING MECHANISMS

(1) Using the inventory of linking mechanisms (Exercise 3.1), consider all the possible linking mechanisms between service organizations. Check all those that your organization currently uses with one or more other service providers, and add others if they apply.

(2) In a different color, circle those numbers that require more work and check those that are not currently in use but should be.

(3) On the Linking Mechanism Worksheet that follows (Exercise 3.2) list all the linking mechanisms operating between your organization and another particular service provider. What could be done to increase the range of linkages? How might these increase your organization's marketability with other input and output publics? To what extent might it reduce your need for funds or increase your access to them?

We will be referring to these notes later on.

On completion of this exercise, you will have located the place of other service providers in your agency's "organization set." This is a term that sociologists sometimes use to identify those organizations that shape an agency's behaviors. The term is drawn from the concept of role/role-set behavior in which a role incumbent's behavior is shaped by the expectations of other role performers whose actions are essential to appropriate performance of the first incumbent's responsibilities. It is not as complicated as it all seems. A stage actor's performance is often shaped in part by the performance of other actors and by members of the audience. A new kid on the block is soon led to know what is expected of him. As children become teens and then young adults, they let their parents know what they now expect parenting behavior to be. A new teacher will soon learn what the norms regarding homework and examinations are, from other members of the instructional staff and from students in the classroom. Although role performers have their own ideas of what behavior may be appropriate, if those ideas are too far out of sync with those of members in the role set, there is likely to be strain, often leading to conflict and the breakdown of smooth working relationships. The same is true

Exercise 3.1
INVENTORY OF POTENTIALLY USEFUL LINKING MECHANISMS

A. MEETING IMMEDIATE CLIENT NEEDS

___ 1. Cross-Referrals
___ 2. Case Consultation
___ 3. Case Conferences
___ 4. Client Teams
___ 5. Case Management
___ 6. Joint Intake, Screening, Diagnosis
___ 7. Case Management by One Agency
___ 8. _____
___ 9. _____
___ 10. _____

B. MEETING AGENCY PERSONNEL NEEDS

___ 1. Staff Outstationing
___ 2. Co-Location of Staff
___ 3. Loaner Staff Arrangements
___ 4. Joint Training and Staff Development
___ 5. _____
___ 6. _____
___ 7. _____

C. GATHERING, EXCHANGING, AND DISSEMINATING INFORMATION

___ 1. Joint Community Needs Assessment or Special Studies
___ 2. Information Clearinghouse
___ 3. Joint Data Gathering or Management Information System
___ 4. Joint Program Evaluation
___ 5. Interorganizational Consultation or Technical Assistance
___ 6. Joint Public Relations, News Releases, and Community Education
___ 7. _____
___ 8. _____
___ 9. _____

D. INTEGRATING PROGRAMS AND ADMINISTRATION

___ 1. Joint Standards and/or Guidelines
___ 2. Sharing Facilities and/or Equipment
___ 3. Joint Program Design
___ 4. Joint Program Operation
___ 5. Purchases of Service
___ 6. Joint Budgeting
___ 7. Joint Fund-Raising
___ 8. Joint Funding (Allocation)
___ 9. Standardized Procedures
___ 10. _____
___ 11. _____
___ 12. _____

Exercise 3.2
LINKING MECHANISM WORKSHEET

Name another service organization with which your organization is regularly involved: _____
List the range of linkages currently in place between them.

_____   _____
_____   _____
_____   _____
_____   _____

What others might be added? Add them in a different color.
How might you induce the other organization to engage in a wider variety of exchanges with yours?

What changes in the way in which your internal publics work might be necessary? What inducements are necessary? What kinds of supports?

What are the implications for funding, for other resources, and for your relationships to various resource suppliers?

What are the implications for your relationship to current consumers or to potential consumer publics?

between organizations. Entering into an exchange relationship with another agency may increase an organization's resources and improve its services, but it also increases its obligations to those organizations.

By defining the place of other organizations in our organization's "set," we are also defining our place in their organization sets. What is true between one agency and other service providers is also true between service providers and funders, legitimating bodies, consumer publics, and so on. Look over the inventory once again. Which of these linking mechanisms apply to your organization's relationships to a funding source? To a consumer population? To a legitimating body? What other linking mechanisms exist between your organization and theirs?

Can you think of an example of a linking mechanism that brings each of these types of publics together? Here are a couple of examples: (1) a housing *task force* links the Area Agency on Aging (funder) with staff of several agencies, including the Senior Citizen's Center with which you may be affiliated (service provider), influential citizens from the local community (general public) and the mayor's office (auspice provider or legitimator), and representatives of the area's elderly (consumers); (2) a *fund raising campaign* for the Handicappers' Workshop (service provider) includes members of the agency's board (legitimators), members of several foundation boards and the United Way trustees (potential funders), representatives of local agencies with which the Workshop is already involved in a number of exchanges, former clients, and other handicapped individuals (consumers).

WHAT IS EXCHANGED

Any of the linking mechanisms discussed are likely to remain in effect so long as they are perceived to be functional by those who are the parties to them. By "functional," I mean that they produce benefits to each of the parties; benefits that are perceived to outweigh the costs involved. For example, in a "purchase of service agreement," the agency purchasing the service may benefit by reducing the drain on its personnel caused by having to duplicate and conduct the service purchased, providing services in local communities that are more proximate to where clients live, and may be fulfilling its mandate under the law at a relatively low cost.

The agency whose services have been purchased benefits through the influx of funds that make it possible to operate, to keep staff employed, and to provide those services that are consistant with its mission and mandate. But there are costs as well. The supplier organization may be unable or unwilling to impose standards on the service agency if it is dependent on that agency for the services it provides. By funding one organization, it is limited in its capacity to fund others. The amount of time spent in monitoring and overseeing the work of its service providers may be uncomfortable and unpleasant for its staff. The service agency may also view this monitoring as unpleasant. Moreover, it may find itself dealing with clients it is unprepared to serve properly at a cost that exceeds the amount provided for in the contract.

Exchange relationships between organizations, whether voluntary or mandated by law, are likely to remain in effect only as long as the parties to it view the benefits as outweighing the costs in the short or the long run. "We put a lot of bucks into the Urban League," a United Way planner told me, "without seeing much payoff over a number of years. But then we are not interested in immediate payoffs. We're here to help the community grow and develop over the long haul. The Urban League is now one of the finest in the country. It involves not only all segments of the Black community, but has established effective links with business and industrial interests throughout the state. We used to supply it with 80 percent of its budget. Now our funds hardly account for 5 percent. I call that a success story . . . not because we're saving money, but because the community is being better served and we had something to do with it."

Clearly, one of the benefits involved in an exchange relationship may be the satisfaction that the persons who are partners to it have in accomplishing an objective. There may also be intrinsic rewards in the relationship itself. "Sometimes I am not sure we help our clients all that much," explains a school psychologist, "but I wouldn't give up our Wednesday afternoon case conferences for anything. I find it one of the most stimulating professional experiences I've ever had."

There are other benefits to association as well. Some years back, I was approached by the new vice president of a foundation with the request that I submit a proposal to train a leadership cadre to be selected from among practitioners in a particular field of service of concern to the foundation. On the surface of things, the foundation was looking for expertise and was willing to pay for it to get a particular job done. But when one dug a bit below the surface, it was possible to identify some other reasons for the request. I happen to work at a prestigious university, and the involvement of the University of Michigan in the project was likely to confer some prestige on the foundation, which was relatively new to the field of service it had selected to try to influence. The new vice president needed some quick show of movement, and involving a major university was important in the consolidation of his position within the foundation. Our mutual understanding of these motivations increased our ability to negotiate a contract and a relationship with which both parties to the exchange were happy. Incidentally, it did not hurt my career, either, to get the grant—a point not missed by the foundation.

Some years later, I approached the same foundation with a proposal for another project. I was given a polite ear, but not much more. By now the foundation had established itself in the field and had other agendas, of which we were not a part. Our relations continue to be cordial, and there is much respect between the actors representing each organization, but the relationship is distant—on hold, so to speak.

TIMING

Clearly, the initial relationship was a matter of timing. We were in an important place in the foundation's "organization space" when it was first starting up; we were much less important at a later date. It makes little sense to apply to a federal agency for a grant using last year's list of priorities if those priorities have shifted. Like the All Neighborhood Center described earlier, it may be necessary for your organization to shift its programs and priorities in response to changing times.

The extent of those changes must be related to a careful consideration of what such changes might imply over the long as well as the short term. I was once affiliated with an academic institution that was staffed primarily by experts in social welfare and in the delivery of social services. In response to the interests of various funding organizations, it broadened its personnel base to include economists and experts in the health services field. Like the original members of the staff, the new members were committed to knowledge development and dissemination. The result was that the institution was successful in getting new grants in the area of health services when funds for research and training in areas more traditionally associated with welfare had dried up.

But there were other consequences as well. The new members of the institution had their own ideas about where it should go, and eventually they outnumbered and outvoted those who had come earlier. Moreover, the new personnel were well connected with resource suppliers, who also had ideas about what they wanted from the institution. Within only three or four years, the organization had moved into a new set of external relationships, in effect had changed its place in both the academic world and the human services.

In both examples, an organization shifted its programs and priorities in the direction of changing opportunities. Both have grown, despite occasional setbacks or retrenchments. Neither is in danger of collapse because of funding cutbacks. In the

ANC example, the agency's commitment to the neighborhoods it served was unwavering, even if its services changed over time. In the academic example, the institution's commitment to research and knowledge development never wavered, although its fields of interest shifted considerably.

In both examples, internal publics (staff and board members or trustees) had something to do with where the organization was to seek external support. Conversely, those external resource suppliers had some ideas of where to go within the organizations they wished to support for the expertise they needed or for the access they sought to that expertise. The same was true in the example of the foundation that sought out the University of Michigan to conduct a leadership development project. In all three cases, the suppliers of funds were in important places in the recipient organizations' environments. But the service providers (ANC, the unnamed academic institution, and the University of Michigan) also filled important places in the funders' environments. Understanding this point and acting on it will increase your leverage, your influence with resource suppliers.

As I will point out later, in the discussion of relationships to philanthropists and to industrial and business concerns, it is not enough to go with hat in hand to convince a potential donor of the worth of your organization and its programs, or of the needs of your clients. These concerns may have no place in that organization's space. What you must do is locate a place for your organization in the potential donor's space and make that organization aware of the benefits to be reaped through an exchange relationship with your agency.

REVIEW

Service agencies occupy "space" in the environments of other organizations and key publics, just as those publics occupy space in agencies' environments. The ability of your organization to establish mutually beneficial exchange relationships with key publics will depend on the space in their environment your organization occupies. The continuation of those relationships will depend on the extent to which the exchanges are perceived by the parties involved to produce benefits that outweigh the costs involved.

With reference to service-providing organizations, a wide variety of linking mechanisms have been identified that make it possible for each of the partners to the exchange to utilize the other as a resource of resource supplies. This increases the range of resources available, thus increasing the likelihood of improving services. It may reduce the need to duplicate such services at greater cost to the agencies involved. Establishing interagency exchanges may be a strategy for reducing your organization's dependence on funding sources while increasing its interdependence with other kinds of suppliers.

SUGGESTIONS FOR FURTHER READING

Aiken, Michael, et al. (1972). *Coordination of services for the mentally retarded.* Madison: University of Wisconsin Press.

Broskowski, Anthony, et al. (1981). *Linking health and mental health: Coordinating care in the community.* Beverly Hills, CA: Sage.

Community Life Association (1975). *Pooled funding as a method of achieving human services coordination.* Hartford, CT: Author.

Gans, Sheldon P., & Horton, Gerald T. (1975). *Integrating human services.* New York: Praeger.

Lauffer, Armand (1982). *Getting the resources you need.* Beverly Hills, CA: Sage.

Rossi, Robert, Gilmartin, Kevin J., & Dayton, Charles W. (1981). *Agencies working together.* Beverly Hills, CA: Sage.

CHAPTER *4*

From Problems
to Programs

THE TROUBLE WITH OUR FUND RAISERS . . .

> The trouble with our volunteers is that they just aren't committed enough to the agency and its programs. I'm talking about the solicitors in our fund raising campaign. If they really understood what our needs are and if they really cared, we wouldn't have such a high burnout rate.
>
> In the past, we've tried to train them. It works with some, but not with others. Some solicitors just don't know enough about kids with special needs to be able to make an intelligent pitch. Others are just inept when it comes to pouring on the pressure.

You've probably heard similar complaints. Substitute "direct service" volunteers for "fund raisers," and you are likely to hear similar complaints about their lack of commitment, knowledge, and skill. If you talk to the volunteers, they might also agree that they need to know more about the agency or how to make a proper pitch. But they are likely to complain that agency staff expect too much, or don't really know how to deal with volunteers who have other concerns in their lives as well. One of the problems with problems is that they are perceived differently by people who see them from different vantage points.

THE PROBLEM WITH PROBLEMS

Another problem with problems is that they are often phrased so as to include, within their definitions, proposed solutions. This would not be a problem if the defining process were more systematic and inclusive, and if the full range of possible solutions was explored. Although this ideal is probably never achieved, it is possible to be both systematic and inclusive. In this chapter we will examine some tools that you may find useful in your efforts to be more systematic in program design. You will find that they are applicable both to the design of a service program (for which funding and other resources may be necessary) or to a resource development program, such as a fund raising campaign, the establishment of a grantseeking capacity, or the expansion of linkages with key publics upon which your agency or service programs may be dependent.

We'll begin with an examination of the assessment process that leads to problem definition, and we will explore the implications of defining problems in different ways. Suggestions about where you might look for direction in translating problems into goals, goals into operational objectives, and objectives into programs and services will be offered.

A problem may exist in the here and now, or it may be anticipated to exist in the future unless some course of action is taken, modified, or halted. "Assessment" is a process of identifying problems as well as capacities for dealing with those problems. The problems addressed in human service agencies are generally perceived as being lodged in a *population,* in the *service-* or *resource-providing system,* or in the ways in which services and resources are *managed.* In effect, what we have is not so much a problem *with* problems as it is a problem *of* problems—the problem of how they are to be defined.

When we speak of a "population," we may be referring to individuals, an organized group, or a larger collectivity, such as all those who live in an area or all who are actual or potential consumers of an agency's services. Individuals may be resource suppliers, for example, funders, staff members or volunteers, or representatives of other organizations.

When problems are perceived as lodging in a population, they are generally defined as the result of one of the following: (1) insufficient or erroneous knowledge; (2) debilitating attitudes; or (3) lack of technical competence or personal skill. For example, potential clients may not know where to go for service. Thus lack of client participation in job training, substance abuse counseling, or family planning may be due to lack of knowledge about the availability of such services, or of what these services might provide. Some potential clients may be unaware that they have problems. Some persons may be fully aware of their problems and the availability of services, but may not know how to apply for help.

Other potential clients may be suffering from *debilitating attitudes:* the fear of facing up to a problem; the reluctance to seek help because of apathy or loss of self-confidence; the feeling that nothing will make any difference anyway; or the belief that the service providers are biased and would not understand.

Still other potential clients may not have the skill to deal with their problems or may not have acquired the ability to represent themselves adequately or to manage their ways through the service system. Clearly, service programs aimed at these people would differ from those intended to deal with the problems of insufficient knowledge or debilitating attitudes within a potential client population. The situation is addressed according to the way in which the problem is defined.

The same would be true in dealing with other types of populations or publics. Internal resistance to change or to establishment of a new service approach can be analyzed in the same way. For example, agency staff may not possess the requisite *skills* to serve a lower-income population with drug abuse problems. They may not *know* the severity of the problem or how it affects other services and programs conducted by the agency. Or they might be *biased* against certain client groups, defining them as deviants when it might be more appropriate to see them as victims.

Similar questions may be asked regarding other issues that affect staff. Does the staff's reluctance to engage in promotional activities on behalf of the agency or its clientele have its roots in lack of knowledge about the utility of promotion, lack of skill in relating to the media, or a general feeling that promotional activities are somehow beneath their dignity? Are volunteers reluctant to work with the elderly because they fear the aging process or because they are uncomfortable with their own mortality? Do volunteers need training in the skills required for solicitation of funds, or are they simply unaware of the need for their help or how to find out where their energies might be put to good use?

Officials in funding organizations such as government agencies and foundations may also be unaware of what your agency does or of the severity of the problems it is trying to address at the local level. Funders, too, can suffer from debilitating attitudes, as when they refuse to examine a request from an agency because of a bias against grassroots efforts such as those of BAT. They may not possess the skills to communicate effectively with some groups because of cultural or ideological differences and perhaps even language difficulties.

In some cases, these problems may not be serious at the moment, but shifts in public perceptions, government policies, or economic conditions are likely to increase their severity in the future. Let us turn our attention now from populations to services and resources.

A useful way to begin might be to focus on the extent to which services are (1) *available,* (2) *accessible,* and (3) *sufficient.* Sufficiency is sometimes defined in terms of *effectiveness, efficiency,* and *responsiveness.* The neighborhood service organization described in Vignette 3 (Chapter 3) was able to take on more functions when it became clear that services were needed but not *available* from other providers. Sometimes, however, services are available, but they are not *accessible.* For example, a community mental health center might close its doors at 5:00 p.m., at precisely the time most neighborhood residents get off work. Another agency might be culturally inaccessible, because the technical jargon—the language its practitioners use—is foreign to the population in need of service, or because class differences give the agency an appearance of being a foreign element imposed on the local population.

"A difference that makes no difference is no difference," Charles Pierce, a nineteenth-century American philosopher, once said. Some services are both available and accessible, but they do not have much *impact* on the lives of recipients. Others are *inefficient,* costly to both the client and the provider agency in money, time invested, and opportunities lost. Finally, too many services are *unresponsive* to the interests of various publics, conducted in such a way as to be *unaccountable* to those who should have some say in their planning, delivery, or evaluation.

Clearly, questions about these aspects of service delivery can be asked by agency staff about the resources needed to provide services. Are the needed dollars, facilities, or technical experts available? Are they accessible? Are they sufficient to get the job done? When other service agencies are defined as resources for our own agency or its clients (as was the case when we examined linking mechanisms in Chapter 3), you might find yourself asking questions about availability, accessibility, and sufficiency. You might also find yourself asking questions about knowledge, skill in establishing and maintaining linkages, and attitudes (yours and theirs).

When management issues are examined, our focus of attention might be internal to the agency itself or external to it. Internal management problems might be defined as to low productivity, poor interpersonal relationships, abuse of authority, and lack of innovation. All these are clearly related to the other problems we have been discussing. When attention is focused externally, the concerns might be with the resource development and orchestration, continuity, consistency, and comprehensiveness of services.

For example, a mental hospital might have an excellent patient rehabilitation program, but the program becomes ineffective if there is no continuity of care following discharge. An agency might have a perfectly adequate budget, supported by many sources, but may have no guarantee of the consistency of that support, that is, that it will be available a year or two from now. The *comprehensiveness* of services is the extent to which different services complement each other. Suppose a family under stress presents the following issues to an agency: the father is laid off; the mother is an alcoholic; the teenage son has had repeated brushes with the law; the twelve-year-old daughter may be suffering from a chronic disease and low self-image; and younger children are doing poorly in school. Services aimed exclusively at one or another of these problems may be ineffective unless others are dealt with at the same time.

The comprehensiveness of a service may also be measured by the extent to which different resources are available in sufficient quantity to complement each other. For example, although funds may be available to provide a given service, if the expertise required to conduct service activities is not, or if staff and volunteer energy is low, the funds may have little bearing on the agency's success. Resources must be properly orchestrated, each complementing the other, for a program to be successful. Sometimes, one resource (such as facilities and in-kind services) can be substituted for another (such as money), but if the right mix cannot be brought together in some comprehensive manner, the resultant program is likely to be less than was hoped for.

The issues mentioned above might be called *here-and-now* issues—they focus on *what is*. In *anticipatory* assessment, one asks the same kinds of questions, but the focus is on the extent to which these problems are likely to be felt in the future. For instance, one might make projections on the basis of anticipated or unanticipated changes. What might be the likely drain on existing services should unemployment double or triple in the next five years? Would one wish, then, to focus on the debilitating attitudes of our clients or on their lack of marketable skills? Or, assuming current trends and the completion of the legislation processes aimed at shifting responsibilities from the public to the private sector, and from federal to state and local jurisdictions, to what extent might one anticipate continued problems of program availability, accessibility, accountability, effectiveness, or efficiency?

The advantage of anticipatory assessment is that it permits practitioners and program planners to think ahead rather than to catch up with problems after the fact. It enables you to make decisions now that are likely to head off problems and their consequences for the populations for which your organization is mandated to provide services.

The following steps might serve as a guide for doing anticipatory assessment. Begin by examining current or anticipated laws, regulations, or policies. For example, your state mental health, corrections, and social service departments are probably well into the process of deinstitutionalization. What are the goals in terms of numbers or proportions of the population currently institutionalized that are to be returned to the community over a three-year or five-year period? Calculate the anticipated size of the legally eligible population for the period you have selected. This might be done on the basis of the figures supplied by a state agency or other available demographic data. If the information is not known, you may have to get it through interviews with knowledgeable persons. Find out what the funding sources for community-based services might be and the anticipated amounts that will be available by a given date.

Now estimate the number of persons who will be in need of various types of services—those your organization currently provides as well as those it does not. Make a comparison between this anticipated client population and the actual numbers of clients who currently receive services from your organization. Segment them according to the categories discussed earlier: geographic, demographic, functional, and psychographic.

Examine the conditions that currently prevail in response to your clients' current needs, and those that are likely to prevail in the future. These conditions may include estimates of the impact of the economy (that is, availability of jobs, availability of housing), the likelihood of consumer responsibility (for example, growth in self-help groups and other forms of networking), and interest on the part of other service organizations to serve the same populations.

Based on these estimates, is demand for your organization's programs likely to increase, decrease, or remain stable? How so? Finally, examine what you would have to do to prepare yourself and your organization for this state of affairs: increase your capability to provide certain services; reduce your efforts or the size of your operation; shift staff and resources from one program to another?

Although there are many unknowns, these are not imponderables; they can and should be thought about. Expanding, downsizing, and shifting priorities may all be in order. Your best estimates will help you determine whether a change in your fund raising and grantseeking strategy is in order.

There is yet a third approach to assessment. *Normative* assessment begins with an image of a desired state. Ask yourself what kind of services you would like to see in place three or five years from now, or what kinds of capacities you would like clients, staff members, or target populations to develop. What kind of funding pattern would you like to see in place? Begin by deciding what a minimally acceptable service program might look like, perhaps in terms of such issues as availability and accessibility. In effect, what you would be doing is developing a "competency" model that describes the desired state of affairs.

When a planning and allocating body, such as a United Fund, establishes minimum standards for service agencies, it establishes a competency model. Professional associations and accrediting bodies such as the Child Welfare League of America and the American Hospital Association do the same. For assessment purposes, designing the model is only the first step. You would then examine where the population or the service system is now in relation to the norms you have specified. You might do the same in relation to the funding pattern that would have to be operable in order to support services described. The gap between current reality and the desired state of affairs will direct you in your program development efforts. Once you have uncovered present levels of competency and compared them to the norms you desire, you would then specify your objectives and set priorities on the bases of salience (importance) and feasibility.

Once a normative model has been established, it becomes a standard against which the current reality is examined. For example, in designing a "full-service" family agency you would concern yourself with the types of services to be made available, their accessibility, effectiveness, efficiency, and so on.

The list below contains some of the key terms in this discussion. Look them over. How can they help you in defining a problem to be dealt with in your plan or proposal for change? How can they help you in a fund raising effort?

Focus of Attention	Issues to Be Addressed
populations or individuals	lack of knowledge
	lack of skill
	debilitating attitudes
services	availability
	accessibility
	effectiveness
	efficiency ⎫
	accountability ⎬ sufficiency
internal management	productivity
	interpersonal relationships
	authority
	innovation
external management	continuity
	consistency
	comprehensiveness

These terms may help you move from a broad and overly generalized definition of a problem to what planners often call "operational definitions"—definitions that serve as guides to action. This will become clear when we reexamine the complaint about unmotivated volunteers with which the chapter opened. The quote was taken from a set of notes I took several years ago, when I was in the "consultation and training business."

"Let's take some of the key terms you used," I suggested to the agency administrator with whom I was consulting. "What do you mean by 'committed enough'?"

"Well," he explained, "they don't show up at meetings, and quite a few never follow up on the solicitor cards we give them."

"Good," I responded, "Now we're moving in the right direction. What else?"

"Well, there's motivation."

"What would motivate volunteers?" I asked.

"A feeling of accomplishment, I guess," he replied, "and some recognition for a job well done."

"Now we are really getting somewhere," I told him. "We are getting at some of the components of the problem, and beginning to think of solutions."

Getting somewhere is what problem solving is all about. Properly phrased, problem statements lead to the establishment of goals and these, in turn, lead to performance objectives. Let's define these terms too.

BEING CLEAR ABOUT WHERE WE'RE GOING

Goals are broad statements of intent and purpose that both energize and legitimate a process. The 1981 edition of *Webster's New Collegiate Dictionary* defines a goal as "the end toward which effort is directed." It is the aim of that effort: the purpose of the actions taken. Goals give direction to the effort. They energize because they give participants a sense of shared purpose, a common target at which to aim. They legitimate because they explain to others the purpose of those efforts in language that conveys a social good, a general benefit or a benefit to particular populations or organizations that are considered deserving or in need.

Goals are phrased in general terms that cover relatively long time spans. For this reason, they may never be fully reached. Since they serve as energizers and legitimators, this is perfectly appropriate. It may be desirable for goals to change over time if they are to continue to energize. Like problems, goals can be stated in terms of (1) populations, (2) services or resources, and (3) management. Examples of population-oriented goals include the following:

- Graduates of the school will be committed to ongoing and continuous education and professional development.

- Community leaders will be aware of the special needs of disabled persons and will be committed to their normal integration into all aspects of community life.

- Solicitors will be motivated to attend all necessary meetings, learn to make the right pitch, and follow up on donor cards. (Is this one goal or three?)

Service-oriented goals might include the following:

- All children in need will have available to them permanent and supportive family placement.

- A 24-hour suicide and family violence prevention self-help clinic will be established to serve residents in the south central district.

. Management-oriented goals might include the following:

- A management information system will be introduced to increase access to needed information by all agency staff and collateral providers.

- Rehabilitation services will be provided in a continuous manner, and coordination mechanisms will be established with the schools, the courts, employers, and other relevant organizations.

Objectives are derived from goals. They spell out in performance terms what is intended. Objectives can be viewed as "subgoals," stops along the road to achieving a more general goal. Unlike goals phrased in general terms, the objectives are specific, time oriented, and measurable. Objectives can be phrased in terms of (1) operations, (2) activities, or (3) outcomes. For example, suppose we were to begin with the goal of establishing a 24-hour suicide and family violence prevention clinic. Here are what some of the objectives of the clinic might look like:

- *Operations objective:* Thirty volunteer staff members will be recruited, trained, and assigned to monitor telephone and walk-in operations in numbers sufficient to handle all requests for service.

- *Activity objective:* By the end of the first year, four self-help groups will have been organized to operate with minimal assistance from the agency, and between two and six others will be in various stages of development.

- *Outcome objective:* The rate of repeat suicide attempts in the south/central district will be reduced 25 percent within a twelve-month period.

Any goal statement is likely to generate a number of performance objectives. Some of these will be feasible within the limitations of the agency, its technology, and its resources. Some will not. Before moving on, try your hand at writing goal and objectives statements. These will be helpful to you when we go over the "branching tree" design model later in this chapter.

EXPLORING THE RANGE
OF PROBLEM SOLUTIONS:
INTERVENTIONS AND THEIR COMPONENTS

You are now ready to *zero* in on possible programs and the activities they comprise. An approach I have found useful in exploring all the alternatives is the use of a "branching tree." It actually begins by spreading out rather than zeroing in. The branching tree is a form of idea inventory or brainstorming on paper.

EXERCISE 4.1
WRITING STATEMENTS OF
GOALS AND OBJECTIVES

(1) Start off with a brief description (a paragraph or less) of a current or anticipated problem or a desired state of affairs. Use the conceptual terminology discussed above.

(2) Identify one goal from that description. If you began with the description of a problem, the goal can be phrased as the absence of that problem or its converse. If you began with a normative statement, the goal will be implicit within it. Write the goal in a single sentence.

Does the goal speak to populations, services, or management? Should it speak to some that are? Are different goal statements needed for each, or are some not relevant to the problem you wish to deal with or the programs you are beginning to think about? Make whatever adjustments may be needed.

Do you think it clearly spells out the direction or aim of the activities that will have to be undertaken to accomplish the goal? Is it an energizing statement? Will it serve to legitimate subsequent efforts? If not, make whatever adjustments are needed.

(3) Now derive the performance objectives from the goal statement. Remember that the objectives can be phrased in terms of operations, activities, impact, or all three. They should be specific enough to serve as the basis for monitoring or evaluating operations, activities, and outcomes; that is, they should be measurable and time specific.

It is a relatively simple procedure, although it may take quite some time to carry out. Like other rational models, it is best used to explore all of the possibilities before you decide what to do and how. It starts with problem definition, then breaks down each general problem into its component parts. For each subproblem a goal is selected, and this goal is used to generate operational objectives. There may be a number of alternative interventions (e.g., service programs) that can be used to achieve a given objective. Sometimes, several interventions in combination may be necessary. Once you have identified these alternatives, the final step is to identify the components of each intervention (i.e., what has to be done or put into place in order for it to come off). The process works somewhat as shown in Figure 4.1, below.

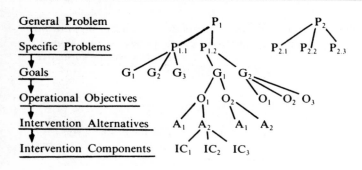

Figure 4.1 The Branching Tree Process

Space does not permit following each of the branches in the figure out to its conclusion. In looking over the example, you will find that the longest branch is $P_1 - P_{1.2}G_1O_1 - A_2 - IC_1 + IC_2 + IC_3$. Had all the branches, starting with P_1 and P_2, been carried out fully, we would have ended with several hundred intervention approaches. You will probably need a chalkboard or newsprint to complete all the branches. Use the schematic presented in Exercise 4.2 as your guide.

If you completed the exercise, you may have generated 600 or 700 alternative program or intervention components. How will you choose between them? The following judgment criteria may be useful: (1) frequency of appearance, (2) feasibility, (3) complementarity with organizational mission, (4) likelihood of contributing to objectives without negative side effects or consequences, (5) acceptability to various publics, and (6) compatibility. Let us take one at a time.

Certain program *components* tend to *appear frequently* at the ends of different branches. On one tree, for example, one might find "counseling," "outreach," "transportation," "volunteer training," or "support groups" appearing many times.

Exercise 4.2
THE BRANCHING TREE

(1) Start with one or more general problems. For example:

P_1 | Many of the elderly in Corktown have difficulty with personal management. This is especially severe with the single aged.

(2) Then break it down into its component parts; make the problem more specific in relation to targeted groups of the elderly. These specific problems might include:

$P_{1.1}$ | Nutritional Deficiencies

$P_{1.2}$ | Poor management of personal budgets.

$P_{1.3}$ | Inability to do basic housekeeping or to perform household repairs.

$P_{1.4}$ | Difficulty in getting about for purposes of shopping or getting to service providers.

(3) Use these more specific problems to establish your goals. For example, "nutritional deficiencies" might result in your determining that:

G_1 | Older people, particularly those isolated in rural areas, will be fed nutritiously.

(4) Now it is time to define your performance objectives. The following might be included:

O_1 | Eighty percent of the persons in the target area will receive information about diets and how they can manage nutritious eating programs on a limited budget.

O_2 | Prepared foods, at an affordable cost will be available close to home to 500 people by the end of the second year of the project's operation.

(5) How might these objectives be reached? Let us take the second objective. Service alternatives might include:

A_1 | Meals-on-Wheels Home Delivery.

A_2 | Congregate meal sites at local schools and churches.

A_3 | Cooperative cooking programs in conjunction with the Coop Food Buying program.

(6) Each of these requires a number of intervention components. The meals-on-wheels alternative, for example, might require:

IC_1 | Outreach and case finding of potential elderly participants.

IC_2 | Sites at which food can be prepared.

IC_3 | A nutritionist who can design menus and supervise meal preparation.

IC_4 | Volunteers for food preparation and transportation to homes.

SOURCE: Adapted from an approach developed by Yeheskel Hasenfeld.

Exercise 4.2

SCHEMATIC GUIDE FOR BRANCHING TREE PROGRAM DESIGN

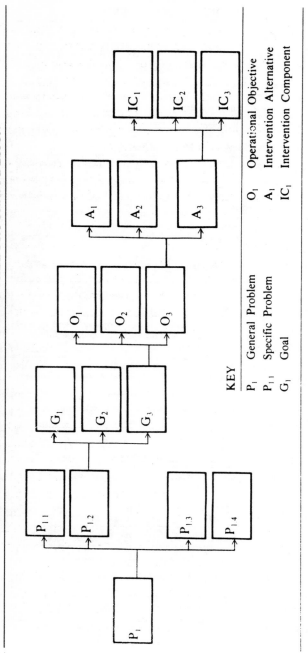

KEY

P_1	General Problem	O_1	Operational Objective
P_{11}	Specific Problem	A_1	Intervention Alternative
G_1	Goal	IC_1	Intervention Component

Using the sample track as a guide, design your own branching tree, specifying all the choices possible. Note that space limitations do not permit tracking from more than one antecedent on each component or branch below.

Any one of these components may appear at the ends of branches that have different origins. You might discover that volunteer training contributes to the conduct of several interventions, to the achievement of several objectives, perhaps even to the accomplishment of several goals and to the resolution of more than one problem. The training of volunteers will not be the only thing that needs doing, but it may contribute to the accomplishment of many objectives.

Feasibility is the likelihood that a particular program component can be put in place. How available are the needed resources of money and credit, facilities, trained or committed staff, political influence, organizational and personal time and energy, and legitimacy?

Are the program components you have tentatively selected compatible with the organization's history and sense of *mission?* Or are they such wide departures from the norm that they are likely either to generate resistance or to move the organization into new and untried paths for which it may not be ready? Are they functional for the organization? That is, will they contribute to achievement of its program missions? Its staff and board aspirations? Its need for resources and community support?

Some program components, although rated high on feasibility and frequency of appearance, may nonetheless contribute little to the achievement of *program goals* that are considered paramount. In such cases, they may divert the organization from investing its energies and other resources where they count the most. Even those that do contribute directly to the achievement of priority goals may lead to undesired side effects or have unanticipated consequences. For example, a one-time food distribution effort may generate such high demand that the agency may find itself permanently in the food business although that was never its intention. A volunteer program, once established, may place demands on the paid professional staff for support and ongoing training to such a degree that little time is left for them to do what they prefer—working directly with clients.

	1 Frequency of Appearance	2 Feasibility	3 Complementarity With Missions	4 Contribution to Objectives	5 Acceptability	6 Compatibility
High						
Somewhat						
Low or Minimal						

Figure 4.2 Program Component Decision-Making Guide

There is also the question of *acceptability*. Are the program components acceptable to various key publics—agency funders, clients, board members? If not, are they likely to generate conflict, or just indifference? Can you live with the indifference or deal with the conflict? Are other components so clearly acceptable that they will overcome disagreements over those that are not?

Finally, there is the question of the *compatibility* of one component with another. In some instances, a "meals on wheels" program for the elderly is fully compatible with a congregate meal facility. Each may serve a different population, or both may serve similar populations on different days. The two programs may complement each other through joint use of facilities, paid staff, and volunteers. But in other situations, the two may be incompatible—because of differences in the populations served, ideological disagreements on the approach used, competition between the two for scarce resources, or other reasons. A fund raising campaign aimed at soliciting large donations from a very few wealthy and prestigious people may be incompatible with a large-scale grassroots effort that includes generating small donations through raffles, bake sales, walkathons, and so on.

The chart presented in Figure 4.2 will be helpful in making decisions about intervention components. For example, on completion of the branching tree, should you find a component rarely present and judge it to be infeasible and in any case not complementary to the organization's missions, you might eliminate it from consideration. If an item is rated high on all or almost all the variables, you might consider it seriously. When an item scores high on some variables and none or minimal on others, more careful examination will be necessary. For example, an outreach program aimed at teen substance abusers may be right on target (high) on contributions to objectives and on feasibility. But it may be low on complementarity and on acceptability to some of the organization's constituencies. What to do? At this point there is no formula. Personal value judgments, staff and board preferences, the availability of funds and other resources—all these may lead to a go or no go decision.

BUILDING ON THE
EXPERIENCES OF OTHERS

The branching tree exercise begins almost as if your program could be designed on a *tabula rasa*. This is both its advantage and its disadvantage. There is, of course, no tabula rasa. Precedent, experience, and convention will dictate what problems you will address, how you will address them, the goals you will set, and the programs you will put into place. The variables discussed in reference to the program component decision-making guide (see Figure 4.2) may, in some cases, predetermine your programs and related activities. "The best we can do," an experienced administrator recently told me, "is tinker around the edges, making improvements here and there." That may or may not be true. It is true that the choices made are likely to be better if the full range of alternatives has been explored. It is likely to be based on an even sounder foundation if it also includes the consideration of successful approaches used elsewhere.

There are many places to go for information. In the chapters on grantsmanship, proposal writing, and fund raising, I will be recommending a wide range of consultant organizations and written materials that you may find helpful. For the moment, I want to keep the discussion to sources of information on service programs.

Funders often know about projects similar to yours. Federal agencies, for example, often publish abstracts or summaries of recently funded projects. The Rehabilitation Services Administration sends one-page abstracts on the projects it funded in the previous year along with an application kit for currently available grants. The Community Mental Health Centers Branch of the National Institute of Mental Health periodically abstracts descriptions of projects it has funded and publishes them in a summary book. The National Clearinghouse on Aging is funded by the Administration on Aging to disseminate information on selected projects that have been identified in each state as being worthy of emulation. The Children's Bureau has funded a network of national and regional centers to promote innovation in child welfare. It sponsors a national center at the University of Michigan School of Social Work that disseminates information on request.

Up-to-date information is often found in the professional literature—the journals and periodicals published in your field. National associations conduct local, state, regional, and national meetings at which presentations on innovative and successful projects are reported. Large foundations and companies in the private sector frequently publish reports on demonstration projects they have funded and that they feel should be duplicated; these projects may accrue prestige to the funder. Local agencies often learn about projects in other localities by contacting the national organizations with which they are affiliated.

Project SHARE, located at 5600 Fishers Lane, Rockville, Maryland 20852, is a good source of information on community development and social action projects. It publishes monographs on practice, annotated bibliographies, and "fugitive" literature—reports on programs and projects that may appear only in the annual reports of the sponsoring organizations.

Why reinvent the wheel if you can learn from someone else's experience? Why not build on that experience, improve on it, or modify it to your particular objectives and to your local circumstances?

FROM SERVICE PROGRAMS TO RESOURCE DEVELOPMENT PROGRAMS

You will recall that "program" has been defined here as a patterned and purposeful sequence of events and activities. The same approach that we have explored for design of a service program is applicable to the design of a fund raising program, a promotional campaign, or any other resource development effort.

This will become clearer as you progress through the next six chapters, in which the focus will be directly on tapping resources from government, foundation, private and voluntary sector, and general community sources.

REVIEW

Problems are sometimes so ill defined as to be relatively useless in determining goals or specifying objectives. One approach to this problem with problems is to be clear about your focus of attention. When the focus is on individuals or populations, the issues to be addressed might include lack of knowledge or skill and the consequences of debilitating attitudes. When the focus is on resources or on services and service programs, the issues might include their availability, accessibility, effectiveness, efficiency, and accountability (or responsiveness). When the focus of attention is on internal management issues, one might address productivity, interpersonal relationships, authority, and innovation. When it is on external management, the concern may be with continuity, consistency, and comprehensiveness.

These terms can be used to define problems in the present or to spell out problems that are anticipated in the future. They can also be used to specify a desired state of affairs, in effect, a competency model that spells out how individuals, services, resource orchestration, or management should function. They also provide the data and conceptual bases upon which goals can be determined. Goals are statements of intent; they point a direction in which we intend to move and they provide the legitimation for such movement. For program design purposes, goals must be broken down into performance objectives. Derived from goals, performance objectives specify the operations to be conducted, the activities that might be necessary, or the outcomes that are desired. In turn, performance objectives make it possible to explore alternative approaches to achieving them. These "intervention" approaches, as they are called here, might just as well be called "services," "political actions," or "fund raising activities," depending on the nature of the intervention comtemplated.

A branching tree model was used to explore alternatives, and these were evaluated on the basis of frequency of appearance, feasibility, complementarity, contribution to objectives, acceptability, and compatibility. While the model is a helpful way to explore a wide variety of alternatives, wherever possible, it should be used in conjunction with an examination of the experiences of others who have faced similar problems or sought comparable conditions.

SUGGESTIONS FOR FURTHER READING

Blakely, E. J. (1979). Goal setting for community development—Case of Yuba City, California. *Rural Sociology, 44*(2), 434–436.

Brody, Ralph (1982). *Problem solving: Concepts and methods for community organization.* New York: Human Sciences Press.

Craig, Dorothy (1976). *A hip pocket guide to planning and evaluation.* Austin, TX: Learning Concepts Publications.

Dale, D., & Mitigui, N. (1978). *Planning for a change.* Amherst, MA: Citizen Involvement Training Project.

Glidewell, John C. (1976). *Choice points.* Cambridge: MIT Press.

Kilmann, R., Pondy, L. R., & Slevin, D. P. (Eds.). (1976). *The management of organization design: Strategies and implementation.* New York: Elsevier North Holland.

Lauffer, Armand (1982). *Assessment tools: For practitioners, managers, and trainers.* Beverly Hills, CA: Sage.

Lauffer, Armand (1982). *Getting the resources you need.* Beverly Hills, CA: Sage.

Lauffer, Armand (1984). *Strategic marketing.* New York: Free Press.

Lippitt, R., Watson, J., & Westley, B. (1958). *The dynamics of planned change.* New York: Harcourt Brace Jovanovich.

Magee, John (1964, July/August). Decision trees for decision making. *Harvard Business Review,* pp. 126–128.

Mager, Robert (1972). *Goal analysis.* Belmont, CA: Fearon.

Neuber, Keith, with Atkins, William T., Jacobson, James A., & Reuterman, Nicholas A. (1981). *Needs assessment: A model for community planning.* Beverly Hills, CA: Sage.

Rein, Martin, & Morris, Robert (1983). Goals, structures and strategies for community change. In R. Kramer & H. Specht (Eds.), *Readings in communities organization practice.* Englewood Cliffs, NJ: Prentice-Hall.

Resnick, Hyman, & Patti, Rino (Eds.). (1980). *Change from within: Humanizing social welfare organizations.* Philadelphia: Temple University Press.

Young, R. C. (1966). Goals and goal setting. *Journal of the American Institute of Planners, 32,* 76–85.

Zander, Alvin (1962). Resistance to change: Its analysis and prevention. In W. G. Bennis, K. D. Benne, & R. Chin (Eds.), *The planning of change: Readings in applied behavioral sciences.* New York: Holt, Rinehart & Winston.

CHAPTER 5

The Bucks Start Here:
Seeking Government Funds

**VIGNETTE 4: WHEN YOU'RE PLAYING
THE FUNDING GAME,
KNOW THE FUNDER'S RULES!**

*Here's the way I look at it: Why write a proposal unless you know
in advance that you're likely to get it funded? Yes, I know there are
a lot of contingencies in this game. But it's just that; it's a game.
And like any game, it requires a win strategy. You sometimes lose,
but it's not because you made the wrong moves. It's because there
were certain things beyond your control. You can't always beat the
odds, but you can make them more in your favor.*

*I've got a few simple rules of thumb. The first is to make sure you
know what the funder wants or how to get him or her to want what
you want. That requires lots of contact with the funder long before
you write your final proposal. First of all, it requires finding out
who is the right person to talk to. Pick up the catalogue of Domestic
Federal Assistance. Check on the right program. And if you can, get
a federal telephone directory to find out who the administrative officer is in a certain granting program. If you don't have the directory,
call the phone number in the catalogue, or write to find out who the
grants officer is for the program you are interested in. In psyching
out government agencies, I find that picking up the telephone and
calling the right person may be all that's needed to establish a contact. Sometimes, though, it's useful to have an introduction arranged
by a friend who has had a project funded by the agency.*

I've sometimes gone directly to Washington just so I might meet an official I'm anxious to build a relationship with. I've found govern- ment people pretty open to a drop-in visit or a telephone call from people in the community. Of course, drop-ins are a little risky if their schedules are tight. But still, even when money is tight the feds are pretty generally happy to see one of us community types . . . if we know what we are about. Sitting off there in Washington or in a regional office can mean living in a cut-off and rarefied atmosphere. Those people need the infusion of information and insight and, I might add, a feeling of support and understanding from people out in the real world. Most of the feds realize that if they talk only to themselves, they'll fall into a rut. They're thankful to have contacts around the country. Besides, if you can give them a few facts about what kind of impact their programs are having, they use those facts as ammunition in their negotiations with higher-ups in the bureau- cracy or in contacts with legislators and legislative committee staff.

Going on a "fishing" expedition does not mean going unprepared. For example, a couple of years back, I went to talk to an official of the Administration on Aging. I knew this guy was interested in self- help programs. I also knew he had a bad back. I commiserated with him over lunch about his bad back and told him I had one, too. Pretty soon we got onto home remedies, evaluations of a local sur- geon we both had some dealings with, and so on. This gave me an opening to mention the use of a lay service network. He'd never heard the term before, but he caught on real fast. He told me about how he'd been part of lots of lay networks himself.

The problem as he saw it was that some people don't have access to other people who could help them. "That's right," I agreed, "espe- cially elderly people. The older people are, the fewer contacts they have. Their friends move away, die, or become immobilized. It's just because they don't have enough family, friends, or neighbors who can help them that they're in particular need of professionalized services. But the professional services are expensive. There ought to be some way in which we can rationalize funding the lay service net- work in order to increase potential for self-help at the community level and reduce the drain on agency services."

Well, the guy really bit the hook on that one. Not too much later, after several preliminary drafts of a proposal, he told me to go ahead and submit the final one. Notice, I said after *the submission of preliminary proposals. I wasn't going to submit a final proposal until I knew that this was what he wanted and that he'd back us up with his review panel.*

If I can avoid it, I never submit a final proposal without first getting comments on one or more preliminary drafts. I keep those preliminary drafts short, concise, and to the point. I figure that if the feds want me to add more, they'll tell me. After all, if I fill a proposal full of garbage, they're not going to be willing to read it. So I let them tell me if they feel I've left things out.

And then I write that proposal the way the funder thinks it should be written. Usually I will ask how they want it. Sometimes a funder will say that I'm too academic in what I've written, that I should use simpler language and more illustrations. Sometimes they'll tell me that I'm too folksy, and I should make it more sophisticated in tone. Whatever they suggest, that's the way I write it.

Of course, things aren't always that easy. Sometimes you're going along real well when the funder hits you with a bombshell. Too many proposals are being submitted and you're competing with a lot of other people for a large share of a very small pot. Maybe there's been a cut in the appropriation and the funder will ask you if you can make do with $30,000 instead of the $80,000 you'd asked for. A time like that is when I have to make some hard decisions. Do I let it go at that and take my chances, or do I bring in the rest of the troops? Once when a funder called me to say there would be less money available for my project than she had anticipated, I pulled out a game plan that was a little bit risky.

First I was silent on the phone for about a minute and a half. This gave me a chance to collect my thoughts, and it worried the woman on the other end of the line. Then I told her I'd been silent because I knew how difficult it must have been for her to call me, and how aware I was of her own commitment to the program. I wanted her to know that I understood how she felt. Then I told her how I felt. I mentioned that, based on our previous contacts, I'd made certain promises to local people. Several agencies were ready to get involved in the cooperative venture. I spoke of how a lot of our local influentials were going to feel about the project's being sliced down to one-third of our request. "What should I tell people?" I asked. I was anxious for her to know that I was going to be talking to our local people, and that she might get some pressure from them. I didn't want it to come as a surprise.

"Tell them what you think you have to tell them," she told me, "and I'll see what I can do from here." I thanked her for calling. Immediately I called the chairman of my board. We figured out which local people had the most influence with our congressman and with people in H.H.S. [Department of Health and Human Services]. We had these people place calls to Washington, telling them how disappointed people were at the cut in funds and how much local support there was for the project.

Two days later, I got a call from my friend in Washington. "You sure have a lot of people on your side," she said. "Submit a new budget. This time cut it by about 25 percent. We can give you that much." Well, that was better than cutting it by two-thirds. I thanked her and said I was sorry if some of our local people had gotten too excited about the cut and put the pressure on. "Well, there has been some pressure," she admitted. I made a note to do something for her later on. A couple of weeks later, I made sure that her superior got word from some of our local influentials about how helpful they thought she'd been. Six months later, knowing I'd have other dealings with her, I wrote a letter thanking her for having done something else for us and sent a copy to her supervisor. Those little gestures help.

Of course, you've got to be careful who you put the pressure on. It can backfire, especially when you use congressmen or staff. The people in the bureaucracy don't like to be pressured by the people on Capitol Hill. And people on Capitol Hill don't like to be bothered with little projects. They don't want to use up their influence on every request that comes around. You've got to know when an issue is hot, how much resistance there'll be toward what you want, and how much of a stake the congressman or senator is going to have in that particular activity or in getting the funds for his or her locality. Sometimes it's better to use a staffer in a congressional committee than a congressman. Staffers have their own lines to the bureaucracy.

Still, you want to be careful. Line up too many guns on your side, let it seem as if you're politicking a grant through instead of having it reviewed on its own merits, and you're likely to be dropped like a hot potato. What I mean is, know your funder and know what it takes to get a project through. If you've got a mismatch, you might as well know early and not bother.

One more word of advice. Remember that you are the petitioner. *You are the one asking for money. That can put you in a dependent position, not the best place to be if you want to be in control of your own destiny. Get yourself into a position where the funder needs you for something. Help the funder make a contact with somebody in another bureaucracy that you know well. Pass on some information that will be useful in his or her work. Some funders like to collect reprints. Invest a few dollars. Send reprints of articles that you know the person will be interested in. Indicate you ran across this in some of your work and that you thought it might be helpful.*

Don't ever let it seem that you're buying a gift. I make it a rule never *to take a potential funder out for lunch or a drink. Some feds are really uptight about those things. I once made the mistake of trying to buy a drink for a woman who works in the Office of Education. She nearly slapped me. First of all, it was a sexist thing to do. Second, she wanted to make sure she wasn't beholden to me for anything. It was different when I sent her a copy of a report on something our local community college had done that I knew would be of interest to her. She didn't interpret that as a personal favor but as a professional courtesy.*

You've got to know what rules the other person is playing by.

VIGNETTE 5: MATCHMAKING—
MAKING GRANT MONIES
WORK MORE EFFICIENTLY

Officially, I'm a grants officer and planner in the State Department of Mental Hygiene. The most exciting and probably the most important planning I do is the providing of technical assistance to local organizations and citizens' groups that apply for financial support. My particular area of expertise is in development of community placements. I don't view my technical assistance function narrowly. Some would disagree with me, but I feel it's not enough simply to help somebody to fill out the forms in proposal or project design. I think of my function as one of opening up possibilities—opening up

*people and agencies, as a matter of fact, to new ideas and new rela-
tionships. When I perform a technical assistance function, I think of
myself as an educator, a consultant, a community developer.*

*Perhaps the most significant thing I've done is to foster exchanges
among agencies and between the professional people and interested
lay people in the community. Because of my years of experience
here, I know lots of folks. I know what they're interested in. I'm
sort of a broker—matchmaker, you might call me. I match people
who've got ideas in common or problems in common.*

*Being a matchmaker is no easy task. First of all, the parties you're
trying to link up don't necessarily want to be linked up; or at least
they don't know they want to be. Second, there is no guarantee that
bringing people together to work on a common problem is going to
result in any amelioration of the problem or in any permanent relationship. I'm getting ahead of myself. Let me take a couple of steps
back.*

*My technical assistance role begins when some agency or group ap-
proaches the community placement officer with a project in mind or
with a problem it wants to work on, and asks specifically for some
consultation or staff assistance; or when the preliminary draft of a
proposal for funding is submitted. When someone writes or calls for
a proposal packet, we send out information indicating technical assistance on project design is available.*

*A third possibility is that the state-level staff or one of our regional
planning councils has decided that there's some project or program
it wants to get off the ground. I take a look at the agencies and organizations in the community that might be able to take on the project. Then I arrange a preliminary meeting with the appropriate
persons to explore the possibility of their submitting a proposal.*

*Regardless of who initiates the contract, preliminary sessions are for
getting acquainted. Sometimes I know exactly what I want to do and
what I want to get out of the other party. But I generally don't spill
the beans right at the start. I feel out their readiness. I educate them
and bring them along until they're ready to hear what I've got to
say. I give them chances to say no before we get down to business.
It works the other way, too. Sometimes they know exactly what they
want to get out of me. A frontal attack is not always the best strategy on their part.*

What we strive toward is a mutuality of perspective. It's like a dating game. Each party tries to test out how far the other is willing to go until they reach some point of accommodation. Sometimes one party is not at all interested, in which case the other side becomes more aggressive or more seductive. It's important to know where each side is coming from.

When I get into this testing-out business, I may have a specific thing in mind that I want the agency or organization to do; or I may want to find out what the agency's capacity is; or I may want to help the agency to identify what it wants to do. In the same way, the persons I'm dealing with may already know what they want; or they may be trying to find out what the department's priorities are and what kinds of resources we have available; or they may just want to test themselves out against some future possibilities. Technical assistance is like consultation. You have to know what you have and are willing to offer and what the other side needs or wants to get.

One problem I've noticed with other planners is that they sometimes try to railroad something through, as if they were in some superordinate position over their constituent agencies. I think that's arrogant. I'd rather view myself as a professional helper trying to give an organization the kind of help it needs to do its job better—or, on behalf of some population that needs service, trying to help an organization change the way it does its job. It's a temporary relationship, and it should be a relationship of equals, although I know damn well that sometimes the other party's got the clout because they've got something I want. Most times I've got the clout because they want something I've got.

What I'm saying is that it's important to understand your own motivations when you're giving technical assistance, and to understand the other party's motivations in accepting it. Sometimes I'm responding because there's a call for help. At other times I'm responding because I think the system out there is unproductive, or that there are sufficient inadequacies and inefficiencies in the service system to require some change. Sometimes I get involved because I'm advocating on behalf of people that need the Office of Community Placement's help.

Whatever the motivation, the process often includes more than just the two parties initially involved. If an agency seems to need a better

idea of what clients are interested in, I may arrange for meetings be-
tween the agency's administrative staff and some representatives of
consumer groups such as the Greenacres Alumni Association, a self-
help group of ex-mental hospital patients from the Midland area.
Let's assume for a moment that the party requesting technical assis-
tance is a psychiatric facility. I may feel that the hospital doesn't
have the staff capabilities to pull off a project it is interested in. I
may suggest a collaborative relationship with the community college
or the department of recreation, or the Catholic family service
agency.

Sometimes my technical assistance results in a project proposal. If
my assistance has been useful, that proposal is going to be funded. I
don't stop at project design. I may help the organization find appro-
priate alternative sources of funding, may make a few well-placed
phone calls to open the right doors, may even help the agency locate
the right staff or the right kind of help for staff retraining and re-
treading. And, after the project is funded, I make sure to pass on
my information on the project to whomever at the state level is going
to be responsible for monitoring it or providing further technical
assistance.

FINDING OUT WHO'S BUYING

As the above vignettes illustrate, funders and applicants both
have a stake in the grants or contract award process. From the
funder's perspective, good applicants and good applications are
at a premium. Federal, state, or local government agencies are
mandated to support legislated programs. In the vast majority
of cases, they are not able to conduct those programs with their
own staff, and so are required to seek organizations and individuals who can do the government's business or through
whom public policy can be executed.

It may not be possible for all funders to provide the extensive
technical assistance and consultation described in the second
vignette, but it is highly likely that funding agencies will provide
you with at least the written materials that will guide you in
your proposal preparation or in seeking alternative funding
sources. These materials may be extensive when supplied by

federal agencies, somewhat more modest from state agencies, and minimal or nonexistent from local government sources. However, this is not always the case. The federal government has been in the grants and contracts business for a long time and has developed highly standardized procedures, but some of its agencies may be in transition or may be underfunded and understaffed. This is even more true at the state level.

State agencies are, for the most part, in a period of transition as they move to assume a larger share of the responsibility for allocating tax dollars raised within the state or for the reallocation of federal dollars. Local government sources may or may not have standardized procedures. By "local government" I mean county, city, township, or other substate district. Such sources will, however, tend to be more knowledgeable about local needs and may provide the most extensive technical assistance. Some local organizations, such as community development corporations, for example, are responsible for the allocation of federal and local monies to community groups and agencies. The corporation's staff may do much more than provide technical assistance. It may involve citizens in needs assessment and in plan making and then advocate on behalf of those citizens with its own board or allocations committee.

How can you find out where funds are available and for what purposes? How can you uncover what you or your organization has that a funder might be interested in supporting? Figure 5.1 illustrates one way—sometimes the availability of funds is advertised.

Government programs are so varied in size, scope, and style that they deserve to be the subject of another book. In fact, they have been the subject of many. If you are interested in a federal award, a good book with which to begin your search is the *Catalogue of Federal Domestic Assistance*. It is available from the Superintendent of Documents each year in May and has a fall supplement with additional supplements projected. Its price has been relatively low in recent years, but, as is the case with other government publications, it is likely to skyrocket over the next decade. It can be found, however, in most

CITY OF ANN ARBOR
Community
Development Program

REQUEST FOR PROPOSALS

The City of Ann Arbor, Michigan is requesting submission of proposals for public services and energy conservation programs from nonprofit service providers. This solicitation is made in anticipation of the availability of Fiscal Year 1983-84 Community Development Block Grant (CDBG) entitlement funding from the U.S. Department of Housing and Urban Development.

Proposals are to be targeted to serving lower income residents of Ann Arbor. Proposals are requested for the following services:

Basic Community Services

Dental Services
Medical Services
Legal Services
Recreation
Family Support Services
Social & Educational Programs.
   Counseling, Advocacy

Other Public Services

Legal Assistance & Education
Services for the Handicapped
Services for Family Public
   Housing Tenants

Economic Development Programs

Child Care Scholarship
   Administration
Job Development & Placement
Pre-Employment Training

Services for Senior Citizens

Visiting Nurse
Transportation
Newsletter
Public Housing Tenants
Social Services

Energy

Low Cost/No Cost Home Visits

All proposals must be submitted on forms provided by the City. Proposal packets may be obtained from the Community Development Department, City Hall, 100 N. Fifth Ave., on or after Tuesday, May 31, 1983, 8:00 a.m. to 5:00 p.m., Monday through Friday. A pre-submission meeting to answer questions regarding the proposals and submission requirements will be held Friday, May 27, 1983, at 9:00 a.m. at the Northside Community Center, Taylor and Plum.

The City reserves the right to reject any or all proposals or to negotiate with the selected bidders to contract amounts consistent with the public services and energy budgets, adopted by City Council on May 19, 1983.

ALL PROPOSALS MUST BE SUBMITTED BY JUNE 21, 1983, AT 5:00 P.M. EST AT THE COMMUNITY DEVELOPMENT DEPARTMENT, CITY HALL, 100 N. FIFTH AVENUE, ANN ARBOR, MICHIGAN 48107.

Authorized by: William V. Hampton, Acting Director, Community Development

May 24, 25, 26, 29, 1983

Figure 5.1 Sample Newspaper Announcement of Availability of Funds at the Local Level

public and university libraries and in the library or bookstore of your local federal building. The catalogue includes profiles of every federal funding source available to "assist Americans in furthering social and economic progress." It tells you which federal agency sponsors what programs, the legislation under which they are established, the criteria of eligibility for applicants, the deadlines for application, and the funding levels; it also provides contact names and often the telephone numbers of key officials who can provide you with additional information.

Federal agencies issue awards as contracts and as grants. Despite President Reagan's first-term efforts to distribute domestic assistance funds directly to the states in the form of block grants, most federal dollars are still administered through categorical programs; that is, there are specific categories of funds available to deal with needs and problems of various populations—such as the aging, children, or adolescents—and regions of the country. There may be subcategories of programs serving children with health needs, children with developmental disabilities, or children in need of permanent placements.

These categories sometimes overlap with problem areas such as substance abuse, chronic mental illness, and hypertension. Sometimes the categories deal with such service arenas as primary or secondary education or community development. You do not need to understand the entire system to apply for funds. You only need to know which category fits the kinds of programs or services your agency is interested in. For that, the index to the *Catalogue* will be most helpful. Figure 5.2 presents a sample page from the *Catalogue,* dealing with RSVP. Look it over and ask yourself what additional information you will need. From whom can you get it?

Some state agencies also publish catalogues. These will be available from the governor's office or from the state agencies through which programs may be funded: public welfare, health and mental health, housing, corrections, and so on. Unfortunately, the information you seek may not be so easy to uncover. If there is neither a catalogue nor some other listing, you may have to find alternative sources of information. A good place to start might be your state League for Human Services or-

72.002 RETIRED SENIOR VOLUNTEER
PROGRAM
(RSVP)

FEDERAL AGENCY: ACTION

AUTHORIZATION: Domestic Volunteer Service Act of 1973, as amended, Title II, Part A, Public Law 93-113.

OBJECTIVES: To establish a recognized role in the community and a meaningful life in retirement by developing a wide variety of community volunteer service opportunities for persons 60 years of age or over through development of community oriented, cost-shared projects.

TYPES OF ASSISTANCE: Project Grants.

USES AND USE RESTRICTIONS: Grants may be made to established community service organizations to assist in the development and operation of locally organized senior volunteer projects. This local community service organization, known as the RSVP sponsor, develops a wide variety of volunteer service opportunities throughout the community in hospitals, schools, courts, daycare centers, libraries and other volunteer stations. The sponsor also arranges for transportation for the RSVP Volunteers as needed. Grants may be used for staff salaries and fringe benefits, staff travel, equipment, space costs and related expenses, and for volunteer out-of-pocket expenses, primarily for transportation. JOINT FUNDING: This program is considered suitable for joint funding with closely related Federal financial assistance programs in accordance with the provisions of OMB Circular No. A-111. For programs that are not identified as suitable for joint funding, the applicant may consult the headquarters or field office of the appropriate funding agency for further information on statutory or other restrictions involved.

ELIGIBILITY REQUIREMENTS:

Applicant Eligibility: Grants are made only to public and private nonprofit organizations including State and local governments.

Beneficiary Eligibility: Retired persons aged 60 and over.

Credentials/Documentation: The applicant must furnish evidence of: capacity to operate direct community service programs; experience and interest in the needs of older adults; and the ability to develop strong community financial and programmatic support. Costs will be determined in accordance with OMB Circular No. A-87 for State and local governments and OMB Circular No. A-122 for nonprofit organizations. A nonprofit agency must submit certification that it has (1) legal authority to receive a grant and operate the program; and (2) proof of its status as a nonprofit organization.

Figure 5.2 Sample Page from the *Catalogue of Federal Domestic Assistance*

APPLICATION AND AWARD PROCESS:

Preapplication Coordination: Organizations interested in exploring the possibility of developing a local RSVP project should contact the appropriate ACTION State Program Office. ACTION issues application forms A-263 and A-1018 to applicants who have established their eligibility. Applications are subject to State and areawide clearinghouses review pursuant to procedures in Part I, Attachment A of OMB Circular No. A-95 (revised).

Application Procedure: Applications are submitted to the ACTION State Program Office, with a copy to the State Office on Aging. State Offices on Aging have 45 days to review and make comments on applications. This program is subject to the provisions of OMB Circular No. A-110 for nonprofit organizations or OMB Circular No. A-102 for State and local governments.

Award Procedure: Grant awards are made by the Regional Directors of ACTION. Notification of awards must be made to the State Central Information Reception Agency in accordance with Treasury Circular 1082.

Deadlines: None.

Range of Approval/Disapproval Time: 120 days after receipt of application by ACTION.

Appeals: No formal appeals for denial of initial grant application, but regulations provide for hearings on terminations and suspensions, and opportunities to show cause in case of refusal to refund.

Renewals: Annual continuations.

ASSISTANCE CONSIDERATIONS:

Formula and Matching Requirements: The nonfederal support of the budget during the first year will not be less than 10 percent. Grantees are expected to increase the local share of the project cost by an added 10 percent the second year and to assume a minimum of 30 percent financial responsibility for the total project budget at the beginning of the third year and each year thereafter.

Length and Time Phasing of Assistance: Grant support and budget periods are normally for 12 months, with continuation application filed annually; disbursements are made quarterly, or monthly for grants exceeding $120,000 annually.

POST ASSISTANCE REQUIREMENTS:

Reports: Quarterly Financial Status Report, Project Progress Report, Quarterly Federal Cash Transaction Report.

Audits: ACTION grants are subject to audit by ACTION representatives and other authorized Federal personnel; does not replace required audits by local grantee.

Figure 5.2 Continued *(continued)*

Records: All financial records including receipts, disbursements, and vouchers for Federal and nonfederal costs; copies of all contracts; personnel records; and job descriptions must be available for a period of three years from date of submission of Final Financial Status Report.

FINANCIAL INFORMATION:

Account Identification: 44-0103-0-1-506.

Obligations: (Grants) FY 80 $26,217,000; FY 81 est $27,717,000; and FY 82 est $28,691,000.

Range and Average of Financial Assistance: $10,000 to $450,000; $36,810.

PROGRAM ACCOMPLISHMENTS: As of September 30, 1980, a total of 274,00 Retired Senior Volunteers were serving in 707 RSVP projects in the 50 States, the District of Columbia, Guam, Puerto Rico and the Virgin Islands.

REGULATIONS, GUIDELINES, AND LITERATURE: 45 CFR Part 1209, ACTION Handbook 2650.2, Policies and Procedures for Business Management of Domestic Project Grants, ACTION Handbook 4405.92, Retired Senior Volunteer Program Operations Handbook and "RSVP - Retired Senior Volunteer Program" (ACTION Flyer No. 4500-1), "RSVP - Retired Senior Volunteer Program" (ACTION Pamphlet 4500.9).

INFORMATION CONTACTS:

Regional or Local Offices: ACTION Regional Offices and ACTION State Program Offices. Refer to Appendix IV, Regional Offices.

Headquarters Office: Director, Older Americans Volunteer Programs, ACTION, 806 Connecticut Avenue, N.W., Washington, DC 20525. Telephone: (202) 254-7310.

RELATED PROGRAMS: 13.633, Special Programs for the Aging-Title III Parts A and B-Grants for States and Community Programs on Aging; 13.365, Special Programs for the Aging-Title III Part C-Nutrition Services; 13.645, Child Welfare Services; 49.005, Community Food and Nutrition; 72.001, The Foster Grandparent Program; 72.008, The Senior Companion Program.

EXAMPLES OF FUNDED PROJECTS: 1) New Jersey - RSVP's are trained as senior advocates to assist other older persons in securing benefits under Social Security and health care programs. They also provide assistance in the preparation of income tax returns. Other volunteers who are retired pharmacists have started a program called "Project Spirit" to help older persons combat prescription drug abuse. 2) Minnesota - Minneapolis RSVP's work at a Crime Victim Assistance Program in conjunction with the Police Department. They gather reports of elderly people who have been crime victims. The volunteers then counsel and assist the victims in follow-up. 3) Vermont - Handicapped RSVP's have been recruited whose skills are utilized in making wooden sliding boards to be used to transfer stroke victims from bed to chair,

Figure 5.2 Continued

and rehabilitation loom devices for nursing home residents. These volunteers also repair sleds for emotionally disturbed children. 4) Ohio - RSVP volunteers help to prepare and deliver nutritious meals to senior citizens under the Mobile Meals Program and, in addition, some have developed a program of monthly blood screening. The volunteers not only take the readings but have set up the administrative end of the program. 5) Connecticut RSVP volunteers provide tutorial services in the public school system and are assigned as consumer advocates to the State Department of Consumer Protection. These RSVP consumer advocates have conducted a survey on the prices of medication and provide information on generic drugs to the elderly.

CRITERIA FOR SELECTING PROPOSALS: 1. Demonstrated need for the program in the community to be served; 2. Evidence of community support for the program; 3. Goals and objectives that are clear, measurable and time-phased; 4. Assurance that program requirements will be complied with; 5. A potential sponsor has the following characteristics: a. Is a public or private nonprofit organization; b. Has authority to operate and administer the proposed project; c. Has the capacity to manage and operate community service programs; d. Has a good working relationship with other community service agencies and organizations especially those dealing with older persons; e. Has the capacity to develop sources of nonfederal support; f. Has a governing body or agency board which understands and endorses the nature and purpose of the program.

Figure 5.2 Continued

ganization, the state chapter of the National Association of Social Workers (NASW), or another relevant advocacy group.

Such voluntary planning bodies as the United Fund and sectarian organizations (e.g., Catholic Charities) may be in a good position to point you to the appropriate state address. Their staff do more than raise funds locally and allocate them to member agencies; they also help those member agencies and others to seek funding from appropriate public sources. Consider also going to other organizations like your own: hospitals, group homes, spouse abuse shelters, and so on. Chances are that your organization is already affiliated with a public or a voluntary coordinating body—a council on aging, a community mental health board, or a coordinating council for children at risk. Who on the staff or the board of that organization can help you in your search?

If your organization is affiliated with a national body such as the American Hospital Association, the Family Service Association of America, or the National Council of Settlements and Community Centers, you may be able to get both technical assistance and written guidance from that body. Some years back, for example, the Child Welfare League of America published four guidebooks to help member agencies unscramble complexities of Title XX funding, cutting through the maze of federal and state guidelines.

Any of these organizations—local, state, or national—can also guide you to local and state sources of funds, and may have materials available on the successful experiences of organizations similar to yours in other locales. Suggestions about useful sources of information on local, state, and federal funding are found at the end of this chapter.

BUILDING RELATIONSHIPS WITH GOVERNMENT FUNDERS

As you complete Exercise 5.1, you will begin the process of building relationships with a funding organization and with one of the staff persons responsible for the allocations or technical assistance process. Remember, they are likely to be as interested in getting to know you as you are in finding out more about them. What kind of information are you ready to share? What can you say about

the kind of organization you represent;

its clients or members;

the services it provides or is contemplating;

the reasons you are seeking support;

the amount you are seeking and for how long;

the other sources you are also considering and the commitments made by those sources, if any;

income from fees, fund raising events, and campaigns;

the nature of your staff;

community involvement or support for your project; and

the needs or problems you intend to address.

If you are asked about any of these items on the telephone, can you give an answer succinctly, in one or two sentences? If you are asked to provide such information in a letter or preliminary outline, can you do it in two pages or less?

Part of the relationship-building process occurs through the exchange of information. Part of it occurs through the kinds of interpersonal relationships that are built up during that communication. The two persons quoted in the vignettes at the beginning of this chapter are clearly experienced in the grants and contracts processes. You may not have had as many experiences, and you may not be as clear as they are about what

---

EXERCISE 5.1
GETTING INFORMATION ON
GOVERNMENT FUNDING SOURCES

(1) Look over the Government Funding Source Inventory. Pick a federal, state, or local government agency with which you want to become more familiar. If it is a federal agency, you might wish to begin your information search by using the *Catalogue of Domestic Federal Assistance*. Some of the information may also be available from a colleague in your organization or in another organization with which you interact.

(2) Fill in the inventory with the information at hand. If there are blank spaces, where should you go for additional information? Will a telephone call or a letter yield that information? If so, be prepared to ask the specific question you want answered. Get the data and complete the form.

(3) Now do the same for funding sources from the other two levels of government.

Exercise 5.1
GOVERNMENT FUNDING SOURCE INVENTORY

1. **Level of Government**
   _____ Local
   _____ State
   _____ Federal
   _____ Other
   _____

2. **Name of Agency** _____
   _____
   Address _____
   _____
   _____
   Telephone ( ) _____

3. **Contact Person** _____
   _____
   Title _____
   _____
   Special Information _____
   _____
   _____

4. **Functional or Program Area in Which Awards Are Made**
   _____
   _____

5. **Geographic Areas** _____
   _____
   _____

6. **Types of Organizations to Which Awards Are Made** _____
   _____
   _____

7. **Populations to Be Served by Awards** _____
   _____
   _____

8. **Current Priorities, If Any** _____
   _____
   _____

9. **Restrictions, If Any** _____
   _____
   _____

10. **Funding Cycle** _____
    _____

11. **Funding Information**
    Assets $ _____
    Number of Awards available _____
    Average Award Size $ _____
    $ Range of Awards $_____ to
    $_____

12. **Matching Fund Requirements**
    ___ _____
    _____
    Can In-Kind Resources or In-direct Costs Be Used? _____
    _____

13. **Kinds of Support Given**
    _____ Block Grants
    _____ Categorical Grants
    _____ Formula Grants
    _____ Contracts
    _____ Purchases of Service
    _____ Other _____
    _____

14. **Uses Awards Can Be Put To**
    _____ Basic Research
    _____ Assessment or Evaluation
    _____ Programs and Services
    _____ Client Support
    _____ Staffing
    _____ Capital Expenditures
    _____ Space/Equipment Rental
    _____ Training and Trainee Support
    ___ Technical Assistance
    _____ Planning
    _____ Coordination
    _____ Demonstration or Start-up
    _____ Ongoing Support
    Other _____
    _____

15. Materials Available
_____ Application Kit
_____ Summaries of Previously
       Funded Projects
_____ Guidelines
_____ Sample Proposals
_____ Other _____
_____

16. Review Process Used _____
_____
_____
_____

17. Due Dates for Proposals _____
_____
_____

Review Results Transmitted by
_____

18. Persons Currently or Recently
Involved in the Review Process
_____
_____
_____
_____

19. Types of Assistance Available
_____ Written Materials
_____ Telephone Consultation
_____ Written Response to
       Written Material
_____ In-Office Consultation
_____ On-Site Visits and Con-
       sultation
_____ Other _____
_____
_____

20. Names of Decision Makers and
Program Persons Who Should
be Involved in Proposals to this
Source Including Client or
Community Representatives
_____
_____
_____

21. Recent Awards in Area of
Interest
a. Award _____
    Organization and Address
    _____
    _____

    Contact Person _____
    _____
    _____

b. Award _____
    Organization and Address
    _____
    _____

c. Award _____
    Organization and Address
    _____
    _____

d. Award _____
    Organization and Address
    _____
    _____

22. Actions (to be) Taken
a. Phone Contacts _____
    _____
b. Written Contacts _____
    _____
    _____
c. Interviews or Meetings _____
    _____
    _____
d. Other _____
    _____
    _____
    _____

Inventory Compiled by   Date

works and why. Look over the two vignettes once again. This time, read them carefully to uncover practice principles that can guide you in your search and in relationship building. A practice principle is just that, a *guide* to practice or to action.

For example, in the first illustration, you might paraphrase the first sentence in the form of a practice principle:

> Don't write a proposal unless you know in advance that you have a fighting chance of getting it funded.

How many more can you find?

EXERCISE 5.2
LISTING OF PRACTICE PRINCIPLES

(1) In simple declarative sentences, list all the practice principles you can find in the two vignettes, one beneath the other. Number them.

(2) Discuss them with colleagues and others who may have had considerable experience in the grantsmanship process or in working with government funding agencies. Ask them which of these are realistic or which they have found most useful.

(3) Based on their comments and on your own reactions, cross out those that you think are not adequate to guide you. Add others. Circle the numbers of those you think should guide you but that you may not yet feel comfortable in following. What must you do to increase your comfort or your capability?

SOME PERSONAL RECOLLECTIONS

I want to share a few experiences with you that may help add to your inventory of practice principles. In the late 1960s the National Institute of Mental Health (NIMH) determined that it would promote the development of continuing education (CE) activities among the mental health professions: social work, psychiatric nursing, psychiatry, and psychology. Announcements appeared in the *Federal Register* that grant funds would be available to professional schools, professional associations (for example, the AMA and NASW), community mental health centers, and state mental health agencies. Subsequently, application information was mailed by NIMH to deans and directors of those organizations. Sixty three-year grants were awarded. The University of Michigan School of Social Work was one of the recipients.

A few years later, the school applied again to NIMH for another CE grant, this time to establish a mental health skills laboratory in the Detroit area. We were not funded. The original seed grant had been intended to help the school establish a capacity to do continuing education without continued federal support. From our perspective, the Detroit project was a new and different program. NIMH did not see it that way. Although Detroit-area agencies were in need, we just did not have the capacity to extend our services to them without external support.

We were not the only interested party, however. Although the original proposal had been rejected, we were in a good position to promote a new application. In the original project design, we had involved representatives of nineteen mental health agencies and the Wayne County Community Mental Health Services Board. The original proposal was modified and resubmitted by the board, which also committed itself to an increasing share of financial responsibility. The lab was to be finally self-supporting at the end of three years. It was to be governed by a council to be made up of representatives from each of the participating mental health agencies. The school was to provide initial staffing, on contract, until the new lab was on its feet. There were no difficulties in getting the new project funded. Can you identify additional practice principles from the above? I will share another experience.

At about the same time we were working on the lab, the Administration on Aging (AoA) was beginning to gear up for the establishment of Area Agencies on Aging throughout the United States. This was 1972. What turned out to be the 1973 Amendments to the Social Security Act—which included Title III, the basis upon which area agencies were to be established—had not yet been passed by Congress. But the administration was confident that the bill would go through and wanted to be ready. You could not establish 600 or more regional planning agencies around the country without trained staff. AoA officials began looking around the country for universities that might be able to do the training once planners were hired. They looked first to universities that had both well-established institutes of gerontology and well-established schools of social work.

Michigan was such a place. One of our faculty members was also on one of AoA's advisory panels. He arranged to leave a book and a few articles on planning recently written by Michigan faculty with AoA staff. They got the hint. We were one of the universities solicited to submit a proposal. We were also one of the three to receive a grant. For the next two years we worked closely with AoA staff on the design and implementation of the training program. As in any partnership, it was not always smooth sailing. The university staff saw itself fulfilling the obligations of a grant, with considerable flexibility in the way in which it should operate. AoA staff tended to view us as contractors, responsible for delivering a product at an agreed-upon time and for a predetermined cost. Despite some tension here and there, the partners completed the terms of the agreement and evaluated the relationship as being satisfactory. It was satisfactory primarily because the consumers of the training program, newly appointed area planners, found what they had learned to be directly applicable to their work.

In contrast to these examples, in 1982 I submitted a proposal to train public welfare officials in grantsmanship and in work with the private sector. Federal guidelines were published by the Office of Human Development in the *Federal Register*. The funds to be allocated had been collected from previous established categorical funding programs, and were to be awarded on a competitive and discretionary basis. The amounts available were not large; the deadline was only six or seven weeks from the time of publication of the guidelines. The review criteria were not clearly described.

Nevertheless, because money was tight, about 8000 applications were submitted. Fewer than 10 percent were funded.

No one received any technical assistance. It was not even possible to find out who was responsible for providing information on specific programs for which funding was announced. I should have known better than to apply. A colleague in another state who did receive an award later complained to me, "It's been a nightmare all along. The feds want to know everything we are doing but they don't have the staff to monitor events properly or even to understand what is going on. Never saw a disarray like this in my life."

In the AoA and NIMH examples, federal agencies had clear ideas of what they wanted accomplished and were ready to invest in technical assistance and other supports in order to increase the likelihood of grantee success. In the last example, the government's intent was not clear, nor was it properly staffed to achieve whatever its objectives may have been.

Similar situations often prevail, for at least a limited time, during administrative changeovers, particularly when the new administration—at the federal, state, or local level—has different priorities than a previous administration. They are also likely to occur when responsibility is shifted from one agency to another or from one level of government to another. The states, for example, strongly resisted efforts by the Reagan administration to shift responsibility from the federal to the state level for the funding of what had been categorical programs through newly envisioned block grant mechanisms. The state agencies just did not have the staffing capacities to both allocate funds and provide adequate technical assistance.

Despite the difficulties that changes in accustomed ways of doing business may present, they also provide new opportunities. Disarray or confusion in a funding agency may provide you and your organization with an opportunity to share information on local needs or on the severity of a problem that should be addressed. You might do so at a public hearing, through reports sent to government officials, perhaps indirectly through a state senator, a city council member, or their staffs. This can be your opportunity to shape the direction of future funding patterns.

How well are you positioned to take advantage of an opportunity when it presents itself, or to turn a predicament into an opportunity?

REVIEW

Both funders and recipients of funding awards have a stake in each other. Funders are often on the lookout for organizations or individuals who can perform the work they have been entrusted to support. Petitioners can reduce their dependency on funders if (1) alternative sources of supply are available; (2) they can indicate a capacity to do what the funder needs done; and (3) they can provide the funder with access to other needed resources—populations, legitimacy, and so on. This is especially true of government funding agencies that are required by public mandate to provide assistance in areas of social and economic development.

The most comprehensive source of information on federal programs is the *Catalogue of Federal Domestic Assistance.* It is a good starting point in your search for the appropriate agency or funding program. Some states also publish similar catalogues. You may have to search out listings by program or population served from various state agencies. If there is a state office for the League for the Human Services, you might get leads there. Other places to get information are professional associations, the staff of coordinating councils and planning agencies, colleagues in other agencies, and so on. There are also a number of advocacy groups, search services, and consulting firms available to help.

Most government funding organizations provide applicants with written guidelines and/or application forms. Some provide extensive technical assistance and consultation in the program development and proposal writing stages of the process. Some continue to provide technical assistance along with their monitoring activities after a project has been funded. The more established the funding source, the closer it is to your organization geographically and functionally, the more personal and extensive the services are that your organization may expect.

SUGGESTIONS FOR FURTHER READING

Start with these government sources.

Catalogue of Federal Domestic Assistance: Published annually in May, the *Catalogue* has semiannual and sometimes quarterly supplements. The most comprehensive source of information on federal granting programs, it describes agencies, funding programs, sums available, where to get additional application information, and so on. It is functionally indexed by agency, program name, subject matter, popular designation, and eligible grantee. The *Catalogue* can be purchased from the Government Printing Office, but you may be able to get it free through your congressional representative's office. You will also find it in most public libraries.

United States Government Manual: Published each year, includes (as up-to-date as possible) names, addresses, and phone numbers of key government granting agencies. Sources as above. Order from Government Printing Office.

Federal Register: A daily publication that contains detailed information on proposed rules, guidelines, and other important financial information on specific grant programs. The *Register* tells when grant monies are to become available, amounts to be spent. It provides current information on new programs that may not be in the *Catalogue.* Most major libraries subscribe. Order from Government Printing Office.

Commerce Business Daily: The is the federal government's shopping list and want ad that announces contract opportunities and grants over $25,000. Even if you do not contract with the government directly, you might be able to subcontract with an organization or company that does. Order from Government Printing Office. Check current prices.

Agency Publications: Do not stop there. Use agency publications to get on the mailing lists of all appropriate funding agencies in your field. Get the news before it happens! No sense in hearing about an award after it has been made. Get on the mailing lists of the relevant federal, state, and local agencies.

You may also be able to get useful information from a number of newsletters and magazines. For instance, Capitol Publications, Inc., Suite G-12, 2430 Pennsylvania Avenue, Washington, DC 20037, publishes the following newsletters weekly, except the last week in December:

Health Grants and Contracts Weekly

Federal Grants and Contracts Weekly: Selected Project Opportunities for the Educational Community

Morris Associates, Inc., 1346 Connecticut Avenue, NW, Washington, DC 20036, publishes the following:

The MH-MR Report (semimonthly)

Health Systems Report (weekly)

Find out about other sources in your area of interest. Check with your professional association, another agency, a national organization you may be affiliated with.

Several books may also be useful to you:

DesMarais, Philip. (1977). *How to get government grants.* New York: Public Service Materials Center.

Stephen Nowland et al. (Eds.). (1975). *How to get money for the arts and humanities, drugs, alcohol, human services, and health.* Radnor, PA: Human Resources Network, Chillon Book Co.

Other materials from the Human Resources Network:

How to get money for conservation and community development (1975).
How to get money for youth, the elderly, the handicapped, women, and civil liberties (1975).

How about other state and local sources of information? Check with your state League for the Human Services or with the staff of a state legislator who is actively involved in promoting legislation or overseeing programs in your area of concern—child welfare, protective services for the elderly, health care, and so on. Go directly to the agency that is responsible for those services. Contact the appropriate official and ask about contract or grant programs for organizations like yours. You may have to go through a few different offices before you reach the right person, but do not be discouraged. They may not know how to find you either. Get whatever literature they provide. Ask for summaries of recent grants of contracts awarded.

The materials you are seeking might be located with a semi-independent contractor. For example, the state Department of Labor may contract out with a private firm for all of its training activities, and this firm may subcontract out on a competitive basis to organizations like your own. A city council may allocate its funds for neighborhood development and other services indirectly through a community development corporation (CDC). If that is the case, the CDC is the one to address for information on available funds.

CHAPTER 6

Building on a Strong Foundation:
Seeking Foundation Grants

VIGNETTE 6: A REJECTION SPURS A NEW PROGRAM ON

We started out as an offshoot of the Women's Crisis Center. The center is mostly volunteer run: women raising each other's consciousness, helping each other when the going gets rough. For some women it's really rough. Three years ago, when the economy went sour, we noticed an increase in calls from women who were complaining of all kinds of abusive treatment at home. Some desperately needed to get away. None of the other services in town could provide them with even temporary shelter. We were able to help some by putting them up in private homes or in hotels, and the Y took a few. This cost a lot and it just wasn't safe.

What we needed was a safe house. But the federal government had just cut its program subsidies to spouse abuse shelters so it didn't look like we were going to be able to get government dollars. The Weelington Foundation had a reputation for concerns about child abuse and also for supporting family development activities. It seemed like a natural.

It didn't take long to write up a proposal. One of our board members had located a piece of property that we thought was sufficiently isolated to provide safety. And we got all sorts of advice from other safe houses around the state on how to staff and manage the facility. We thought we had a pretty good proposal. And one of the founda-

tion staff members encouraged us to submit. "If it strengthens families, we're interested," Frank Santier of the foundation told me. "Send it in."

We did. We got turned down. I was stunned. I called Mr. Santier and asked the reason. "There are two," he explained. "One is substantive, the other is a matter of form." On the substantive matter, he continued, we had emphasized the needs of the women for safety and had described services aimed at providing them with greater independence. Many of them, our proposal emphasized, needed to get away from their husbands at least temporarily, if not permanently. "The foundation," he told me, "is interested in promoting family stability and development; not family dissolution. The husband is the villain in your proposal and the wife, the victim. We see them both as victims."

That really got me thinking. Were we so militant as women that we had forgotten that a marriage is made up of two persons? If we followed the Weelington Foundation's logic, would we have to redesign our program, offer services to men? Wouldn't they resist services, especially if offered by a Women's Crisis Center? Should we consider some kind of court-ordered program? But wouldn't that mean we would have to get women to press charges and wouldn't that be defeating in terms of family stability?

We needed some help on this if we were to go back to the foundation. Some of my colleagues and some of our board members didn't want anything to do with the foundation. They thought we could go our own way and find funding elsewhere. I wasn't so sure. I thought the foundation was on to something with its criticism. I decided to visit the foundation office and explore our interests with them some more.

I brought along Marci Maslow, a staffer on the Child Guidance Clinic that had received funds from the foundation in previous years. Marci is one of our active volunteers. She came in part to give me moral support, in part to give me legitimacy, in part to give me some ideas.

I was really surprised. Frank Santier and Rosabeth Mitchel of the foundation staff gave us a full hour and a half. In that discussion we explored all kinds of possibilities to complement the safe house project: men's discussion groups, referral of spouses to the community mental health center and to the family and children's agency, employment counseling. Problem was, the project was getting too big for us to handle. "We'll have to see what part of all this we can carve out for ourselves," I concluded the meeting and thanked them both for their time.

We did submit a new proposal. And we did get partial funding. The rest was raised through a capital drive and through an expanded allocation from the United Way; several of the other United Way agencies vouched for us and for the need to set up a shelter.

Oh, yes. The matter of form. *Our original proposal had been 38 pages long. It was loaded with details on the facility and how we would manage it, on the documentation of the problem, and so on. The second proposal was only 8 pages long. It had very few details, but it did spell out how we were going to contribute to family stability and development. And it did spell out our capability of doing the job in collaboration with other local human service agencies. The reviewers were satisfied; they didn't want to be bothered by details.*

As Rosabeth Mitchel told me before we resubmitted, "Staff at the foundation may be interested in lots of details, and if you get funding we'll want regular reports. But our lay people are the ones who make decisions. They are busy people. We can't expect them to read a proposal if it's more than five to eight pages in length. They don't want details. They trust us to get them. They want to deal with policy issues. Don't overwhelm them with more than they need."

VIGNETTE 7:
WHY JUST A POSTCARD?

I've always been interested in neighborhoods and in empowerment. A few years ago a federal grant for neighborhood involvement might have been a real possibility. Today, it's out of the cards, especially for the kinds of purposes I was interested in. So I figured our best bet was to look for foundation support.

I started my search by going to the community library. It happens that we have one of the Foundation Center's "cooperating collections" here so I felt pretty sure we could get the information we needed. The search began with a review of the last couple of years' issues of the Foundations Grants Index. *The index comes out once* *a year and it refers to descriptions of grants in the amounts of $5000 or more made by about 500 foundations. Whenever I found something that fit, I checked out the more detailed description of the grant in one of the issues of the* Foundation Center News, *a journal that comes out six times or so each year.*

Well, I got a few good prospects. But it wasn't enough. So I decided to invest a little more time and a few bucks. The Foundation Center started a printout service a couple of years back called COM-SEARCH. It prints out names of foundations and projects in a whole gamut of different subjects.

I found several categories of printout subjects that seemed to fit our interests: films, documents and audiovisuals (we were thinking of involving residents in videotaping the community), mental health, public health, orchestras and musical performances, the aged, the handicapped, Blacks, Hispanics, environmental protection, crime and law, civil rights, and community and urban development. These are the subjects of printouts published each year, so you can't tailor a printout to your own specs. Still, by looking each one over, I was able to spot a number of foundations that dealt with several topics of interest to us.

Having located 67 likely prospects, I sent them each a two-page letter describing briefly what we intended to do and asking whether or not the foundation might be interested. The letter, I might add, was textbook perfect. It even included a Xerox of a photograph of one of our neighborhoods as an eye-catcher.

I got 65 responses, most of them on mimeographed postcards; all of them turndowns. No explanation, no nothin'! Why just a postcard?

FOUNDATIONS HAVE AGENDAS

The message in the above vignettes is clear: Foundations have agendas, and they are not about to provide funding to groups, individuals, or organizations whose requests do not complement those objectives. Before you decide to modify your agenda significantly, however, you should know something about foundations and about what they fund.

In 1983 foundations allocated somewhat less than $3 billion to nonprofit organizations and charitable causes. That is no small amount, but, proportionately, it is not all that much either. Of the more than $60 billion in nongovernmental allocations to nonprofit organizations, over 80 percent came from individuals, almost 10 percent through bequests, about 5 percent from corporations, and (as the $3 billion figure implies) less than 5 percent from foundations. The contributions of foundations to what is generally called the voluntary sector, though substantial, are not necessarily decisive. Moreover, these contributions are spread out among a number of subcategories of the voluntary sector: education and research (e.g., colleges, school-related activities, research and development); culture (fine arts performances, museums and historic preservations, libraries, broadcasting); religion (churches and religious publications); health services (hospitals, nursing homes, preventive and public health activities); community development (conservation, environmental protection, public education, social action); *and* human services (including financial assistance, legal aid, special programs for youth, the aged, families, and so on).

According to the authors of the *1982 Foundation Grants Index,* 369 of the nearly 19,000 bona fide private foundations studied gave 45 percent of the grants awarded in the previous year. (There may be as many as 30,000 to 40,000 private foundations in America.) About one-fourth of those foundations accounted for half of the number of grants and 77 percent of the funds allocated. *Education* and *health* have, in recent years, each accounted for 20 to 25 percent of the money allocated, and *human service agencies* for about 16 percent. This has changed dramatically since 1981. Today the human services receive one out of every three or four dollars allocated by foundations. The reasons for the change are not hard to find. The recession in the early 1980s, with its high unemployment rate and the substantial cutbacks in federal funding for social services that accompanied it, put enormous pressures on foundations to respond to human needs at the local level. Research-related activities were cut back, as was support to hospitals and other health providers on the assumption that Medicare and

Medicaid funds would substitute. In addition to increased funding for human services, contributions to community cultural activities also reflected a rise from about 14 percent of the allocations to over 17 percent. In both cases, grant funds were clearly earmarked for local giving.

Although this may be a hopeful sign to some local agencies, foundation dollars are limited and will never be able to make up, in any substantial way, for recent cuts in public programs. Moreover, increased demand on their resources and aggressiveness on the part of local applicants have forced many foundations to reevaluate their policies and funding strategies. "It's taking us longer than we thought," explained a foundation officer to me, "but we have just got to complete our reassessment if we are going to be fair to those who may wish to apply." Different types of foundations have different interests. And within each category of foundation, interests and priorities are likely to differ further.

The term "foundation" tends to be used somewhat loosely. Because it connotes a certain amount of prestige, its use has been adopted by fund raising groups, organizations that provide direct services, pressure groups, and not a few outright rackets. The term "private foundation," on the other hand, has come to have a very specific connotation. *Private foundations,* according to the 1969 Tax Reform act, must have charitable, religious, educational, scientific, or cultural purposes.

TYPES OF PHILANTHROPIC FOUNDATIONS

There are a number of different types of foundations, each with its own characteristics. Many general-purpose philanthropic foundations are identified as *private foundations.* These have broad charters and often rather large endowments. The large ones operate independently and are professionally staffed. Many private foundations will support only pioneering or innovative programs and will be reluctant to support projects or organizations for long periods of time. Although in times of emergency some have been known to bail out a supplicant, they are more apt to see themselves as responsible for providing seed money to launch new programs that will in time become self-supporting. Some of the largest—the Ford Foundation, for example—also concern themselves with initiating social experiments that are likely to have an impact on public policy and ultimately on public expenditures. Other large foundations include the Robert Wood Johnson, Rockefeller, Kellogg, and Carnegie foundations. Medium-sized foundations include the Mott and Edna McConnel Clark foundations. Although no longer connected to industry, many of their initial donors were large industrialists. Thus the Clark Foundation's portfolio began with a large bequest of funds from Avon Products, and the Mott Foundation built its portfolio around a donation of General Motors stock.

These foundations, however, operate fully autonomously, *independent* from the businesses and even the individuals who founded them. They have their own boards of directors that make the final decisions on any grants to be made, and for this reason they are often referred to as *independent* foundations. The key people in the grants process are the staff members responsible for given areas of concern (e.g., child welfare, job training, community education).

These staff members are the ones with whom you will have contact, and they will screen proposals before any are to be submitted to the board. They also recommend whether or not a grant is to be made and the size of the award. Although some of the staff members tend to be national or even international in the scope of their interests, others will be both knowledgeable about and responsible for the foundation's involvement in the local community or with such functional concerns as aging or youth. A number of foundations that had previously identified themselves as general-purpose foundations have through their reevaluation processes become special-purpose foundations.

In contrast, *community foundations* are set up exclusively to serve a specific geographic area, usually a city, and sometimes its adjacent townships. Cleveland established the first community foundation in the years immediately preceding World War II. There are now more than 300 others throughout the United States. Today they account for about 3 percent of all foundation assets and allocations in the United States. Initially established to ensure proper stewardship of trusts and bequests, community foundations now actively seek funds from individual and corporate donors who prefer to have their philanthropic responsibilities administered by professional foundation managers. Several report allocations from local government sources as well.

Community foundations are concerned primarily with local needs. At one time they tended to sponsor only such cultural programs as the local philharmonic or a summer "concert in the park" series. Today they are increasingly involved in human service and community development activities. These include downtown reconstruction, the building of pocket parks, and the support of social services for which other funds may not be readily available. Community foundations frequently seek to use their funds as venture capital to attract other grants, possibly from government or industrial sources.

Community foundations' trustees include prominent citizens who make all final decisions. Some make genuine efforts to represent all segments of the population. However, as with independent foundations, staff are often gatekeepers and the primary decision makers. Although many trustees and staff may be savvy about local needs, they may also need to be educated. Your success as a fund raiser will be much improved if the staff are knowledgeable about your agency's services and the needs of the populations you are concerned about. It may take a while before you can properly position your organization to make an application. Media and public awareness campaigns may increase your chances considerably.

Family foundations make up by far the largest numbers of private foundations in the United States. They vary greatly in size and areas of interest. Their endowments are generally under $5 million, and many may be only in the $10,000 to $200,000 range. Although some have boards, the preferences of family members who make major contributions generally prevail. Few have professional staffs; some family foundations are administered by a trustee, who is probably a private attorney, a local banker, or a trust corporation with many other responsibilities.

Some family foundations are clearly tax shelters. The goal may be to provide university scholarships to worthy students, but recipients may be limited to friends and relatives of the family. Many have religious purposes. Some are connected with social agencies, the primary supporter of an endowment program for specific projects in those organizations. Family foundations are sometimes on the lookout for good prospects—people and organizations to fund. Once on a family foundation's list, you may remain on it indefinitely. But getting on that list is another matter. It may require knowing someone in the family or knowing someone who knows someone. Because most do not have professional staff, they may not know how to deal with most unsolicited proposals; some will not even acknowledge receipt of your inquiry.

Recent concern with corporate America's social responsibilities has focused attention on *company (-sponsored) foundations.* You are probably aware that corporations are permitted to make charitable contributions of up to 10 percent of their pretax earnings, and frequently they establish foundations to administer those funds. As with the others, company foundations are tax-exempt and nonprofit entities. Although separate from their parent companies, their boards tend to consist almost exclusively of company officers. Examples include the Alcoa Foundation, the Sears Roebuck Foundation, the Exxon Education Fund, and the Aetna Foundation. You will not only recognize the company names, but may be aware of some educational or cultural programs sponsored by these foundations.

About 5 percent of the assets owned by American foundations fall into this category. Today most of the funds allocated tend to be confined to communities where the parent company has its officers or plants. In general, grants are made for the support of institutions or agencies that benefit the company's employees, its stockholders, or others with whom it has business relationships. Some corporations have used foundations to enhance their public images through the sponsorship of cultural and other programs. We will come back to this concern in the next chapter.

In some communities, corporation executives have banded together to increase the size of their giving programs. The Ford Foundation, in fact, has encouraged corporations in cities throughout the United States to increase their giving by offering matching funds that deal exclusively with economic development at the grassroots level. In San Francisco, several executives have organized a "2% Club" that is actively involved in inducing corporations to contribute more to the local community.

All of these foundations can be categorized as *nonoperating;* that is, they fund programs that other organizations take operational responsibility for. In contrast, there are a growing number of *operating foundations* that solicit funds for their own purposes and give those funds to pet projects and programs they themselves sponsor or operate. Examples include universities that set up foundations to raise money and reallocate to university building or scholarship funds, homes for the aged, local philharmonics, museums, and the like. It is unlikely that these foundations would be receptive to your organization's interests unless they clearly further those of the foundation.

FINDING OUT ABOUT FOUNDATIONS

While there is a great deal of information about foundations in general, you will find that it can be somewhat difficult to get information on specific foundations. The larger ones will tend to have annual reports, special project summaries, and even information packets aimed at encouraging eligible applications. Most foundations, however, are either unstaffed or understaffed. And unlike government bureaus, they are not required by law to establish clear guidelines and criteria or to provide technical assistance. You may consider yourself lucky even to get a mimeographed "thanks for your inquiry" postcard from some. While IRS regulations have opened their books to public scrutiny, foundations are not required to make it easy for you to scrutinize them. Making themselves inaccessible or unresponsive is one way of reducing the demand for their generally limited funds.

There are, fortunately, a number of general references and a wide variety of periodicals as well as some search services available to you. A good place to start is by examining the materials developed by the Foundation Center. Another is by examining your own state foundation directory. A third is by subscribing to appropriate journals, special interest associations, and commercial search services. None of these may be as useful as information you might get from a colleague or a friend who has had the good fortune of being funded by a foundation. But be careful: Word-of-mouth information can be unreliable. Foundations change priorities; they often are faced with eligible requests for funds that total ten or more times the sums available.

The Foundation Funding Source Inventory (see Exercise 6.1) can help you in your efforts to get accurate and up-to-date information on foundations in which you are interested.

EXERCISE 6.1
GETTING INFORMATION ON
FOUNDATION FUNDING SOURCES

(1) Look over the Foundation Funding Source Inventory. Pick a foundation with which you want to become more familiar. If you are not sure where to start, try the resources available from a nearby Foundation Center Cooperating Library, or get the information from one of the four Foundation Center Offices (New York, San Francisco, Washington, D.C., or Cleveland). For the address of the nearest Cooperating (Library) Collection, call (800) 424-9836.

(2) Fill in the inventory with the information you have collected. If there are too many blank spaces, contact the foundation directly, or use an available search service.

Exercise 6.1
FOUNDATION FUNDING SOURCE INVENTORY

1. Type of Foundation
   _____ Independent, General
         Purpose
   _____ Independent, Special
         Purpose
   _____ Community
   _____ Family
   _____ Company
   _____ Operational
2. Name of Foundation _____
   _____
   Address _____
   _____
   Telephone ( ) _____
3. Contact Person _____
   _____
   Title _____
   _____
   Special Information _____
   _____
   _____
4. Functional or Program Areas
   in Which Awards Are Made ____
   _____
   _____
5. **Geographic Preferences or**
   Restrictions _____
   _____
   _____
6. **Types of Organizations to**
   Which Awards Are Made ____
   _____
   _____
7. **Special Characteristics of**
   Populations the Foundation Is
   Most Interested In (ethnic,
   economic status, religion)
   _____
   _____
   _____
   _____
   _____

8. **Current Priorities, Special**
   Interests _____
   _____
   _____
   _____
9. **Restrictions, If Any** _____
   _____
   _____
10. **Funding Cycle** _____
    _____
11. Funding Information
    Assets $ _____
    _____
    Number of Awards Available
    _____
    Average Award Size $ _____
    $ Range of Awards $ _____
    to $ _____
12. Matching Fund Requirements
    _____
    Can In-Kind Resources or
    Indirect Costs Be Use? ____
    _____
13. Uses Awards Can Be Put To
    _____ Basic Research
    _____ Assessment or Evalua-
          tion
    _____ Programs and Services
    _____ Client Support
    _____ Staffing
    _____ Capital Expenditures
    _____ Space/Equipment Rental
    _____ Training and Trainee
          Support
    _____ **Technical Assistance**
    _____ **Planning**
    _____ **Coordination**
    _____ **Demonstration or Start-up**
    _____ **Ongoing Support**
    Other _____

14. Materials Available _____
    _____ Application Kit
    _____ Summaries of Previously
          Funded Projects
    _____ Guidelines
    _____ Sample Proposals
    _____ Other _____
    _____

15. Names of Other Foundations
    with Similar Scope or In-
    terest _____
    _____

16. Review Process Used _____
    _____
    _____

17. Due Dates for Proposals _____
    _____
    _____
    Review Results Transmitted by
    _____

18. Persons Currently or Recently
    Involved in the Review Process
    _____
    _____

19. Types of Assistance Available
    _____ Written Materials
    _____ Telephone Consultation
    _____ Written Response to
          Written Material
    _____ In-Office Consultation
    _____ On-Site Visits and Con-
          sultation
    _____ Other _____
    _____

20. Names of Decision Makers and
    Program Persons Who Should
    Be Involved in Proposals to this
    Source Including Client or
    Community Representatives
    _____
    _____

21. Recent Awards in Area of
    Interest
    a. Award _____
       Organization and Address
       _____
       _____
       Contact Person _____
       _____
       _____

    b. Award _____
       Organization and Address
       _____
       _____
       _____

    c. Award _____
       Organization and Address
       _____
       _____
       _____

    d. Award _____
       Organization and Address
       _____
       _____
       _____

22. Actions (to be) Taken
    a. Phone Contacts _____
       _____
       _____

    b. Written Contacts _____
       _____
       _____

    c. Interviews or Meetings _____
       _____
       _____
       _____

    d. Other _____
       _____

Inventory Compiled by   Date

THE FOUNDATION CENTER AND
THE RESOURCES IT HAS AVAILABLE

Because information on foundations was so difficult to come by, the Foundation Center was established in 1956. Its offices were located in New York, where many of the largest foundations were located. Its support currently comes from some 100 or so large and small foundations throughout the United States. The center helps grantseekers to sort among nearly 20,000 active foundations for those that might be most interested in their projects. Foundations support the center because they, too, want grantseekers to avoid taking a hit-or-miss approach. A more targeted search process relieves foundations of the need to distribute basic information to everyone who requests it.

The center publishes reference books on foundations and disseminates information through a nationwide public information and education program in the interest of matching foundation interests with nonprofit organization needs. It will not direct you to particular foundations, nor will it arrange introductions, but it will provide you free access to information at its New York office or at any one of its three branches (Cleveland, San Francisco, or Washington, D.C.), and through its 105 Cooperating (Library) Collections. These are located throughout the United States, often in university, community college, or public libraries, or in the offices of supporting foundations. To find out where the nearest collection is, call toll free (800) 424-9836. You will find that the reference librarian will be more than helpful in guiding you to the appropriate sources. Collections include Foundation Center materials and scores of other books, articles, and periodicals.

The center publishes five general directories and the *Foundation Grants Index Annual,* plus a number of COMSEARCH printouts. You were given some idea of what these services can do for you by the second vignette at the start of this chapter. I will share some additional information about these sources of information with you, and my guess about why the grantseeker quoted received only "thanks, but no thanks" postcard replies.

Let us start with the directories. The single best source on corporate, independent, and community foundations is the *Foundations Directory,* now in its ninth edition. New volumes come out every few years. In the latest edition you will find information on between 3000 and 4000 foundations, including those that give grants that total $100,000 or more each year and whose assets exceed a million dollars. These are the sources of almost 90 percent of all grant dollars allocated by foundations. The directory is organized by state, with foundations listed alphabetically. It is also cross-indexed so that you can locate the foundations that are the likeliest prospects for your grant application. Information on assets, numbers of awards and sizes of awards, key officials, and, in fact, much of what is included in the inventory in Exercise 6.1 will be found here. But the information is skimpy.

You may also want to examine two other directories: *Source Book Profiles* and *Corporation Foundation Profiles.* The 1982 edition of the *Source Book Profiles* includes three- to six-page entries on the 1000 largest foundations, including 200 company and 25 community foundations, breaking down each one's giving by subject area, type of grant, and type of recipient. The *Corporate Foundation Profiles* includes similar data on the company foundations, plus financial data on 300 or so additional corporate foundations. Fifty or so of the corporate profiles are updated each year.

Two other directories may be of interest to you. The *National Data Book* includes virtually all of the currently active grant-making foundations. Foundation entries include name, address, financial officer, and fiscal data—and an indication of whether or not a particular foundation issues an annual report. Included are all foundations that give more than one dollar per year in grants; for example, 87 percent gave under $100,000 per year. Some of these are the small foundations in your community or state that might be likely prospects for a small award.

The *Foundation Grants to Individuals* directory zeros in on the 950 or so foundations that cumulatively give almost $100 million in grants and awards to individuals each year. Over 44,000 people receive grants from these foundations for educational assistance, study abroad, research, or special projects in the arts, sciences, and humanities. You have probably heard of the Guggenheim Foundation. How many more are you aware of?

Before we turn to the *Foundation Grants Index,* a word about the *Foundation Center News.* The *News* is a professional journal of interest to all those in the philanthropy business, published by the Council on Foundations on a bimonthly basis. It can be ordered from the Council at 1828 L Street, NW, Washington, D.C. 20036. Foundation officers read it to find out what is going on and to chart trends in giving. You might find it useful for the same purposes. About half the pages in each issue describe grants (reported to the center) that were made within the last month or two in amounts of $5000 or more to nonprofit organizations. The *Index* comes out each year and helps you locate the appropriate description of the more than 22,000 grants described in the *News.* The *Index* cross-references grants by foundation, by geographic area, and by interest or subject matter. It is the quickest way to locate information on foundations that made grants in areas of interest to you during the previous year.

If your head is reeling from an information overload, let me suggest another way of cutting through the enormous amounts of information available through the center. Try locating the appropriate COMSEARCH printouts. *Geographic Printouts* list and describe actual grants made to organizations in two cities (Washington and New York), eleven states (California, Illinois, Massachusetts, Michigan, Minnesota, New Jersey, New York, North Carolina, Ohio, Pennsylvania, and Texas), and four regions (the Northeast—Maine, New Hampshire, Rhode Island, Vermont, Connecticut; the Southeast—Florida, Georgia, Alabama, Mississippi, Louisiana, South Carolina; the Northwest—Washington and Oregon; and the Rocky Mountains—Arizona, New Mexico, Colorado, Utah, Nevada, Idaho, Montana, and Wyoming).

Special Topics Printouts list the 1000 largest foundations in the United States by asset size and by annual grant award totals; the 600 largest company-sponsored foundations; and the 1450 operating foundations that administer their own projects or programs. There is also a new series of COMSEARCH printouts, *Broad Topics,* covering grants for (1) arts and cultural programs, (2) business and employment, (3) children and youth, (4) higher education, (5) hospitals and medical care, (6) museums, (7) science programs, (8) social science programs, (9) women and girls, (10) international and foreign programs, and (11) minorities.

Probably the most targeted information is to be found in the new series *Subject Printouts.* You can obtain a complete list from the Foundation Center. These are organized under topic headings such as communication, education, health, and cultural activities. Under a particular heading—welfare, for example—there are subtopics: housing, civil rights, and community development. Unfortunately, you cannot just punch a few key variables into a Foundation Center computer in order to get a personalized printout tailored to your specific concerns. But the standardized COMSEARCH printouts will certainly help you identify the likeliest prospects. Why, then, did this approach not work out for the author of the second vignette?

A MORE PERSONALIZED APPROACH

It has been my experience that buckshot approaches rarely work. Photocopied, "to whom it may concern"-type letters are likely to get mimeographed or photocopied responses. I have found that it often pays to place a call first, ask the receptionist for the appropriate project staffer or other person to talk to, and then to talk to that person—much as I recommended you talk to government officials. Foundation personnel are not as obligated as government officials to give you time, nor will they necessarily refer you to another, more appropriate funding source. However, if you are on target, you will know right away. Your letter can then be addressed to a specific person. It can be tailored to the kinds of initial feedback that person gave you, and it can refer to the foundation's current interests and priorities—those that complement the focus of the project you will be proposing.

Remember that many foundations, especially the smaller ones, have no paid staff. They may be managed by a part-time volunteer, often a member of the family that has put up the money, and so will find it difficult to respond to your inquiries. Although well staffed, the larger foundations may be so inundated with requests that they will respond only to certain types of inquiries. I have found that many foundations do not consider fully fleshed-out proposals without prior contact. Nor will they respond to long and detailed inquiries. You might find the following tips helpful. They come from my own experiences, but if yours are different, follow your own instincts.

Tip 1: When approaching a foundation cold, use the telephone first and then keep your correspondence brief. Your cover letter should be no longer than a single page. It should include information on who you are, why you feel your project is important to your organization, and why you think it might be of interest to the foundation. Attach a one- or two-page description of the project for which you would like funding. You might prefer including two or three descriptions as bait. This will give you some idea of what the foundation is biting on this year. But don't allow the total number of pages to exceed two or three.

Tip 2: In your one- or two-page proposal outline, specify the objectives you are trying to reach, how you want to reach them, and how long it will take to get to where you want to go. Point out the significance of the project for those persons being served as well as for others who may want to replicate the project elsewhere. Indicate how much the project might cost. And mention something about the accountability or evaluative procedures you'll be using. Pitch to the specific interests of the foundation. If you know a foundation is interested in health *research,* for example, don't submit a *training* proposal for physicians and nurses.

Tip 3: If at all possible, avoid going in cold. The smaller foundations especially like to deal with people or organizations they know. If they publish annual reports, these should tell you who has been funded in recent years. Check with someone else who has received a grant from the foundation. Get a sense of what the foundation's real priorities are. And, if possible, get an introduction to a foundation board member or to the foundation's executive officer or grants manager through someone else who has already had a successful experience with the foundation.

You will have additional ideas of your own or may have gathered them from colleagues who have had experience in dealing with foundations. Develop a set of tips or practice principles to guide you in your search and in your relationships to foundations. Use Exercise 6.2 as a guide.

EXERCISE 6.2
LISTING OF PRACTICE PRINCIPLES

(1) Review the practice principles you identified for working with government funding sources. Which of these apply to foundations? Which would have to be modified or eliminated?

(2) Identify additional practice principles in this chapter and add those from your experience or the experiences of colleagues.

(3) Draw up a new list of practice principles appropriate to work with foundations, or add to and modify the list you designed for government sources, indicating (a) which are universal, (b) which apply only to public sources, and (c) which apply to foundation sources.

REVIEW

There are more than 30,000 philanthropic foundations in the United States. Of these, over 20,000 provide grants and other funding to nonprofit organizations. A relatively small number —about 100 of the largest foundations—account for roughly one-fourth of the funds awarded. There are several kinds of philanthropic foundations. The vast majority, about 19,000, are generally defined as private, general-purpose, or specific-interest foundations. Although many have national or international agendas, most orient their funding activities to local communities or to specific types of organizations. Such *independent foundations* as Ford or Mellon are among the best known.

Community foundations are a growing phenomenon; these are exclusively local in their orientations. They allocate funds generated from bequests, corporate donors, individual benefactors, and even local government allocations.

Company (-sponsored) foundations are perhaps the fastest growing category in terms of assets and funds allocated. Their assets currently account for approximately 5 percent of all foundation assets. Awards tend to be made in ways that complement the sponsoring company's interests, serve the employees of the company, or deal with issues in communities in which the company has plants or headquarters. *Family foundations,* often identifying themselves as private foundations, tend, in fact, to be exceedingly private. They are generally very limited in their focuses, even if their official statement suggest broad interests or general purposes. Many aim at support of religious or ethnic causes, organizations or individuals with appropriate backgrounds and characteristics. *Operating foundations* are of a different order. Although some are fully funded, many engage in fund raising activities. Grants are allocated to programs and projects administered by the foundation itself.

The Foundation Center was established almost thirty years ago for the express purpose of making information on foundations more accessible to grantseekers, the academic community, and the general public. Its headquarters are in New York and it has three regional branch offices. In addition, it supports a growing network of cooperating collections: reference materials generally located in public libraries or in university, community college, and foundation office libraries throughout the United States. Many of these resources are published by the center itself. These include a journal, five directories, computer printouts, and an index.

Foundations tend to have very limited and highly targeted agendas. Unfortunately, many do not publicize their efforts, and specific information or guidelines may be hard to come by. Proposals that do not articulate directly with a foundation's concerns, or that arrive unsolicited and unannounced, may go unheeded. This poses a special challenge to the grantseeker to get accurate, up-to-date information, and to put his or her organization in position to be sought after and welcomed by appropriate foundations.

SUGGESTIONS FOR FURTHER READING

Start with publications of the Foundation Center. These can be found at one of the 105 or more Cooperating Collections or at one of the Center's four offices, or can be ordered directly from the Center at 888 Seventh Avenue, New York, NY 10106.

The Foundation Directory (9th ed.)

Source Book Profiles

The National Data Book

Corporate Foundation Profiles

Foundation Grants to Individuals

The Foundation Grants Index Annual Volume

plus COMSEARCH printouts by *Subject Matter, Geographic Area, Broad Topics*

In addition, you can order the following publications from the Foundation Center:

Kurzig, Carol. (1981). *Foundation fundamentals: A guide for grantseekers.*
Includes information on what foundations are and how they work, how they fit into the total funding pattern for nonprofits, who gets grants, and how to find a foundation with an interest in your field. It also includes a proposal research checklist and suggestions on how to present your ideas.
1982 Foundations Today (1982, April).
A 24-page state-of-the-art report documenting increased emphasis in social service and the arts.

The following items are available from the Public Service Materials Center, 355 Lexington Avenue, New York, NY 10017:

Dermer, Joseph. (1980). *Where America's large foundations make their grants*
Lists over 750 foundations, and most but not all of their grants. Arranged alphabetically by state, with grants listed by subject area. Includes deadlines.
Dermer, Joseph. (1973). *How to get your fair share of foundation grants*
Tells what is expected in a proposal, how to research and approach foundations, based on advice of nine experts in the field.
Dermer, Joseph. (1973). *How to raise funds from foundations*
Offers help in avoiding common pitfalls and suggests planning procedures

and approaches that have worked well for others. Includes an especially useful section on resuming contact with a foundation that has initially turned you down.

Foundations that send their annual reports (1976).

For those of you interested in foundations outside the United States, check out the following directories, both of which list foundations by country and will give you information similar to the Foundation Center's *Foundation Directory.*

Directory of European foundations. (updated periodically) New York: Basic Books.

Pinpoints American organizations that receive funds from foundations in Europe.

International foundation directory. (n.d.) Detroit: Gale Research Co.

Foundations in more than 40 countries are described.

Additional information on foundations that fund specific areas of interest are also available, sometimes from national organizations and associations. For example, you might want to check the following items, some of which may lead you to government sources in addition to foundations:

Robinson, Philip (Ed.). (1979). *Foundation guide for religious grant seekers.* Missoula, MT: Scholars Press.

Millsapps, D. (Ed.). (1978). *National directory of arts supported by business corporations and foundations.* Washington, DC: Washington International Arts Letter.

Dodge, A. B., & Tracy, D. (Eds.). (1978). *How to raise money for kids.* Washington, DC: Coalition for Children and Youth.

Katzowitz, L. (1978). *Researching foundations.* Los Angeles: Grantsmanship Center.

Struckoff, E. C. (1977). *The handbook of community foundations: Their formation, development and operation.* Washington, DC: Council on Foundations.

Directories on foundations that are located in your state are available from a number of sources. These may be published by the League for the Human Services or by a state agency. The easiest way to locate the directory is by contacting the state attorney general's office. This office is responsible for granting the foundation a license to operate and gives it the preclearance to operate on a tax-free basis. The governor's office and a state legislator's office are other places to contact.

CHAPTER 7

The Business of Business Is Business
Seeking Private Sector Funds

VIGNETTE 8:
FROM REDLINING TO REDEVELOPMENT

They accused us of redlining. It wasn't true. It is true that the banks were redlining, refusing to provide mortgage or improvement loans to people in high-risk neighborhoods. We're an insurance company; we did not see it as in our interest to make mortgage loans. But we were selling insurance in every neighborhood, regardless of the risk. High-risk policies cost more; but that's business. We've always had a commitment to the communities in which we have national or regional headquarters. So we were willing to take the risks, even lose money on some of the policies we sold.

Still, as the neighborhoods close to the inner city were deteriorating, costs were getting higher. Some businesses were suffering badly. Boarded up storefronts were a common sight. Thefts increased as some of the more stable residents moved away and as some of the major institutions, the churches and banks, pulled out. A major fire or two seemed to break out every week. We suspected arson in some business establishments and in some deteriorated apartment buildings. And as everyone knows, health problems are most severe in poverty areas. There is no question that neighborhood deterioration was costing us money.

And we did have to close some of our offices or pull out some of our agents. But we never refused a bona fide request for insurance. We weren't redlining, even if that's not how CORP saw it. CORP is a network of neighborhood associations that calls itself the Commu-

*nity Organization and Rehabilitation People. They lumped us to-
gether with the banks, picketed our offices, issued damaging press
releases. Frankly, it wasn't good for our public image.*

*And it didn't fit our image of ourselves as a community-spirited
company. A number of the executive staff were pretty defensive,
wanted to counterattack in the press. Interestingly, the board wasn't
defensive at all. We had a number of church, business, and labor
people on the board who felt strongly about the attacks on the company. They felt even more strongly about profits. And they believed
just as strongly in our social commitments as a company and as an
industry. The problem was that profits, image, and commitments
seemed to be out of sync. "As you know, the archdiocese provides
some support for CORP," one of our board members pointed out.
"We know they tend to be seen as extremists, but we've always
found them to have done their homework. If they are targeting this
company, we should examine the charges seriously."*

*The board chairman agreed. He established a task force to recom-
mend a course of action. One of its recommendations was to sit with
representatives of CORP. I participated in the first meeting. I was
empowered to offer CORP a grant for training local residents in
community development techniques and for increasing CORP staff.
At first they thought we were trying to buy them off.*

*"Look," I explained, "we are not about to abandon the city. Unsta-
ble neighborhoods cost us money, and we are fully aware that they
create tragedies for the people in them. If you can help stabilize the
neighborhoods, we all stand to gain." They agreed to think on it
and we set up a series of planning meetings. At the second session,
CORP came in with a number of demands. Money for organizers
wasn't enough, they argued. They wanted us to invest in building
rehabilitation projects: fixing up homes and redeveloping shopping
centers. "Why not use your investment portfolios to reduce your insurance risks?" they asked. They offered to take us on tours of several neighborhoods to show us what was needed and to meet some
of the people we would be investing in. We went.*

*After several more meetings, we agreed to put up $4 million for
short-term rehabilitation and new construction loans, if CORP, with
our help, could induce banks to put up the money for long-term
loans, and if CORP could establish local neighborhood nonprofit
corporations to manage each project. It took about six months to*

put the deal together. CORP insisted we also reopen neighborhood-based insurance offices. We did.

We're now three years into the experiment. None of our loans have defaulted. Once the banks were threatened with lawsuits for redlining and saw that we were willing to put our money on the line, several agreed to enter into cooperative agreements on long-term financing. From our perspective, the experiment has increased our profits and reestablished our image as a forward-looking, community-oriented company. It's good business.

Income from the sale of policies has grown enormously; and outlays in terms of payments on claims has decreased considerably. Most important, three of the seven neighborhoods we are currently involved in have stabilized, and three of the others seem to be turning around. We may be too late on the seventh, but we've got some new ideas there, too.

NEW PARTNERSHIP WITH
THE PRIVATE SECTOR:
SOME FACTS, LOTS OF FICTIONS

According to some proponents of the "new federalism," cuts in federal government appropriations to such human service programs and nonprofit organizations as those in the education, culture, and health business are necessary not only to balance the budget, but to shift the locus of responsibility to the more proximate levels of government and to the private sector. However, states, municipalities, and county governments have not been able to pick up the slack. In many sections of the country, particularly the older industrial areas, a shrinking tax base has resulted in even greater cuts to programs. Let us look at some of the figures.

Mental health service budgets in some states have been cut by as much as 40 percent over a three-year period beginning in 1980. Cuts in Title XX social welfare funds have reduced services to the disabled, to children, to youth, to other disadvantaged populations. Ethnic and racial minorities have been hit the hardest. The voluntary sector, which had revenues of approximately $180 billion in 1980 (about half of which went to educational, cultural, and human service programs) has been on the defensive ever since.

Those revenues had been provided in roughly the following proportions: one-half from user fees or third parties; one-quarter from all forms of charitable giving; and one-quarter from government sources. Government funding for entitlement programs, such as medical care, are difficult to cut. Medical care, moreover, is heavily funded through user fees and third-party insurers. But social service and community development programs, which are funded almost entirely through categorical and discretionary grant programs, are relatively easy to cut. Thus legal aid services, which were in disfavor with the Reagan administration, suffered disproportionately. Federal budget cuts are expected to cause private and voluntary nonprofit organizations to lose approximately $27 billion between 1981 and 1984, of which $5 billion will be cut from social service programs.

Changes in the tax structure make the situation even more bleak. The 1981 tax reform bill reduced the maximum deduction an individual could take from 70 percent to 50 percent. A donor who in previous years might have made a charitable contribution of $10,000 would have been out of pocket only $3000 since he or she could have deducted 70 percent of that gift. Today a $10,000 donation would put the donor out $5000. The 1981 tax law also lowers the corporate incentive for making charitable contributions by reducing corporate tax liability. Although business enterprises continue to be permitted to contribute up to 10 percent of their pretax profits for charitable purposes, historically the actual amounts given have been a fairly stable 1 percent or less. This percentage is hardly expected to increase without proper incentives. Cumulatively, government cuts and changes in the tax laws are expected to cost nonprofit organizations almost $46 billion by 1984.

To darken the picture even further, any reduction in profits by many major corporations is not likely to induce them to increase charitable contributions. Some of the programs most severely hit by federal cutbacks are among those least popular with business leaders. Legal aid services for the poor, for example, have resulted in a number of public action law suits against corporations. Even with the best of goodwill, business could not easily step into the breach left by organizations that have folded because of inadequate financial support. Businesses at the local level are not likely to have the expertise to do needs assessment or services planning, or to conduct human services programs for people in need. Nor is it their business to do so.

So where are the incentives for the new partnerships between the private and the public sectors or the private and the voluntary sectors? The incentive is not likely to be purely philanthropic. In most situations it will have to be in the direct self-interest of the corporation. The example in the vignette at the start of this chapter is a case in point. The insurance company reduced its payments while increasing its premium income; it made a profitable investment as well.

Partnerships between social agencies or community groups and business enterprises must be true partnerships. Asking for a handout is not the way to build a partnership. Building on the concerns of both partners can be. What follows is a list of other examples that may stimulate you to consider opportunities in your locale.

In Arlington, Virginia, a developer who sets aside a certain percentage of flats for low- and moderate-income families in a middle-income development receives special dispensation of zoning ordinances governing the height or density of apartment buildings within the development.

In the Detroit area, a mental health center offered to provide drug counseling services to workers in an industrial plant, to be reimbursed in part by a third-party payer (a medical insurer), and later went on to interest the industrial firm in funding prevention programs in the schools attended by employees' children, thus improving productivity and morale in the plant.

In Baltimore, a citizens' movement sparked by the Roman Catholic archdiocese induced the Baltimore Gas and Electric Company to raise $200,000 from the private sector, which the city department of social services distributed to those of the city's poor who could not pay their utility bills. It cost BG&E, but it also saved money by eliminating the need to shut off utilities to those who could not afford to pay their fuel bills. People would have suffered, and the unpaid bills would probably have totaled more than the money raised and distributed.

Food banks in a number of communities throughout the United States have profited as a result of the Tax Act of 1976, which stipulates that corporations may donate equipment or stock to charitable institutions for the ill, for infants, or for the needy. In some cases a social agency may issue vouchers for food that are redeemable at a supermarket. In other cases the supermarket donates dented cans, day-old breads, or slightly wilted vegetables to a distribution center, saving itself money through a tax write-off.

Shared housing arrangements, mediated by a family service agency, resulted in private and public grants for the rehabilitation of several privately owned buildings in a northwest community. The landlords benefited through the program by having needed repairs made to their buildings and by full occupancy, even though they charged reduced rents.

Tax reductions are offered by the District of Columbia to those neighborhood businesses that agree to employ and to train area residents, in particular the young, the elderly, and the disabled.

In St. Louis, a group of business leaders raised several million dollars, which were then matched by the Ford Foundation, for the sponsorship of minority business enterprises. These businesses received technical assistance from both the private sector and voluntary and public agencies. The sponsors benefit from more employment, less crime, and a decrease in other problems that would have resulted in property tax increases.

In many of these examples, the initial idea for the project or program came from staff members or volunteers connected with a social agency. Some of these are what have recently come to be known as "nonservice" approaches. The term is an unfortunate misnomer. It is intended to imply complementary or alternative services without direct cost to the initiating organization. Thus, in Arlington, the county does not have to build or subsidize as much public housing as might otherwise be needed. In Baltimore, the public welfare department does not have to provide heating subsidies to those who cannot afford to pay their utility bills. Government grants or loans are not needed to launch some of the new business ventures for minorities and other disadvantaged populations in St. Louis, and the technical assistance provided reduces the likelihood of failure or default. The insurance company's support of neighborhood renewal increased resources available while increasing the company's profits.

This is not to suggest that there are no costs involved. Of course there are. But the costs are hidden, often absorbed by the private sector, which benefits in terms of reduced taxes, increased income, or reduced outlays. You can get additional information on these nonservice approaches by writing to the Program for Nonservice Social Welfare Initiatives (SRI International, 333 Ravenswood Avenue, Menlo Park, California 94025) or to Nonservice Initiatives Project (Public Technology, Inc., 1301 Pennsylvania Avenue, NW, Washington, D.C. 20004).

INVESTIGATING THE OPPORTUNITIES IN YOUR AREA

As these examples suggest, there is no standard way of investigating grants or nonservice contributions by business enterprises in your community. Direct grants or other contributions from corporations do not operate the same way as company foundations. These foundations, where they exist, were established in order to divorce philanthropy from ongoing business operations and, by so doing, protected gift giving from fluctuations in corporate income. It unlinked corporate giving from direct corporate interests.

Direct corporate interests, on the other hand, are the key to getting increased support from the private sector. And this should be the focal point of your investigation of opportunities for private sector support and involvement. Universities have operated on this principle for a long time. For the past 35 years or so, one of the primary beneficiaries of corporate philanthropy was educational institutions, particularly universities. The endowment of chairs and the provision of scholarships to prestigious institutions or to local colleges and universities were seen by donors not only as good public relations, but as good business. Corporate contributions resulted in a more highly trained pool of recruits and in research activities that were often of direct benefit to the corporate sponsor.

This limited, although relatively successful, effort on the part of higher education to gain corporate support did not come without considerable effort. Nevertheless, support continues to be ad hoc, isolated, and relatively sporadic and arbitrary. Successful efforts by universities generally depend on successful relationships to a company's chief executive officer and to other management staff. Unfortunately, these managers may not see corporate contributions as being in the company's best interest. Efforts to increase corporate giving have been enhanced somewhat by the Council for Financial Aid to Education, a kind of financial trade association for higher education. Similar trade associations do not yet exist for social welfare agencies, social and community development groups, or other human services. Could you establish one in your community? If you do, remember that it is the private sector's interest, not your agency's, that must be the focal point.

Let's face it. The American public did not buy Chrysler products in 1982 and 1983 because they wanted to enhance the company's profits or because they wanted to bail the company out of a devastating cash flow problem. They bought Chryslers because they were convinced by Lee Iacocca that the company was here to stay, and that it was selling the best product for the price, a product that was well built by a company that was committed to survival. Companies are not about to buy an agency's service for any other reason. Going to an executive officer with hat in hand with a request for funds because the government is no longer willing to support one of your programs, or because the United Way was not successful in its campaign, is no way to generate enthusiasm.

Company executives are concerned with fiscal responsibility and their responsible stewardship of funds. Commercial enterprises are profit oriented. Proposals we make to them should indicate clearly the financial advantages, in the short or long run, that are likely to accrue to the enterprise. Proposals should include clear definitions of the product, its quality, the procedures to ensure production on time, and the accountability mechanisms used to ensure conformity to acceptable standards.

Company concerns with stewardship mean we have to give evidence that our staff are knowledgeable and qualified to do the job we intend to do, and that our board members are responsible, committed, and respectable individuals.

Finding out which company is willing to buy, and what they may be willing to purchase or to engage in directly, may take a great deal of research. The insurance company/community development and the settlement house/supermarket experiences are fortuitous examples of effective partnerships. You will need to research the business enterprises in your community that will be open to general partnerships of equal benefit to your organization and to the publics it seeks to serve.

There are some standard places to start: The National Committee for Responsible Philanthropy (810 18th Street, NW, Washington, D.C. 20006) advocates for the needs of nonprofit organizations concerned with social change. The *Independent Sector* is a journal that also advocates for corporate and foundation contributions to voluntary nonprofit organizations, primarily human service organizations (its address is the Council on Foundations, 1828 L Street, NW, Washington, D.C. 20036). The Public Management Institute (at 333 Hayes Street in San Francisco, California 94102) publishes an annual *Directory of*

Corporate Philanthropy with information on the giving programs of the top 500 businesses in America. It also publishes numerous reference works and conducts training and consultation services. The Conference Board (at 845 Third Avenue, New York, New York 10022) also sponsors workshops and publishes reports on major corporate philanthropic policies and practices. You might also write for a list of relevant publications to the American Enterprise Institute in Washington, D.C. This institute has been conducting research, sponsoring symposiums, and publishing policy papers on related topics.

At the end of this chapter I have listed a number of directories that I think you may find invaluable. They list the most important and largest corporations in the country, and often provide information on the locations of each company, the products they produce, the names of key officers, and sometimes their interests and affiliations. You may find the names of some business leaders who are active on boards or organizations like your own, or who may be alumni of the same university you or your board members attended. Look over the list carefully. Hit the library and do some research.

You may prefer to start closer to home. Read the newspapers carefully. Clip out articles on local corporations and businesses and on company executives who are involved in some activity close to the interests of your organization. Examples might include an executive who has adopted children with special needs, a nursing home that is upgrading its equipment, a corporation with a special program for its retired employees, or a company that donated an older computer to a community college—it may have some word-processing equipment next year that is begging for a recipient.

Do not limit yourself to what the press covers. Visit a local stockbroker. Find out which area companies are doing particularly well or which ones may have been awarded a lucrative government contract. Brokers are also good resources for locating company annual reports that may include references to new products and product lines, philanthropic activities, or the public images a company may wish to project. Those same companies publish newsletters and other house organs that may give you additional information. They may also be willing to carry stories on the things your organization does that may be of interest to the company's employees and to its consumers.

EXERCISE 7.1
LOCATING COMPANY PROSPECTS

(1) Using the suggestions in this chapter and the directories listed under "Suggestions for Further Reading," identify at least five likely private sector prospects for contributions and five other business or professional firms that might be targeted for partnership efforts of some sort. These may include nonservice approaches.

(2) Complete the Private Sector Funding Source Inventory for one corporation and one other type of private sector enterprise. Item 3 refers to products or services (e.g., automobile manufacturer or health care services) that may have some implication for agency needs. Item 4 refers to the firm's needs or interests (e.g., drug counseling or preretirement counseling for employees or opportunities for executives to become integrated into the community). Item 6 might include involvement of officers on social agency boards, or interests in the arts or in population groups such as the elderly or disabled children.

Time now to go back over the chapter and identify new practice principles.

EXERCISE 7.2
LISTING OF PRACTICE PRINCIPLES

(1) Review the practice principles you identified for working with both government and foundation sources in Chapters 5 and 6. Which of these apply to work with the private sector? Which would have to be modified or eliminated?

(2) Identify additional practice principles in this chapter and add those from your experience or those of colleagues.

(3) Draw up a new list of practice principles appropriate to work with the private sector, or add to and modify the set you developed for government and foundation sources. Which of these (a) are universal, or apply only to (b) public, (c) foundation, and (d) private sector sources?

Exercise 7.1
PRIVATE SECTOR FUNDING (OR NONSERVICE) SOURCE INVENTORY

1. Type of Enterprise
   _____ Corporation
   _____ Small Business
   _____ Public Utility
   _____ Professional Firm
   _____ Other _____
   _____

2. Name: _____
   _____
   Address (local) _____
   _____
   _____
   Telephone ( ) _____
   Address (national head-
   quarters) _____
   _____
   Telephone ( ) _____

3. Major Products or Services
   That in Some Way Articulate
   with Agency Interests _____
   _____
   _____
   _____

4. Company Needs or Interests
   that May be Served by the
   Agency _____
   _____
   _____
   _____
   _____
   _____

5. Previous or Recent Gifts
   of Funds, Materials or
   Nonservice Activities
   Relevant to the Human
   Services. Include
   Agencies Involved
   a. _____
   _____
   b. _____
   _____
   c. _____
   _____

6. Executive Officers and Interests
   a. Chief Executive Officer: _____
   _____
   Public Service Interests of
   Affiliations _____
   _____
   b. Community Relations
   Officer _____
   Public Service Interest of
   Affiliations _____
   _____
   c. Other (Title) _____
   _____
   d. Other (Title) _____
   _____
   e. Other (Title) _____
   _____
   f. Other (Title) _____
   _____

7. Materials Available
   _____ Annual Reports
   _____ Newsletters, House Organ
   _____ News Stories
   _____ Special Project Reports
   _____ Other _____

8. Actions to be Taken
   a. Phone contacts _____
   _____
   _____
   b. Written Contacts _____
   _____
   _____
   c. Interviews or Meetings _____
   _____
   d. Other _____
   _____

Data Compiled by _____
_____
Date: _____

REVIEW

Cuts in government funding are not likely to be made up by the private sector, even if boosted by modest increases in foundation funding. Recent changes in the tax structure serve as a disincentive to individuals and corporations to contribute even in the amounts given for philanthropic purposes in recent years. Despite the economy and despite the fact that corporations can gain some tax advantages by contributing up to 10 percent of their pretax profits to qualified nonprofit organizations, the amount given has hovered around or just below the 1 percent mark for many years. There are no indications that this will change in the near future.

Nevertheless, private sector contributions can be increased if they are clearly in the interest of the donor enterprise. Business enterprises are in business to make money, and increased profits can be achieved through increased income or decreased expenditures. Cooperative arrangements with human service and other nonprofit enterprises are likely to be successful if they articulate with these interests of the private sector. A number of examples were given, including some that required direct investments by private sector organizations, those that required contribution of services or of equipment, those that included service to the private sector, and those nonservice activities that required none of these but that resulted in tax or income savings by the company. To a large extent such activities are likely to take place on the initiation and with the creative leadership of the nonprofit organizations who will benefit directly or who may increase benefits to the populations for which they are concerned.

SUGGESTIONS FOR FURTHER READING

Look over some of the following directories. Most are available to your public library or in a university library. Some may be available in the offices of local corporate headquarters:

Directory of companies filing annual reports with the Securities Exchange Commission. Superintendent of Documents, Government Printing Office, Washington, DC 20402.

Once you have identified a company you are interested in, you can request an individual corporate annual report, which may give you more information than any other publicly available source. Updated annually.

Directory of corporate philanthropy. Public Management Institute, 333 Hayes Street, San Francisco, CA 94102.

Gives patterns of top 500 corporations. Updated annually.

Koskowitz, M., Katz, M., & Levering, R. (n.d.). *Everyone's business almanac: The irreverent guide to corporate America.* New York: Harper & Row.

Provides information on who owns what and how much they make.

Middle market directory. May be ordered from Dun & Bradstreet, 99 Church Street, New York, NY 10007.

Lists corporations that have a net worth of $500,000 to $1,000,000. Includes name, address, key employees, sales volume, and other pertinent data. Updated annually.

Million dollar directory. Also available from Dun & Bradstreet.

Contains geographic and alphabetical notations and Standard Industrial Classification codes that identify the types of industry or activities engaged in. Annual.

Reference book of corporate management. Published by Dun & Bradstreet, annual.

A potential gold mine of information on corporate managers in America's largest firms, biographic data that can provide clues to interests and affiliations.

Standard industrial classification manual. Superintendent of Documents, Government Printing Office, Washington, DC 20402.

A taxonomy of types of industries and industrial activities that might provide clues to industries that might have common interests with those of your organization.

Standard & Poor's register of corporations. Standard & Poor, 345 Hudson Street, New York, NY 10014.

Indicates names and locations of corporations and identified growth trends. Updated annually.

Standard & Poor's register of directors and executives. Also from Standard & Poor.

Indicates who leading corporate executives are, interests and affiliations, previous corporate histories. Best used in conjunction with *Register of corporations* and with *Standard industrial classification manual.*

The Fortune Double 500 directory. New York: Time and Life Books, Rockefeller Center.

One thousand corporations are listed in rank order according to a variety of economic indicators (profits, employees, etc.) Annual.

The handbook of corporate social responsibility: Profiles of involvement. (1977). Radnor, PA: Human Resources Network, Chitlin Books.
Names corporations and suggests approaches to use with them.

Thomas register of American manufacturers. Thomas Publishing Company, One Penn Plaza, New York, NY 10001. Eleven volumes.
Lists include products and services according to geographic regions, also manufacturers—their contacts, major officers, products, subsidiaries, and affiliates. The manufacturers' association in your state may publish additional directories. Check with your local chamber of commerce or state commerce department for the address.

There are also a number of books that can help you in your search. Most do not deal exclusively with corporations or with the private sector. Check the references in other chapters for more general texts on fund raising and grantsmanship. Check those that focus on the arts, the aged, or some other issue of concern to your organization.

Two recent articles may point you in new directions:

Whitcomb, Carol A., & Miskiewitz, Maryann K. (1982, Winter). Tapping new resources. *Public Welfare.*

Anstrom, Decker, Schaefer, Donald, Schless, Phyllis, Schottland, Charles I., & Woodson, Robert L. (1982, Spring). Articles in the "Opinion" column: Can the private sector take up the slack? *Public Welfare.*

You can expect a growing literature on the private sector and its relationship to the human services. Keep your eyes peeled to the professional journals and the conference topics sponsored by your professional association, business groups, the Chamber of Commerce, and so on. Ask members of your board or advisory committee to keep an eye out, too.

A brief but loaded manual by Howard Hillman may be all that you need to start the process of identifying, approaching, cultivating, and negotiating with business enterprises for grants and other forms of support. It is available from the Public Service Materials Center, 11 N. Central Avenue, Hartsdale, New York 10530. The center publishes other books, pamphlets, and workbooks that you may find helpful as well.

Hillman, Howard. (1983). *The art of winning corporate grants.* Hillsdale, NY: Public Service Materials Center.

Check with local medical, dental, and legal associations or their state offices for memberships, firms, clinics, and the like. These may be listed in the Yellow Pages of your telephone directory. Some information may be available from additional directories. Marquis Who's Who, for example, publishes a *Directory of Medical Specialists,* and Marindale-Hubbard publishes a *Law Directory.*

CHAPTER *8*

Civic Duty:
Seeking Support from the Voluntary Sector

VIGNETTE 9:
"I GAVE AT THE OFFICE"

I guess you could say I grew up with this organization. My dad was an active volunteer with the old Community Chest between the world wars. The Chest became the United Way back in the early fifties; that's when our symbol changed from a red feather to a torch; we still call our campaign the "Torch Drive."

This is a strong United Way town. We believe in the voluntary agencies we support; and the residents in the area have always been pretty generous. I don't mean to say that running a campaign is easy; I was chairman of the campaign committee for five years before I was elected president of the United Way board; and there's plenty of work to be done. But we've routinized the work. There are few surprises. I'll tell you how the campaign works; then I'll tell you how we make our allocation decisions.

The biggest chunk of money we get comes from individuals—about 73 percent of the wage-earning population in this town and a lot of homemakers give to the United Way. We have arranged for all the major companies to establish payroll deduction plans, and we ask workers to pledge a couple of hours a week to a full day's salary to the campaign. We thought we would lose some from this sector when we suffered an economic downturn in the early eighties. Just the opposite; the base shrank a bit, but we pressed home what our agencies did and how they helped the unemployed, so contributions actually rose 8 to 10 percent each year. It didn't happen without a lot of work.

We have a campaign team in each company; usually it includes top management people and, when there is a union, the union reps. Some companies just pass around the literature we prepare on why funds are needed and what everyone's "fair share" might be. But where we have good volunteers, they actually hold meetings or use coffee break periods to interpret our agencies and what we do. About half the money we raise comes from company employees. These are small gifts, but in accumulation, they amount to nearly $6 million. We do even better with employees in government and in nonprofit organizations in terms of individual contributions. We don't do as well as we could from such independent professionals as attorneys and doctors and insurance agents. Next year we'll borrow a strategy long employed by some of the sectarian fund raising federations such as the Jewish Welfare Federation and Catholic Charities. We'll have doctors soliciting other doctors in their own specialties, and so on.

Altogether about two-thirds of the money we raise comes from individuals, including homemakers and retired people who we get to through neighborhood doorbell-ringing campaigns, and through the mail.

We also get another 25 percent of our funds from major companies. This is an area we could stand some improvement in. Most of the companies that donate give us between 2 and 4 percent of their pre-tax profits. But only about 12 companies account for more than half of what we raise in corporate gifts. Most companies don't give anything, even though the law allows gifts of up to 10 percent. We also get about 3 percent of our money from small businesses, another place we could stand to improve. And every year the community foundation donates around $2.5 million, just above 2 percent of what we raise. The foundation and some of the corporations earmark their funds to specific agencies or projects. A few of the individual donors do too. But, by and large, we make the determination of how the money gets allocated and to whom. The process is also routinized and that's why it is so cost-efficient.

We have six allocation divisions. Each division has about sixty volunteers in it. We try to make sure those volunteers include board members and others who have been active with some of our member agencies, the ones to whom we allocate moneys. We also have professionals from those agencies on the division committees.

Each division deals with a particular service area. For example, the Family Service Division deals with family counseling, child guidance, adoptions and foster care, and so on. The Health Care Division deals with drug and other forms of substance abuse services, with community health clinics, and we've become affiliated with local chapters of the American Cancer Society and the American Heart Association, with whom we do joint campaigns. We also have an Education and Recreational Division, a Cultural Arts Division, a Legal Aid, Protection, and Safety Division, and a Community Development Division. Our Volunteer Recruitment and Training Program is handled separately.

Each division has a chairperson and several committees. One committee reviews staff-prepared reports on needs and previous allocation patterns. It sets target figures for allocations for the current year. Other committees review the specific allocation requests of member agencies and of other petitioner organizations that are not full members but that provide a service that falls under one of our priorities.

If it were just a matter of looking at each agency's request and dividing up the pie, it would be relatively easy. But it's more than that. Agencies have to come in and make their pitch to each of the subcommittees, justifying their expenditures and in particular any deviation from last year's expenditures. In some cases we try to induce an organization to move aggressively into a new area. No one was doing drug counseling with teenagers, for example. So we targeted two member agencies we thought should and could. We negotiated with them for some time, even threatened to cut back some funds from what we thought were nonessential services, at the same time that we offered the carrot of increasing funding if they moved into drug counseling.

The carrot-and-stick method sometimes works, but we try to stay on the carrot side. We study problems, involving agency staff and volunteers in the study process. The United Way planning and technical assistance staff helps the member agency prepare a proposal for a new or expanded service. So when their request comes in, it is something we have already all but agreed should be done.

The problems occur when an agency is doing things that are no longer relevant. It's hard to phase out a member agency or pressure it to change. Their board people and staff are after all on our division committees and boards, too. And if they aren't they've got other supporters who may be.

It can also be difficult for a new organization to get United Way support. We have a pretty high set of standards for professional practice. And a new organization will have to follow our budgetary procedures, agree to limit its own independent fund raising efforts, and will have to engage in activities that the division and the board consider high-priority items.

The Rape Prevention Center is an example in point. It started as a volunteer-run self-help group. It applied for funding for the first time four years ago. But rape prevention was not on our list of priorities at the time, nor were we convinced that the center had the capability of doing what it claimed. So we established a time-limited task force that included members from the Health Care and Family Service and Community Development Divisions to study the extent of the problem and to recommend whether or not rape prevention or counseling services were needed in town, whether these should be conducted under existing agency auspices, whether the center was the right organization to do it, and, if so, from which divisions the allocation should be made. The study process took two years, but in the meantime, the task force recommended an emergency allocation of $2500 a year out of the board's contingency fund to carry the center while its request was being studied.

You've heard the expression, "I gave at the office." And when it comes to money, most people do. But as you can see, they give a lot more in time and in commitment. In addition to volunteering for committee and campaign work, we have about 850 people affiliated with the Volunteer Bureau, through which they get training and are referred to member agencies. They give at the office, but it may not be their own.

VIGNETTE 10:
ALL FIRED UP

About a year ago, we found ourselves in deep difficulty. Not only was our growth threatened by cuts in federal and state grants, and by reduced access to philanthropic foundations, but the organiza-

tion's very survival as a health advocacy center was in danger. The problems were not of our own making. Shifts in national and regional spending priorities and a lagging economy had conspired to define our services as nonessential. But the staff was not about to accept that definition. If the problems were not of our own making, we decided, the solution would be.

One of our major concerns was the prevention of disabling, disfiguring, and life-threatening burns. "It is precisely when times are bad that we have to get our act together," Marvin Kligman, our director, began a staff meeting. "Cuts or no cuts, this is the time when public awareness and prevention activities are all the most important."
"Clearly we can't do it all alone," I found myself responding.
"Right," Marv continued. "Up to now we depended on others for grants and contracts. We're still going to have to depend on others for financial resources, but we are going to have to find new ways of getting the money we need. Let's make a list of those groups and organizations in the community that might care as much about burn prevention as we do."

The list generated by staff included fire fighters; the police; public health officials; individuals; physicians, nurses, and health care professionals; public housing officials; landlords; and a number of other easily definable publics. "Okay," continued Marv, "let's figure out which of these are to be targets of our intervention, and which ones are potential partners in that intervention." Staff members discussed each public. Some, such as landlords, were both targets and potential collaborators. But landlords were not likely to put money out or engage in a fund raiser on behalf of the institute. Health care providers might be individually concerned with prevention and with treatment, but were also not likely to be actively engaged in fund raising activities. Fire fighters, on the other hand, seemed to be a good bet for involvement as partners in raising the public's consciousness as well as suppliers of needed financial resources.

When I first approached one of the fire fighters' associations, I was surprised at the warmth with which they greeted me. I've never really known firemen. Let me tell you, they know their business and they care. They depend on each other in emergencies, they develop a real camaraderie and esprit de corps. And they have no trouble including other people in their inner circles. That's why they are so outgoing and friendly toward school kids when they come to visit the firehouse. And most of all, they know what getting burned means.

The first thing that we did was to provide them with some of our written material on the prevention of fires, handouts that they could use in schools and public presentations. Then we coached them on how to work with the local radio station and the newspapers. But we also leveled with them about our own financial needs. We couldn't continue providing materials of this sort or consult with them without some financial support from the community. I really wasn't expecting it, but the first fund raising effort took place at their annual picnic last May. Fire fighters and their families, other city officials, and, interestingly, people who had been helped by the fire department at one time or another were all there. The chief got up and made a speech, then he introduced me. I spoke for about five minutes about how we all need to work together and I described some of the serious consequences of burns to individuals and their families. The chief came back to the mike and told everybody about the importance of the work of our institute and asked everybody to dig in. I hate to get cute about it, but they were really "fired up." They collected over $500. The fire fighters were ecstatic.

When I met with them a few weeks later, they felt proud of themselves, but as one of the guys put it, "We really can do better but we don't know much about fund raising." That was my opportunity. Together we mapped out a campaign that included the involvement of parent/teacher organizations, the same PTOs with which the fire fighters worked when schools sent children to visit the fire stations in the community. And it included involving burn victims as well as people who had suffered property damage but not bodily harm through fires.

It took only about three months of organizing to put everything in place. The annual picnic is now seen as a fund raising event. They are about to start a semiannual letter-writing campaign. The fire fighters' wives auxiliary has opened up a thrift shop (and would you believe, it got its first major donation from what was left over in a clothing store after a fire).

It turns out that several of the fire fighters were active members of their local Kiwanis and Knights of Columbus chapters. They have started pressing for those organizations also to raise money for burn *victims. Most of these dollars will probably stay in the community, but some may be directed to supporting some of the institute's activities, at least to purchasing some of our written materials.*

This year we expect about $2500 in gifts from that community, but that is not the entire point. By involving people in fund raising efforts, we have actually involved them in a process of consciousness raising. I've spent about twenty working days in that community, and I suppose for fund raising effort that wouldn't be cost-effective. Not the first time around. But it will get more cost-effective as the community is able to take on more and more responsibility for fund raising on our behalf. And as we get more experienced with these approaches, we will be able to replicate them in communities throughout the country. We couldn't have found better partners than the fire fighters.

FUNDING THROUGH THE VOLUNTARY SECTOR

Until the advent of the New Deal in Roosevelt's first term, the vast majority of social services and most of the cultural arts programs in the United States were funded almost exclusively by the private and voluntary sectors. Family service agencies, settlement houses, Ys and community centers, child guidance clinics, sheltered workshops (e.g., Goodwill Industries, the Salvation Army), and others either raised their own funds through local and national campaigns or joined forces with other agencies in federated campaigns.

Although many voluntary agencies also get government support (through contracts and grants) and foundation support (through endowments and grants), most continue to depend on all or substantial support from federated campaigns. By far the largest and most ubiquitous of the fund raising organizations in the United States and Canada is the United Way. Other sectarian or ethically oriented campaigns include those conducted by Jewish Welfare Federations, Catholic Charities, the Urban League, Lutheran Social Services, and so on. Which sectarian federations exist in your community? Are there other federated structures that raise funds for a particular sector of the community: an arts council, a hospital or health federation? Some campaigns, particularly for health and environment issues, may be national in scope.

In recent years voluntary agencies and other nonprofit organizations have begun to develop effective partnerships with different kinds of voluntary associations. Some agencies develop a fund raising arm, sometimes called an *auxiliary* or the *Friends of . . .*, but I am not referring to these. I am referring to the various civic and fraternal organizations in the community—the Order of the Eagles, the Elks Club, the Masonic Lodge, the Knights of Columbus, the Royal Order of the Moose. To these you might add groups such as the Jaycees, Council of Jewish Women, local chapters of the National Organization for Women (NOW), environmental groups, the Junior League, and other associations that are purely local in characters, such as a local Chamber of Commerce. These are often referred to as *service clubs*. Check the Yellow Pages and various local directories for them. You are also likely to find churches, synagogues, and other religious organizations listed, as well as booster clubs, educational organizations, and advocacy groups. Which of these are likely partners in fund raising? From which are you likely to get grants or allocations on an occasional or regular basis? Through which of these could you make connections with larger corporate givers?

The industrial unions are a not unlikely source of support. Even in times of high unemployment, when unions are themselves hard pressed for money, they invest considerable sums in social services for their members, for retired members, and for former members who may be currently unemployed. Unions also have large trust funds through which they sometimes make modest but nevertheless significant gifts, particularly if these gifts result in benefits to the union's members.

How could your agency's services increase the union's bargaining position during its next round of negotiations with industry? For example, when unions were first considering negotiating for mental health benefits, they were in desperate need of service providers with whom they could contract on an experimental basis to test out alternative ways in which those benefits might be structured. What are the hot issues today in your community?

THE UNITED WAY:
A PROTOTYPE "FEDERATED" STRUCTURE

There are over 2200 independent and autonomous United Ways in the United States; each is loosely affiliated with the United Way of America, a national standard-setting and co-ordinating body. Each is incorporated as a tax-exempt, 501(c)(3) charitable organization governed by its own board of volunteers.

According to an April 1983 fact sheet entitled "Basic Facts about the United Way" (available from the United Way of America, United Way Plaza, Alexandria, Virginia 22314),

Contributions to United Ways result in financial support for about 37,000 agencies and service groups providing human care services. Literally millions of people are helped each year by the services supported by United Ways.

United Way volunteers of different ages and incomes and from all segments of the community govern their United Way by serving on boards and committees; plan and conduct the annual fund-raising drive; study human service needs and patterns of service delivery; determine priority needs in their community; review agency services and budgets in order to allocate contri-butions in a fair and efficient manner.

United Ways rank among the most efficient of all charitable organizations. Latest available statistics show the average ad-ministration, allocation, and fund-raising cost of all United Ways is approximately 10 percent of available dollars.

About 4100 professional staff members, according to a 1982 survey, are employed by United Ways and United Way of Amer-ica to support the work of a far greater number of volunteers. Professional staffs of United Ways range in size from about 150 staff members or more in the largest cities to one in smaller communities. In addition, there are literally hundreds of small, local United Ways run entirely by volunteers.

One thousand two hundred and two independent local United Ways are members of United Way of America, the national association, as of March 1983. Dues contributed voluntarily enable United Way of America to provide programs, services and materials in the areas of training, planning, allocations, government and labor relations, fund raising, communications, national agency relations, and research and data collection.

A breakdown of total allocations by all United Way organizations reporting allocations by services shows the following percentages of support: Family Service—26.2%; Social Development—20.6%; Health—17.9%; Recreation—6.7%; Neighborhood and Community Development—8.3%; Protection and Safety—6.9%; Daycare—5.0%; Jobs and Income—3.9%; Education—2.6%; Other—1.9%.

Local United Ways are a major source of support for agencies engaged in health services delivery, health research, and health education. In 1982, approximately $245 million, or 17.9 percent of United Way allocations, went to such causes.

A total of 7.4 percent of United Way allocation is distributed to agencies which are minority controlled—over half of all volunteers and staff being minorities.

United Ways support services for people from all walks of life and all income groups. Services of United Way-supported agencies often viewed as "middle class" or "traditional" reach heavily into the inner-city and ethnic or lower-income neighborhoods. For example:

— Settlement houses and neighborhood centers received $56 million from United Ways in 1982 . . . a majority of the people they serve being nonwhite and poor.

— Seventy-five percent of Boys Club members come from families with incomes of less that $12,000 . . . 44 percent come from families with incomes of less than $8,000, and 13 percent come from families with incomes under $4,000. . . . 46 percent are from single-parent families.

Types of services supported by local United Ways include adoption, advocacy, adult education, alcoholism services, arts and culture, child protection, community health clinics, consumer protection, crime prevention, day care, drug abuse services, emergency assistance and shelter care, first aid, foster care, health research, home and mobile meals, homemaker service, individual and family counseling, information and referral/hotlines, job training, legal aid, maternal and child health, mental health education, rape relief, recreation, rehabilitation services,

services for handicapped, services for older Americans, services for women, social adjustment, development and functioning, special transportation, suicide prevention, volunteerism [reprinted by permission of the United Way].

Although smaller United Ways and sectarian or sectorally limited federations may be entirely operated by volunteers, the medium- or larger-sized organizations are likely to have well-trained staff. These include social planners (often with social work background), fund raisers, accountants, and specialists in particular practice sectors or arenas (health, the arts, community development, and the like). Some have professionally managed volunteer bureaus. The fund raising pattern described in the first vignette is typical of most United Ways. Other federations may rely more heavily on mail and personal campaigns targeted at a more limited segment of the community (e.g., Jews, Catholics, Blacks, or others who support services to targeted groups).

Those large enough to have paid staff all use relatively similar allocation procedures. Councils or divisions are set up to deal with specific areas of interest: cultural and educational programs, social services, health programs, and so on. Each council is made up of volunteers who may have undergone some training before being appointed to the council, or who may have worked on a variety of tasks and on subcommittees prior to their appointments. Each council receives technical assistance from one or more professional staff persons.

The staff also works with "petitioner organizations," those who will be requesting funds to be allocated by the council. This "technical assistance" in the preparation of funding requests is intended to make certain that proper allocating procedures are used and that funding requests are in line with overall funding priorities; these are set by the board, which relies on staff to provide it with information on community needs, particularly those unmet by other sources.

In general, only member agencies can expect to receive an appropriation and this appropriation is made on an annual basis. Member agencies come to expect regular appropriations, generally at the same level as the sums received in the previous year, adjusted for inflation. They are held accountable for the way in which those funds are spent; most report on their programs and spell out the details if their current requests diverge in any way from the previous year's. It is difficult for nonmember organizations to receive allocations.

Nevertheless, such allocations are sometimes made, especially when the community faces a particularly pressing problem and none of the member agencies is prepared or willing to take on responsibility. A grant or allocation to a nonmember organization may also be made on a tentative basis if that organization is being tested for possible full inclusion as a member of the federation. In addition to their regular allocations, member organizations may submit requests for the financing of special, innovative projects. Sometimes the funds requested are designated as seed money and are intended to attract funds from other sources. In a period when the available supply of funds seems to be outdistanced by need, federated agencies are examining their traditional allocation patterns very closely. It has, on occasion, become more difficult for old-time member organizations to receive allocations than for new organizations that are more responsive to current needs.

On the average, United Ways allocate about 10 percent of the funds raised to their own administrative costs. These include expenditures incurred in the campaign itself, in planning and coordinating activities, in research and evaluation, in bookkeeping and in management of the allocation process, and in volunteer training and placement. By any measure this cost is modest. It compares extraordinarily well with the inefficiencies of fund raising efforts in prefederation days, when each agency used to conduct its own fund raising efforts. Sometimes costs were as high as 80 percent of the amount raised. Local Jewish federations are even more efficient, generally allocating less than 8 percent of the money raised to campaigns and related administrative costs.

United Ways perceive themselves as leaders in promoting sound accounting and financial reporting principles. *Account-*

ing and Financial Reporting: A Guide for United Ways and Nonprofit Human Service Organizations was first published in 1974. It is still one of the best guides available. It contains standards, models, and directions for use by United Ways in reporting expenditures and income *and* identifying expenditures and income of the agencies to which the monies are allocated. According to the United Way, "Based on the latest accounting principles of the American Institute of Certified Public Accountants, this guide has become the standard for the nonprofit field. United Ways are committed to full and fair disclosure of all expenses."

The financial records of almost all United Ways are audited annually by an independent public accountant whose examination conforms to generally accepted standards outlined in the accounting guide. All United Ways are encouraged to publish financial reports to the public that provide full disclosure of all revenues (including campaign results) and expenditures.

CIVIC GROUPS AND OTHER LOCAL PARTNERS

Fund raisers have too often neglected the potential of establishing partnership relationships with civic and religious organizations. That is why I chose to include the second vignette in this chapter. I do not mean to suggest that your basic support is likely to come primarily from partnerships with any of these groups—that is unlikely. The health care institute in the example certainly did not. By any measure, the amount it raised, even for one of its programs—burn prevention—was relatively modest. Efforts to replicate the pattern described in other communities might increase those funds, but, again, not without a good deal of investment. That investment, however, had other programmatic payoffs. By engaging fire fighters first, and then local civic groups, the institute staff was actually able to engage in its primary concern: heightening public awareness and raising community consciousness of a severe and dangerous problem.

I had occasion to discuss this experience with the institute's staff only a few weeks before writing this chapter. Several prac-

tice principles emerged from the discussion. I highly recommend them to any organization. First among these is to *broaden
your base of support* so as to minimize your dependency on
one or two sources. When foundation grants become scarce,
for example, it may make more sense to seek support from
industry or the general public, rather than another foundation.
Second, *find another partner or partners,* persons and organizations that will be as concerned as you about raising the necessary funds—partners who may even take on fund raising for
your organization as a major commitment. Third, *use fund
raising activities in such a way as to complement other organizational programs* and services. In some cases, fund raising
activities may themselves become essential services, particularly when they increase public awareness and involve the public in programs of self-help. Can you think of others?

Use the inventory form that follows to collect and record
information on appropriate voluntary sources of support.

RELATIONSHIPS IN
THE ESTABLISHMENT OF PARTNERSHIPS

The extent to which your organization will be successful in
getting an allocation for a federated structure or in inducing a
civic association to direct some of its fund raising and charitable
activities toward your organization will depend on the way your
organization and its capacities are perceived. Let us look at
the United Way as a case in point.

The United Way has carved out a domain for itself. In part,
this is a historical domain, clearly understood by all concerned.
In part, the domain it deals with is a result of the decisions of
its current board and its member agencies. "These are the
organizations and programs we fund," explained a United Way
executive. "There are certainly other worthwhile causes, but
if we took them all on, we would dilute out effectiveness and
do damage to the member agencies who depend on us. When
our priorities shift in response to new needs, if our member
agencies aren't willing to shift some of their services, we may

look for an outside organization and even give it conditional associate membership. Sometimes an outside petitioner is successful in convincing our staff and board that we are not adequately dealing with newly identified needs. That doesn't mean that the organization that pointed up the shortcomings is the one that is going to get funded. We're going to look at the capacity of an organization to do the job for which we allocate money, the people it serves, and who else might be able to deliver the same product for less money. Most of our member agencies have carved out their own turfs and whatever competition may exist between them is kept to a minimum. When a new organization comes around, it sometimes upsets the domain claims already accepted by those who are affiliated with us."

What your organization actually does constitutes its de facto domain, although it may also make claims for expanded domain over other problems, populations, or services in the future. That is, it may position itself to take advantage of changing public awareness or emerging problems in a given area of service.

The extent to which it is likely to receive funding for maintaining partial or absolute ownership over its particular turf

---

EXERCISE 8.1
FINDING INFORMATION ON VOLUNTARY
FUNDING SOURCES

(1.) Look over the Voluntary Sector Funding Source Inventory. Notice that there are two parts of the form. Form A deals with federated fund raising and allocating bodies such as the United Way and sectarian organizations. Form B deals with civic associations that may engage in charitable work, but are not necessarily in the funding business. Decide on one federated structure and one civic association you want to know more about.

(2.) Fill in the inventory for each type of organization. You may be able to get all the information you need from the United Way office, or from the local Chamber of Commerce, which may have a list of civic associations. If you are not sure where else to begin, try the Yellow Pages.

Exercise 8.1
VOLUNTARY SECTOR FUNDING SOURCE INVENTORY
Form A. Federated Structures

1. **Type of Federated Structure**
   _____ United Way
   _____ Sectarian _____
   _____ Other _____

2. **Name of Organization** _____

   Address _____

   _____

   Telephone ( ) _____

   _____

3. **Major Allocations Division**
   a. **Arena** _____

   _____

      Staff Person _____
      Lay Leader _____
   b. **Arena** _____

      Staff Person _____
      Lay Leader _____

   _____
   c. **Arena** _____
      Staff Person __ _____
      Lay Leader _____

   _____
   d. **Arena** _____

      Staff Person _____
      Lay Leader __ _____

   _____ _____

4. **Other Relevant Staff Members and Titles of Lay Leaders**
   a. _____
   _____
   b. _____
   _____
   c. _____
   _____
   d. _____
   _____
   e. _____
   _____

5. **Types of Organizations to Which Awards Are Made**
   _____

6. **Types of Allocations Available for Nonmembers, if any:**
   _____

7. **Membership Requirements or Procedure for Becoming Members** _____

8. **Total Amount of Funds Available**
   for Current Year _____
   Specific Divisions _____
   Nonmembers _____
   Other Category _____

9. **Current Priorities** _____
   _____

10. **Restrictions, if any** _____
   _____

11. **Funding Cycle:** _____
   Campaign Dates _____
   Allocation Dates _____
   Other _____

12. **Allocation Procedures and Key Dates** _____
   _____

13. **Materials Available**
   _____ Application Kit
   _____ Summaries of Previously Funded Projects
   _____ Guidelines
   _____ Sample Proposals
   _____ Other _____

14. **Actions to be Taken**
   a. **Phone Contacts** _____
   _____
   b. **Written Contacts** _____
   _____
   c. **Interviews or Meetings** _____
   _____
   d. **Other** _____
   _____

Form B. Civic Associations

1. Type of Association
_____ Fraternal
_____ Business
_____ Ethnic or Sectarian
_____ Church Related
_____ Other _____
_____
_____
_____

2. Name of Association _____
_____
Address _____
_____
_____
Telephone ( ) _____

3. Officers (Names, Titles, Phone Numbers)
_____
_____
_____

4. Other Relevant Contacts and Their Interests
_____
_____
_____

5. National or State Affiliation _____
_____

6. Kinds of Activities Engaged in by Local Chapter that May Be Relevant to Your Organization's Fund Raising Concern
_____
_____
_____
_____
_____

7. National Fund Raising Priorities _____
_____
_____
_____

8. Restrictions, if any _____
_____
_____
_____

9. Other Local Fund Raising Efforts _____
_____
_____

10. Areas of Your Organization's Concern that Might Also Become the Association's Concerns:_____
_____
_____
_____

11. Actions (to be) Taken
a. Phone Contacts _____
_____
b. Written Contacts _____
_____
c. Interviews or Meetings _____
_____
d. Other _____
_____
_____
_____

Inventory Completed by:
_____
Date: _____

will depend on the consensus by other relevant publics that its claim is appropriate and that you have the capacity to perform adequately. Consumers must consider your organization to be the right address to which to apply for service. Collaborating organizations must be willing to work with your organization, even if there may be some competition between your agency and those collaborators over one or more aspects of your claim. These are the variables you will have to demonstrate when applying for membership or associate status to a federated structure.

Domain consensus defines and sets the boundaries and the jurisdiction of your organization within the larger human services community. It includes formal agreements between your organization and others, and informal expectations that services will be provided in an acceptable manner. Consensus over your organization's domain continues so long as the agency fulfills the functions judged to be appropriate to it and adheres to generally agreed-upon norms regarding standards of quality.

For funders to agree that your organization is worthy of support, they will also need to know something about the severity of the problems to be addressed. They must agree that the population to be served is legitimately in need of those services and that the services rendered are appropriate to those needs. Effective claims to domain reflect the credibility an agency has achieved with its input and output publics. Some agencies may be regarded with mistrust, not because of anything they may or may not have done, but because some of its other publics may be mistrusted. Thus clients may mistrust a social agency because it receives support from a source it does not trust. Some funding sources may not trust a service organization that provides services to consumers who may be considered somehow illegitimate.

An organization's credibility often depends on the credentials of the staff. The way in which these credentials are established will vary from one constituent group to another. "When I first introduced myself to United Way officials," reports the director of an agency, "I established my identity through formal credentials. I interpreted the functions of my agency, and let them know what my responsibilities are. In that first meeting, they couldn't care a hoot about who I was personally, but they did care who I represented and about my, and the agency's, past record. It also helps that I have a Ph.D. It's only after we got to working together that we developed personal relations, mutual obligations that we were both able to build on.

"But it's different when I meet with representatives of civic associations and other community people," she continues. "They don't want to know about my position in the bureaucracy. They want to know what I stand for, personally, who I am as a person. Even more important is who my organization serves: what the needs of those people are. They are less interested in the services and how they are delivered than in the needs to be addressed." And perhaps even more important is the ability of your organization to find common interests with the association and its key members—make your cause their own.

EXERCISE 8.2
LISTING OF PRACTICE PRINCIPLES

(1) Review your last list of practice principles. It should articulate with your fund raising efforts directed at government, foundation, and private sector sources.

(2) Identify additional practice principles in this chapter, and add those from your experience or those of colleagues who have worked with the voluntary sector.

(3) Draw up a new list of practice principles appropriate to fund raising with the voluntary sector, or add to and modify the master list you have already developed. Which of these principles apply only to the voluntary sector?

REVIEW

The voluntary sector is made up of all those organizations that raise money for charitable or community improvement purposes and those that provide services on a nonprofit basis.

Although such voluntary agencies as community centers, museums, and local health clinics may raise their own funds through campaigns and other activities, many are affiliated with federated fund raising and allocating structures. Foremost among these is the United Way. In addition, some belong to sectarian federations or federations organized to respond to the needs of particular populations or to deal with clearly identified sets of programs (health, rehabilitation, and so on). Some voluntary agencies also seek effective partnerships with civic associations. These groups include the Elks, "boosters" clubs, church-affiliated groups, the Junior League, and so on.

The United Way is not only prototypic of other federated structures, but is the standard against which others may be measured. There are more than 2200 autonomous United Ways in the United States, the vast majority of which are affiliated with the United Way of America, which is a standard-setting and technical assistance organization to its local affiliates. United Ways are governed by locally elected boards, conduct annual campaigns, determine priority needs in the community, and allocate funds to member agencies and to others who may be designated as affiliates or recipients. Allocation decisions are generally made by lay persons who examine applications and proposals that are grouped under various councils or divisions (education and culture, family services, health, and so on).

Many United Ways and other federated structures have highly trained professional staffs who perform planning, fund raising, technical assistance, accounting, evaluation, and other functions. The allocation and request processes are generally highly structured. Allocations are made only after considerable study.

The relationships between nonprofit service organizations and the wide variety of civic associations that exist in every American community are much more loosely patterned. They vary from partnership to partnership and from community to community. The example of a preventive health institute working first through a fire fighters' association and then through the fire fighters to involvement of three other civic groups is an interesting one. It suggests how creativity and the right mix of mutual interests between organizations and their members can result in financial support. Just as important, the fund raising activities serve to heighten public awareness of a problem and public involvement in dealing with the problem, very possibly the programmatic objectives of the organization seeking new sources of funds.

SUGGESTIONS FOR FURTHER READING

Start off with some directories:

The directory of the United Way of America. Updated each year and can be ordered from the United Way of America, United Way Plaza, Alexandria, VA 22314.

The national directory of private social agencies. Available from Croner Publications at 211-05 Jamaica Avenue, Queens Village, NY 11428.

Trustees of wealth: A Taft guide to philanthropic decision makers. Available from the Taft Information System, Taft Products, Inc., 1000 Vermont Ave. NW, Washington, DC 20005.

This guide identifies some of the wealthiest philanthropists in the United States, the kinds of organizations they are affiliated with, their philanthropic interests, and so on. It might be a good place to seek information on persons in your community who are active in federated structures and in civic associations.

Eckstein, Burton. (1978). *Handicapped funding directory.* Oceanside, NY: Research Grant Guides.

Provides information about laws pertaining to equality for handicapped persons, publications issued by various organizations dealing with various aspects of the subject, and sources of funding for pertinent projects.

Check also the *Directory of Directories* and the *Directory of Associations* in your public library. These may lead you to other important national addresses that might be good sources of information. The following are among the thousands found in the *Directory of Associations:*

Council of Jewish Federations, 555 Lexington Ave., New York, NY 10017.

Family Service Association of America, 44 E. 23rd Street, New York, NY 10010.

Mental Health Materials Center, Information Resources Center for Mental Health and Family Life Education, 419 Park Avenue South, New York, NY 10016.

National Association for the Education of Young Children, 1834 Connecticut Ave. NW, Washington, DC 20009.

National Association for Mental Health, 1800 N. Kent Street, Rosslyn, VA 22209.

National Association for Retarded Children, Inc., 2709 East, P.O. Box 6109, Arlington, TX 76011.

Sex Information and Education Council of the United States (SEI-CUS), 1855 Broadway, New York, NY 10023.

United Way of America, 801 N. Fairfax Street, Alexandria, VA 22314.

Check also the reading suggestions in Chapters 4, 5, 6, and 7, and the more general sources of information in Appendix B.

CHAPTER 9

Up from Apathy:
Increasing Contributions from Individual Donors

GIVING AWAY THE AMERICAN WAY

There is probably no adult in the United States who has not been solicited for financial donations to a worthwhile cause or organization. Americans are generous givers. The reasons for their gifts are many. The four persons quoted below express fairly typical reasons for giving.

I had to undergo an abortion a few years ago. Let me put it another way. I *chose* to have an abortion. My other children were grown. My health is not the best. I did not want to take any chances for me or the baby. And I did not want to put an added strain to our marriage.

But the interrogation I had to go through at the hospital; the blatantly sexist comments of the attending physician . . . it created even greater anguish than having made the decision in the first place. I felt as if I had to defend myself and my morality.

During the recuperation period in the hospital I had a great deal of time to think. I thought about all those young kids who get pregnant without wanting to and all the poor women who cannot afford to have children or who may be too inarticulate to defend themselves against someone else's view of morality.

Since then I have contributed each year to planned parenthood and abortion rights organizations. I want everyone to have the right to choose and to be protected from misinformation or misguided advice and from external judgment. I'm not an activist and I don't get involved in any other way. But I know that the money I am giving will protect someone else from indignity.

For the first couple of years after I graduated, I gave at least $100 a year to my school's alumni association. That doesn't seem like a lot to me now, but it was a lot to me then. Although I was barely earning $100 a week before taxes, I couldn't do less. For four years I had received scholarship money or some other form of aid without which I could not have finished school. New worlds were opened to me each of those years; I wanted other young people to have the same opportunity.

As the years progressed, I gave more; but I got more, too. The alumni association provides all kinds of membership services; a club with swimming and phys ed privileges, low-cost charter trips, investment advice from those people who handle the university's investment portfolio.

The more I got, the more I figured I owed. I began earmarking some of my savings for the university. I guess I got to be tagged a big giver, even though I wasn't as wealthy as others who were also giving a thousand or more. Being considered in the big leagues didn't hurt my law practice.

As an officer in the alumni association, I do more now than just give money. But I keep getting in return. There's a feeling of satisfaction in seeing the university grow, in maintaining my relationships to faculty I had admired and respected as a student, to making new contacts with people I have things in common with as a member of the community and as an attorney.

My parents didn't have much money but they did have values. Those values still live through me. My present is really my past. I don't want to live forever. My children are all right financially. But you know, two of them intermarried. If I left them all my money and property the government would get it anyway. That's why I am bequeathing money to the church. I may have failed in my lifetime, but others can take over after I die.

They are going to name the new overnight campsite for me. Maybe my great grandchildren will go. They'll know who their great granddad was and what he believed in. Maybe they will believe in the same things. At least someone else's children will. What's it all for unless you can't give a little to future generations?

I know people think of me as a philanthropist, and I suppose I am. But I'll tell you a secret. Anyone in the 50 percent tax bracket gets back half of whatever they give. On top of that, in this state, if you donate to a state institution like a university or a state-supported program for the disabled, you get a 100 percent deduction from your state income tax. My gifts wind up costing me 30 cents on the dollar and I get the satisfaction of giving to the organizations I believe in instead of having the government deciding where it should go.

These sentiments are not unique. Voluntary support for causes and organizations has been the American way since immigrants first came to these shores. Cut off from the extended family support systems of their lands of origin, they established *landsmanschaften* (groups of coreligionists or persons from the same village or area of origin) and free-loan societies, took on collective responsibilities for widows and orphans, established institutions to care for the poor, the sick, the disabled, and the otherwise disadvantaged. The United Way and other federated giving structures discussed in the previous chapter are current expressions of these efforts. Your organization can develop its own fund raising efforts, soliciting dollars directly from individual donors. You may be surprised at the untapped reservoir of funds and goodwill that exists in your community.

There are many reasons for giving. People have a need to do something worthwhile in their lives, to feel that they are contributing to the general welfare, to see themselves as sharing with or taking responsibility for others. They also have a need to belong, to be associated with others they respect and by whom they wish to be respected. Almost everyone likes to be wanted, to be sought after, to be "a part of" instead of "apart from" a group or association they feel is worthwhile. These motivations are supported by a sense of duty, a desire to pay back, and, not uncommonly, a sense of guilt.

There are also instrumental reasons for giving: advancement of one's career or occupational goals; tax benefits for oneself or one's heirs; and perhaps a desire to be remembered or "immortalized" by contributions to a cause that may extend for a long time into the future. No gift can make one immortal, but it can extend one's contributions into the future.

In this chapter, a number of vehicles for giving will be examined, starting with a look at bequests. Then brick-and-mortar campaigns, development programs, endowments, and activity support campaigns will be discussed. A wide variety of "selling" activities and special events that can be used to raise significant amounts of money and perhaps critical consciousness as well will be explored. In Chapter 10, we will look at the way that fund raising programs are organized, with a special emphasis on campaigns. You may want to read both chapters together. You will find many of the references and reading suggestions applicable to both discussions.

WHERE THERE'S A WILL
THERE'S A WAY

"There are three things you need to remember," a tax attorney told me when I was researching this chapter. "First: Where there's a will, there's a way. Second: Most bequeathers have gray hair. And third: Deep down inside, all of us strive after immortality. All the rest is commentary." So here comes the commentary.

Perhaps some people *do* strive after immortality, but others know that their rewards will come from improving the lives of others. They may also be concerned with the future—with those who come after they have gone. They may have a concern with security, not necessarily for themselves, but for those who will live in the future. Their concerns may be for the survival of an ethnic group or a cultural inheritance. They may be concerned about the security of others with whom they have identified in the past. Perhaps some are trying to work out a balance in their lives, overcoming a long-buried sense of loss through an act of expurgating guilt.

Not long ago, I asked an elderly woman what had compelled her to make a bequest to an organization with which I am affiliated. "When I was young, there wasn't a place like this for me," she replied. "But if I were young now, this is the kind of place I would want to come to. I feel towards it almost the way I do toward my warmest childhood memories. When I think about this place it generates a nostalgia for my youth."

A Talmudic quotation comes to mind. It comes from a small book observant Jews frequently read on the Sabbath afternoons, *The Sayings of the Fathers:* "It's not your task to complete the job, nor are you free to desist from it." People who make bequests often do so because they feel obliged to make a contribution, even if that contribution only starts up the process that they will not live to see completed. It is that belief in the future and the desire to contribute to the future that characterizes financial bequests. Perhaps there is in their commitment a share in immortality.

Successful fund raisers are masters at tapping such motivations. I say "tap" instead of "capitalize on" because I believe that is exactly what the process is all about. There is, in all of us, an untapped reservoir of unselfishness and a desire to do good. But many of us do not know how or where to make our contributions, so we go with the institutions that have proven themselves—those with successful track records. That is why most bequests tend to go to the more successful institutions. They go to Harvard more rapidly than they go to a smaller, less known, and much more needy school in a midwestern state. But the mission or purpose of that small college may be much more in keeping with the interests of a prospective bequeather—if he or she only knew of it.

It is not necessary for the donor to pass on before the agency benefits from a bequest. A bequest can be made as a life insurance policy, an annuity, or another income-generating investment from which the agency draws now and from which it will receive a larger indemnity or death benefit in the future. A life-income annuity plan can be written for the donor, with the large sum going to your organization at a later time.

These "delayed gifts" provide tax benefits that may accrue to the donor's estate. The tax laws on estates tend to change frequently. If you plan to embark on a bequest program, consult a tax attorney or an estate planner, perhaps one connected with a bank or trustee organization. Becoming familiar with such people is not a bad idea for other reasons. As you get to know them, they will get to know you—and they will be able to advise their clients about the tax and other advantages of bequeathing money to your organization.

The better professional trustees know your organization, its programs, and its missions, the more likely they will be to suggest just such a bequest when the time is appropriate. Involve these people as partners in the development of a bequest program. They may be as anxious to find you, so as to serve their clients better, as you are to find them and their clients. Making a bequest puts one among the community's elite. Facilitating one may be next best. One thing to remember: Under current tax laws, by 1987 it will be possible to pass or transfer an aggregate of up to $600,000 without having to pay a gift or estate tax. That means you may be focusing on big gifts when it comes to deferred giving.

MEMORIAL AND OTHER SPECIAL OCCASION GIVING

Smaller gifts can be solicited from friends and relatives in memory of a deceased loved one. Typically, this is done through churches and other religious or ethnic associations, but such gifts can be solicited by any organization: museums, libraries, Ys, child guidance clinics. Memorial gifts are generally made by members on behalf of members. The members in your organization may include paid staff, volunteers, and participants on committees, advisory groups, and boards.

But memorials are only one form of special occasion giving. Consider the following also:

weddings and anniversaries

christenings, bar mitzvahs, confirmations

hospitalizations or returns from the hospital

graduations, promotions

special honors

arrivals and departures

And while you are considering these "excuses" to give, consider also making it easier for people to honor friends and relatives. Print up cards (condolences, congratulations, get well) that members can purchase or pick up from your organization. Include a message inside that indicates that a gift has been made in the recipient's honor to your organization or to a special program the organization sponsors. Indicate something about the organization and what it does. One gift may generate other gifts in the future.

EDIFICE COMPLEXES

A more focused and well-orchestrated fund raising effort may be required when the organization needs a new facility or to expand and modify an existing one: offices, a campsite, a chapel, a meeting hall, an athletic facility. Building fund and other capital improvement campaigns have characteristics of their own. First, they require carefully built plans and time-tables. Second, they require considerable consensus on the part of a leadership group that is itself committed to making significant contributions.

There must be consensus around what is to be done, how the new structure or facility is to look, and the purposes it is to fulfill. Unlike some other campaigns and gift programs in which individuals can determine the purposes of their contributions, or in which the organization makes the determination in relation to evolving needs and opportunities, what is often called a "bricks-and-mortar" drive requires that the major givers be committed in advance to the characteristics of the final product.

Almost everyone has an idea of what makes a building beautiful or functional. Some members of churches and synagogues and boosters of public buildings such as museums and community centers have been accused of having an "edifice" complex, that is, of being more interested in the pretentiousness of a new building than in its uses. But if a more modest building would not be sufficient motivation to generate community giving, there may be something to be said for pretentiousness. When working on the basic structure of the building—or some program site, such as a recreation facility—the bricks-and-mortar campaign committee should also consider landscaping, equipment, and upkeep. It may not be sufficient just to raise enough money to "burn the mortgage," it may also be necessary to raise enough to establish a special fund to pay the additional expenditures that the new or modified structure may require. A mortgage may be helpful to start the construction process early, but nonprofit organizations gain no tax advantage from mortgages. The faster the mortgage can be paid off, the less drain there will be on the organization's ongoing operations.

Build upkeep and fuel costs into the building fund target. When fuel prices skyrocketed a few years back, I saw several organizations close at least some of their doors. A new recreation facility, office, or meeting place may not achieve its full potential unless it is well equipped. Consider the purchase of electronic data processing system, items for a physical education plant, art facilities, or other items necessary for the programmatic or administrative functioning of the organization. Many of these items may be donated to individuals or by companies that prefer such in-kind donations to cash contributions. The tax advantages are the same, and it may permit givers to upgrade their own equipment. Your organization gets what it needs, even if the items are not new or the most advanced available.

With the exception of upkeep, capital campaigns must be clearly separated from concerns over operating budgets or ongoing programs. Unlike the others, capital campaigns are time limited—generally two weeks to four years in duration. That does not mean that they should be unrelated to programmatic concerns. It does mean that the fund raising effort should be conducted separately and perhaps aimed at persons who do not currently contribute to other fund raising efforts. Some people like to have their names or those of family members recognized on the new building or facility. Some will contribute to the "Morris Jenkins Wing" because they may wish to honor Mr. Jenkins, without any thought of having their own names associated with the facility. One university, which solicits both big and small givers for its capital campaigns, honors all givers by selling "bricks" for $20 each; and actually lists the contributors of each brick on a plaque located near each building entrance. "Hey," I heard a student remark, "did you know your dad's laid a dozen bricks in this building?"

BUILDING ALSO MEANS "DEVELOPING"

As the nomenclature suggests, *development funds* and *activity support* campaigns are aimed at the expansion or development in some depth of an existing program or the establishment of a new program or service. Funds are not raised for ongoing operations, but for purposes of generating a new approach or reaching a new population. Development funds are generally long term in their orientation. They may be given special names that are easily identifiable and that attract contributions: the "minority opportunities fund"; the "community arts program"; the "Holocaust Memorial Program."

Like capital drives, development funds also require a careful cultivation of various publics long before they are asked to contribute. In addition to individual donors, contributions to development may include business corporations and philanthropic foundations. The appeal to different publics may have to be around special concerns: school lunches, increasing environmental esthetics, the putting in of playground equipment or park benches, providing supports to the disabled or the aging.

Unlike bricks-and-mortar campaigns, development campaigns are not one-shot affairs. They are ongoing. When special funds have been raised for one program, new development campaigns may be established. Former donors may be tapped again and new prospects identified. Like other agency programs, development campaigns can be collaboratively sponsored by several nonprofit organizations or by several industrial and civic organizations working in concert on behalf of a single agency.

WE NEED YOUR HELP NOW

Some activities require *immediate* or *emergency* support. There may be no need for ongoing development or expansion. Such needs generally are based on organizational responses to predicaments or opportunities presented by the environment. Opportunities can become predicaments. For example, a museum may be offered a once-in-a-lifetime opportunity to purchase a rare work of art; or a social agency may find itself the recipient of a professional-quality photo offset system that it has no room to accommodate; and another may be given the opportunity of purchasing the building it has been leasing—at terms it can ill afford to pass up. In the first example, the museum may have to seek special gifts in order to be able to pay for the work and at the same time not dismantle its budgeted long-range purchasing program. In the second, the agency may need additional funds to redo part of its facility to accommodate the equipment. In the third example, the agency needs money to make at least a down payment on the facility.

More frequent, in recent years, have been the strains imposed on agency budgets and services by new and, in some cases, temporary consumer demands. In many parts of the country, social agencies, churches, and civic associations have worked independently or collectively on the distribution of food and emergency relief to needy families and individuals. Food banks and shelters were set up to respond to desperate circumstances. These were not perceived to be regular or ongoing services of the sponsoring or coordinating organization, so development funds were not needed. However, an immediate, and perhaps one-time-only infusion of funds, in substantial amounts, was needed.

These funds can be raised from regular givers—persons who may already have been tapped for development, bricks-and-mortar, or ongoing support programs. They may also come from new sources who are turned on by the opportunity or the predicament presented.

ENDOWMENTS

Before moving on to an examination of sales and special events, I want to explain briefly about endowments. These are funds or income-producing property (real property, stocks and bonds, and so on) contributed for the purpose of supporting a program or service indirectly. Endowment funds are invested. The income from these investments is then allocated to the support of the designated program or service. For example, the endowment of an academic chair may cost the donor $1 million. The income from the investment of those dollars—say $100,000 per year—will be used for the faculty person's salary plus supportive services.

Endowments can also be used for summer camp scholarships, special annual events for staff or volunteers, affirmative action programs, promotional campaigns, the purchase of equipment, the support of cultural events, or ongoing agency operations.

TREASURES FROM TRASH

In addition to soliciting cash, equipment, or supplies for direct use by the organization, your agency may find it profitable to collect or even purchase materials and services for resale. For example, "treasure from trash"-type sales begin with contributions of used household furniture and family clothing. These are then resold through bazaars, garage sales, white elephant sales, rummage sales, auctions, and organization-run gift shops. Making useful items available at low costs to low-income populations, as do many church or service club thrift shops, is in itself an important service.

Generally, little cash is required to be invested by the sponsor. Considerable investment in time and energy on the part of staff or volunteers is required. Sales events can be destructive of normal agency operations if paid staff are too heavily involved. Volunteers, on the other hand, may find bazaars or thrift shops and even yard sales to be rewarding in terms of the social relationships established, the recognition received, and the sense of achievement and accomplishment gained from having completed the work on behalf of others in need. They may benefit as much from these social exchanges as do the consumers of other agency services.

Recognizing this, some agencies purposefully involve clients in such activities. "If the teens wanted to keep using the facilities, we reasoned, they would have to raise some of the funds for rent and renovations. Within six months, they raised half the money needed for a lounge. Senior citizens raised the rest. Would you believe they share its use on different nights? Both groups are now fully committed to the purposes of the agency, and they've gained a new respect for each other."

An agency's primary service may be organized around production and sales. The work of Goodwill Industries and other sheltered workshop or home industries programs are good examples.

WHAT AM I BID?

The donation of items or services by corporations, such as a lease or a discount on an automobile, office equipment, or free concert or theater tickets, may be "resold" by the agency directly or at an auction. Individuals can also donate services to be auctioned off—such as catering a dinner, entertaining at a party, doing someone's income taxes, or typing up to 100 pages without charge.

Art and antique auctions have become increasingly popular over the years. They can be organized around items donated, for which the giver receives a tax benefit, or may include merchandise "purchased" on consignment. An organization with which I have been associated contracts with a commercial auction gallery each year. It is the organization's responsibility to advertise and attract people to the auction. It is the gallery's responsibility to bring the artwork and to conduct the auction, for which the agency receives 20 percent of the proceeds.

Purchasers also receive a tax benefit for their purchases, and frequently are able to buy items at considerably below regular gallery prices. Art auction galleries frequently make their own purchases in large quantities, sometimes early in an artist's career. They also keep overhead low. For this reason, they make money while passing on considerable savings to the consumer. Works of art, antiques, and other collectibles can be certified as genuine by the gallery, thus further inducing the purchase as a sound investment.

SALES ENRICH IN OTHER WAYS

Works of art, oriental rugs, or valuable handicrafts need not be sold only through auctions. A Boston gallery with which I have worked over the years provides local sponsors with an attractive package that includes artwork selected to reflect the consumer's interest and pocketbook. The sponsor receives a complete kit of instructions for the opening night. It includes a slide show about the exhibit, instructions for conducting a wine and cheese party, and flyers and announcements for distribution prior to the opening, describing in pictures and words many of the items to be offered for sale. Sample press releases are also included.

The sale items arrive with instructions for display, and for repackaging and shipping to the next destination. Costs can be covered in advance through the sale of an "ad book" or recruitment of sponsors, who, through gifts of $25 to $50, are listed on the program or invitation to the sale. This initial gift can be applied toward the purchase of any item in the exhibit. Thus the donor has the satisfaction of sponsoring the exhibit, receives recognition for his or her contribution, is assured a discount at the sale, and, of course, acquires a tax benefit. The sponsoring agency sees this not only as a fund raising event, but also as a cultural and educational service to the community.

GET IT AT A DISCOUNT

"Discount days" can be arranged through local merchants with very little time and effort on the part of the recipient organization. It is not uncommon for large food chains to provide charitable organizations with opportunities to make charitable contributions. The organization's members, on presenting the cashier with a coupon, can have 5 percent of their total purchase allocated to the organization. Information on the organization, along with discount coupons, may be made available at the door. Clothing, hardware, book, and record stores may also be induced to allocate 5 percent or 10 percent of sales in any given day, week, or month to a charitable organization or cause. What kinds of arrangements are possible in your community? Should such arrangements be negotiated on a store-by-store basis, or might it make more sense to involve members of the downtown merchants' association or shopping mall associates in planning such an event?

Discount books that provide the purchaser with reduced prices for dinners, movies, or merchandise are popular with merchants and individual purchasers, both of whom expect financial benefit, and possibly a tax benefit. Ad books, which may include coupons, provide similar benefits to the donors. They can be given away at a special event, or sold like discount books.

REACHING THE STAY-AT-HOME

Why not try aiming sales at people who remain at home? For example, Hadassah, a Jewish women's organization, sponsors a "lox box" as an annual event in many American communities. People who purchase the box in advance are assured delivery on a given Sunday morning of a breakfast box that includes lox, cream cheese, bagels, and coffee cake. The activity not only energizes the organization's members and other volunteers, but makes all the participants feel that they are engaged in the communitywide event without ever having to leave their homes. Besides, it tastes good! Jewish organizations and other religious groups have frequently used a "pushke," or home contribution box, in which family members deposit loose change. The box is collected at specific dates and the family involved is often provided with a certificate or a gift of some modest value in return for its contributions.

GETTING THEM OUT AGAIN

The "walkathon" for Tay Sachs Disease netted about $9000 last year. That may not be a tremendous amount, but the money was not the only thing we were after. The money was to set up a one week Tay Sachs screening clinic. But there is not much sense in providing a clinic if no one is going to come, and this could be the case if people are unaware that they might be carriers. That is what the walkathon was mostly for. It educated the public—it heightened awareness, and it reduced whatever shame might be associated with coming to the clinic to be tested. It did just the opposite. It made people ashamed if they didn't come.

Most of us have participated in, paid for, or witnessed other marathons—walkathons, bikeathons, jogathons, even crawlathons. We have participated in other fund raising events in which we received an immediate benefit for our contributions. Examples include the following:

campaign dinners

barn dances and balls

hayrides

mystery bus rides

theater or concert parties

carnivals

fun nights

We have also paid out some money in hopes of getting some back on bingo nights or "Las Vegas" weekends (in our hometowns). Some of these special events may occur on a one-time-only basis. Others will be held as annual events.

These special events do not just run themselves. They require carefully thought-out objectives and highly motivated participants who are ready to raise a targeted amount of money because of a shared sense of commitment. The activity may be seen as primarily fund raising in its orientation, but it may have other, even more significant objectives. The walkathon for Tay Sachs and the involvement of the fire fighters discussed in Chapter 8 were both aimed at raising the public's critical consciousness and altering behavior patterns. In Chapter 10, we will examine how campaigns are organized. Before you move on, complete Exercise 9.1.

You have now conducted a preliminary assessment of what is and what ought to be. In the next chapter, we will examine a number of ways in which your organization might mobilize itself to conduct one or more of the desired activities and to reach the targeted publics.

Now it is time to review practice principles once again. A number of the principles enunciated in this chapter complement those in Chapters 5 through 8. Some may be different. Look over your previous lists and complete Exercise 9.2.

REVIEW

There are a number of reasons people contribute to organizations and charitable causes. These include a desire to belong and to be recognized, to be needed; commitment to an idea, a cause, or a group in need; the tax or other economic benefits that may accompany contribution; the services re-

EXERCISE 9.1
INVENTORY OF FUND RAISING ACTIVITIES AND PUBLICS

(1) Look over the Matrix of Fund Raising Activities and Publics. Columns 1 through 7 are direct fund raising activities in which the public is asked to contribute directly. Columns 8 through 10 refer to indirect approaches in which the public is asked to buy a product or a service or to participate in a special event.

Circle the numbers above the columns that reflect the kinds of activities in which your organization currently engages.

(2) Notice that rows 1 through 15 are left blank for you to fill in. These are the publics that your organization targets for fund raising. These publics might include wealthy philanthropists, local industrialists, persons who have expressed interest in health care on a national basis, a list of persons interested in the arts, alumni of your organization, parents of retarded children, current clients, active volunteers, all persons in the community over 65, residents in a particular neighborhood, disabled persons, coreligionists, and so on.

In identifying those publics, you will be pinpointing a particular funding market, in effect segmenting the market much as your organization does when it targets particular segments of the consumer market for its products or services. List all the market segments your organization currently targets in the left-hand column. These are now the headings of your rows. You may find the segmenting principles we discussed in Chapter 2 useful. You will recall that these included geography, function (i.e., by service or problem need or interest), demography, and psychography (i.e., commitment, involvement, etc.).

(3) Now put a check or an X in the box that corresponds with a public and a fund raising activity. For example, if the first row heading was "Current and Past Board Members," you might put an X under "Bequests," "Building Fund," and "Special Annual Events."

Match all publics and the appropriate fund raising activities.

(4) If there are other publics that are not currently reached but should be, add them in the left-hand column in a different color ink or pencil. Now identify the kinds of fund raising activities that should be used to reach them. Use the same second color pencil or ink.

(5) Finally, go back over the publics you currently reach with one or more fund raising activities. If these should be reached with other activities, check or X the appropriate box. If some of the activities currently used to reach them could stand improvement (those you checked in the original color), circle your original check or X in the second color.

Exercise 9.1
MATRIX OF FUND RAISING
ACTIVITIES AND PUBLICS

Types of Fund Raising / Publics from Whom Funds Are Sought	1 Bequests	2 Endowments	3 Ongoing Activity Support	4 Capital Campaign	5 Development Program	6 Emergency or Immediate Support	7 In-Kind Contributions	8 Thrift Shop, Used-Item Sales	9 Special Sales and Auctions	10 Special Events
1										
2										
3										
4										
5										
6										
7										
8										
9										
10										
11										
12										
13										
14										
15										

EXERCISE 9.2
LISTING OF PRACTICE PRINCIPLES

(1) Review your last list of practice principles. It should articulate with your fund raising efforts directed at direct fund raising and indirect fund raising.

(2) Identify additional practice principles in this chapter, and add those from your experiences or those of colleagues who have worked with direct and indirect fund raising.

(3) Draw up a new list of practice principles appropriate to direct and indirect fund raising, or add to and modify the master list you have already developed. Which of these principles apply only to direct fund raising? Which only to indirect fund raising?

---

ceived or goods purchased through a contribution; and a desire for personal immortality or for the continuance of a group, an idea, or a cause.

Human service agencies and other nonprofit organizations have from their inception built on these motivations to conduct a wide variety of fund raising activities. These fall into two general categories: *direct fund raising,* such as bequests, endowments, development campaigns, capital drives, ongoing activity support, and emergency or immediate needs support; and *indirect fund raising,* through sales, activities, thrift shops, and special events on an ad hoc or regular basis. Examples of each were given throughout the chapter.

SUGGESTIONS FOR FURTHER READING

Start by becoming familiar with several organizations that publish materials of interest to you, or consult with grassroots and other fund raisers:

Barnes Associates, 4800 N. Central Avenue, Phoenix, AZ 85012, provides consultation and training on fund raising and publishes *Barnes Fund Raiser,* a monthly newsletter; and *Fund Raiser's Bonus Books 1 and 2,* which include a variety of ideas.

National Catholic Development Conference, 119 N. Park Avenue, Rockefeller Center, New York, NY 11570. Also publishes a number of guides and a bibliography of fund raising literature.

The American Association of Fund Raising Counselors, 500 Fifth Avenue, New York, NY 10036, publishes a *Directory of Members* that you may find helpful in locating a fund raising consulting firm in your community or in your area of interest.

The Center for Community Change, 1000 Wisconsin Avenue, NW, Washington, DC, provides advice and assistance to low-income and minority community-based organizations.

The Community Congress, 1172 Morena Blvd, San Diego, CA 92110, publishes periodic information on fund raising and related issues, annotated bibliographies, and so on. It is a good source of information on other networks and consumer or grassroots resource development projects.

The Fund Raising Center, 287 McPherson Avenue, Toronto, Ontario M4V 1A4, conducts occasional workshops or provides consultation. It also publishes how-to materials you may find helpful. Start with the following: "Fund Raising Letters"; "Guide to Deferred Giving"; "Organizing Your Way to Dollars."

The Fund Raising Institute, P.O. Box 365, Ambler, PA 19002, provides consultation and training to professional development offices and publishes a variety of guides and how-to materials.

The KRC Development Council, 212 Elm Street, New Canaan, CT 06840, publishes a great many materials of interest to fund raisers and grantseekers. Several are found in the Suggestions for Further Reading in Chapter 10. An interesting first-person account of fund raising for a voluntary agency with lots of examples is found in

Pulling, Lisa (1980). *The KRC Desk Book for Fund Raisers.*

The Midwest Academy, 600 West Fullerton, Chicago, IL 60614, conducts a wide variety of workshops and courses for community organizers and representatives of grassroots organizations. Many deal with fund raising and resource development. One of its publications, *Fund Raising and Local Community Organization,* by R. Craemer, is a good grassroots primer.

The National Council of Philanthropy, 680 Fifth Avenue, New York, NY 10019, is an association of associations that sponsors conferences on fund raising and philanthropy. Its membership includes foundations and corporations as well as fund raising organizations. Check its publications list.

There are several journals you may want to examine and possibly subscribe to. Begin by looking at

Fund Raising Management, published by Hoke Communications, 224 7th Street, Garden City, Long Island, NY.

You will also find the following books helpful. Look them over, and also check with colleagues about what they have found helpful.

Davis, King (1975). *Fund raising in the black community.* Metuchen, NJ: Scarecrow.

Flanagin, J. (1982). *The grass roots fund raising book.* Chicago: Contemporary Books.

Grubb, D. L., & D. R. Zwick (1976). *Walk-a-thons, bike-a-thons and assorted marathons for money.* East Charleston: West Virginia Citizen's Action Group.

Gurin, Maurice G. (1981). *What volunteers should know for successful fund raising.* New York: Stein & Day.

Leibert, Edwin R., & Sheldon, Bernice (1972). *Handbook of special events for nonprofit organizations.* New York: Association.

Mirkin, Howard, R. (1975). *The complete fund raising guide.* New York: Public Service Materials Center.

Musselman, Virginia W. (1969). *Money raising events for community groups.* New York: Association.

Newman, Edwin S., & Margolin, Leo J. (1954). *Fund raising made easy.* New York: Oceana.

Schnecter, Paul (1978). *The art of asking: A handbook for successful fund raising.* New York: Walker.

Schnepper, Jeff A. (1982). *How to pay zero taxes.* Reading, MA: Addison-Wesley.

Sheppard, William E. (1979). *Annual giving idea book.* Plymouth Meeting, PA: Fund Raising Institute.

Stengall, L, & Coone, B. (1978). *Fund raising events: Making woman power profitable.* Washington, DC: National Women's Caucus.

Urech, Ingrid (1976). *Stalking the large green giant.* Washington, DC: National Youth Alternatives Project.

Warner, Irving. (1975). *The art of fund raising.* New York: Harper & Row.

Do not forget to check previous chapters for overlapping resources. Chapter 10 also contains a great many other fund raising references. You can also get written materials from the United Community Funds and Councils of America, 345 E. 46th Street, New York, NY 10017.

CHAPTER *10*
=====

On the Campaign Trail:
Building the Fund Raising Structure

CAMPAIGNING HARD

I suppose the campaign organization is a little like a military organization. Maybe that's why it is called a *campaign*. But in the military you can coerce people to do what you want. In a fund raising campaign you don't threaten and you don't coerce. But you motivate aplenty! People have to believe in what they are fighting for. And they've got to be rewarded and recognized just like a foot soldier. Everybody has to feel like his or her contribution counts. If the solicitors and the planners don't, how are they gonna get the donors to feel that way?

A fund raising campaign is no different from a political campaign. You need both a strong structure and an attractive product. Without these, there's no way you're going to get the commitments you need in order to succeed. Campaigning is hard business. If you're playing to win, you have to play hard.

Both of these quotes are from experienced professional fund raisers who have developed reputations for success. Both stress the nature of the organization of the fund raising effort. Fund raising campaigns will be the focus of this chapter: those aimed at increasing endowment funds, generating bequests, or supporting ongoing activities or new developments. The campaign structure, the way in which leaders are recruited and developed, the organization and the rewards for active solicitors will be examined, and a look at how letter-writing campaigns can be used to open up new sources of support will be presented.

But first, I want to share some additional quotes with you. Again, they come from experienced fund raisers, some who work at the grassroots level, and others who work with the committee's elite. They are stated in practice principles. Look them over. Do these add to those you have already abstracted from previous chapters?

TO WIN AT HORSE RACING

To win at horse racing, you not only need horses that can run, you have to have horses that *will* run. It's the same with solicitors and donors. They've got to have the motivation, or they won't contribute to their utmost.

———————

Don't build a campaign around the hope of finding a "sugar daddy" who will bail the organization out. Broaden the base of the fund raising effort to include large, medium, and small givers.

———————

Some people just want to give gifts and be let alone. But most want to know that others like themselves are also involved and they want others to know they are involved. Develop a network of givers. Let them relate to each other and encourage each other to contribute more.

———————

Let donors know that they and their contributions are needed. But don't build a fund raising effort exclusively on guilt. Involve people in the sharing of the responsibility.

———————

Treat all donors as prospects, but recognize that all prospects are not necessarily donors. Just because someone contributed money or other goods in previous years does not mean that he or she is going to be willing to contribute this year.

———————

Contributors rarely reach their maximums. Most people can give more and/or can be induced to solicit others.

———————

Don't ignore persons who have been irritated by a solicitation or bypass those who refuse to contribute at this time. Build on their concerns, establish relationships, and cultivate them for the next round.

———————

Although campaigns and events may be seasonal, fund raising strategies should be planned the year round. They should be articulated not only with the organization's service programs, but also with its supportive public relations and community education activities.

———————

Reward those who are involved in the fund raising effort. Although involvement itself may be a reward, the benefits of participation may be insufficient to overcome the costs in time and emotional energy. Recognition is the best reward. Show people you care because they care. And always thank people for whatever they do, big or small.

———————

Boost, don't boast. Involve people in the cause; a concern for a population in need; a commitment to a service program. Don't push yourself or your organization.

Keep these quotes in mind as you read this chapter and begin the planning of a campaign or other fund raising activities.

DESIGNING THE CAMPAIGN:
SOME PRELIMINARY CONSIDERATIONS

It is not enough to decide to run a fund raising campaign—or even to decide on the kind of campaign it is to be: bricks-and-mortar, developmental, or whatever. Each campaign must have clearly defined goals. Before beginning the campaign, do some preliminary idea inventorying with others whose involvement is crucial to the campaign's success.

Begin by examining the goals of the campaign. Are they to raise money and nothing more, or do they also include energizing one or more of the organization's publics, increasing public awareness, or building a cadre of volunteers who might become involved in other aspects of the agency's program? How are these goals to be translated into operational objectives?

Goals and objectives should be clarified by key members of the organization's staff in collaboration with lay leaders who have a stake in the organization and who may be required to take primary responsibility for aspects of the campaign. Put the goals on paper. Determine which ones are compatible, and which ones may divert energies from other organizational commitments. Let us assume, for the moment, that the major goal is to raise money for the organization. How much money? What is your target goal in terms of dollars? Is that sum to be reached this year? Or is the target to be reached over a two-, three-, or five-year period?

Who is to be involved in the campaign process—what lay leaders, which of the agency's paid staff? Should outsiders, experts in fund raising, be involved in campaign planning and management? Which publics are to be targeted for involvement as solicitors and as donors? Look at your completed matrix exercise for Chapter 9. Have all the appropriate publics been identified? Consider the following:

- *geographic scope:* neighborhood, community, state, national
- *demographic characteristics of givers:* age, gender, income level or employment, social position, education, race, ethnicity, religion

- *functional characteristics:* alumni (or former users of agency services), persons with problems in common (e.g., hemophiliacs, parents of children with developmental disabilities), professional interests (lawyers, physicians, retired business people, etc.)
- *psychographic characteristics:* sense of identity or belonging, energy, prestige

Once you have made preliminary decisions on these issues, it is time to begin designing and building your campaign structure.

BUILDING A CAMPAIGN STRUCTURE

Most campaigns have a number of structural elements in common. For example, most have a "campaign cabinet" that operates independent of the sponsoring organization or the agency that is to benefit from the campaign's fund raising efforts. A "general chairperson" will work with a small steering committee, often made up of the chairs of the cabinet's subcommittees or task forces. Typically, task forces may be assigned to (1) solicitation of initial or special gifts, (2) general solicitation, (3) prospect development, (4) public relations, and (5) various administrative functions.

Experienced campaign managers suggest that 20 percent to 25 percent of the funds to be raised during a given year be solicited from a "pacesetter" group during the early phases of the campaign, perhaps even before it has been officially kicked off. These funds are referred to as "initial gifts." It is the responsibility of the *initial* or *special gifts group* to solicit persons who have regularly pledged the largest sums in previous years. Special gifts can continue to be solicited from individuals or business firms throughout the campaign.

Pacesetters need not be the wealthiest members of the community. They must, however, have confidence in both the persons soliciting and the organization if they are to be willing to put their money on the line. They must believe that the funds contributed will achieve what the organization has promised, and that other donors will be induced by their examples to contribute sufficient sums to reach the targeted goal. Like all donors, pacesetters may require some recognition for their contributions. Although some prefer to remain anonymous, others may appreciate having their names appear on campaign stationery. This has the added strategic value of legitimizing the organization in the eyes of new or potential donors.

The *general solicitation committee* will aim its efforts at these other donors, those who give medium and smaller sized gifts. Depending on the scope of the campaign, the general solicitation committee may be divided further into a number of groups, each with its own captain. These groups may be organized around different categories of publics: corporations, individuals who give medium-sized gifts, and so on. Or they may be organized around peer groups: doctors, lawyers, other professionals, small business owners, corporative executives, homemakers, and so on. Households may be divided geographically by neighborhood or by size. Or they may be divided according to certain characteristics along ethnic and religious lines. A special category may include former consumers of an agency's services, such as families that have adopted children, persons who have used a hospital's services, parents of young men and women at a university, or alumni. Review the geographic, demographic, functional, or psychographic characteristics just discussed in determining how general solicitations should be targeted.

The *prospects committee* locates individuals who should be added to the list of those to be solicited. A good way to begin a prospect list is to ask for names from board and committee members of the organization, current and former givers, former recipients of service, even agency "partners," such as fire fighters, and their publics—for example, parents of schoolchildren who have visited the fire station. These lists require continual updating as new prospects are identified. Names may be coded according to size of gift anticipated and the history of the prospective donor's relationship to the agency.

The *public relations committee* is not concerned with fund raising per se, but with setting the scene for effective fund raising. It may issue periodic press releases, arrange for feature newspaper articles, and work with the radio and local television people interpreting the campaign and the services it is intended to finance. Typical public relations activities include arranging for the following:

orchestrated letter-writing campaigns to the local newspaper;

printed handouts—posters, bulletins, and the like;

special articles or features for the general press or the house organs of business corporations, unions, churches, and civic associations;

displays in public places such as shopping centers and concert halls; and

speakers who present information to community groups prior to their solicitation.

The necessary supportive services without which the campaign could not proceed are provided by *administrative groups.* Their services include recruiting and training solicitors, auditing, clerical assistance, preparation of reports on the campaign, or monitoring the campaign structure and the activities of its component units.

THE PEOPLE WHO MAKE
THE CAMPAIGN WORK

If to win at horse racing, you need horses that "will run," the same is true of campaign workers. Numbers are not enough. They need the competence, the skill, and the motivation to win. Like donors to the campaign, solicitors and others must be convinced of the importance of the endeavor and that the efforts put in will pay off. But, like any other human service endeavor, campaigns can be slow in starting, and the results can be disappointing.

Good leadership can do much to overcome difficulties. Some leaders have developed their capacities to solve problems or to motivate others over the course of many previous campaigns. Others may start fresh with your organization, drawing on professional and occupational skills or on volunteer experiences with other organizations. If you are the campaign staffer, you may want a balanced leadership group, composed of persons who have been trained through your organization and others who were recruited or borrowed from other organizations and who can bring relevant experiences to the campaign.

New solicitors and other volunteers will need some instruction. Even old-timers need refresher courses and pep talks. The following activities might be considered:

- *orientation sessions* that include written and spoken materials and that introduce the worker to the procedures to be used, the campaign structure and its key actors, the targets to be reached, and the purposes for which funds will be used

- *campaign literature* that is designed for solicitors or other volunteers, and other literature that can be mailed or given to prospective donors.

- *solicitor training,* which may include films and role-play and practice experiences

- *on-the-job supervision and coaching,* which may include observation of more experienced solicitors followed by joint solicitations and eventual "solo flights"

- *small group feedback sessions* at which solicitors and others can be informed of how the campaign is faring, get reinforcement from sharing experiences with others, and so on

Most volunteers need ongoing support and recognition. Many will need to get over inhibitions about requesting funds; others will need to become more realistic about what can be achieved. They may be thinking too high or too low. With sufficient commitment, they can go beyond their own expectations. Some organizations have routine ways of recognizing outstanding solicitors. These include awards and special recognition ceremonies, prizes, feature articles in the organization's newsletter or in the general press, and so on.

GETTING OFF TO
THE RIGHT START, AND
ENDING ON TIME

All campaigns have beginnings and ends. Few campaigns can succeed without well-planned and carefully monitored timetables. The following events might belong on your timetable:

- meetings of the governing board, steering committees, and other committees
- recruitment, orientation, training, and practice sessions for solicitors
- placement of news releases and spot announcements in the news and entertainment media
- mailing of information packets, solicitation letters, and other printed materials
- special events, such as "kick off" campaign meetings, on-going support sessions, and award dinners
- administrative follow through and follow-up, such as thank-you letters and follow-up calls to persons who have made pledges but have not sent in their checks
- interim and final reports

These events must be paced properly so that there is sufficient time between steps to permit people to complete the required tasks. A well-designed timetable accommodates to various "peak" periods in which volunteers are expected to put in the bulk of their time. The timetable can be drawn up in a variety of ways. Look over Chapter 11, on writing a proposal narrative, which describes several types of timetables: Pert networks, Gantt charts, time-frames. Which system would work best for your campaign?

Whatever system you use, it should not only help you to plan the campaign, but it should be used to determine whether or not your campaign is on schedule and the extent to which targeted goals have been met. If you are off schedule, readjustment of the time-frame or a heavy push may be required to get you back on the timetable.

IDENTIFYING PROSPECTIVE DONORS

Ways of determining which publics to target for a fund raising campaign have already been discussed. But some organizations may not be able to develop lists of their own. It is possible to get lists of prospects from other sources. The fund raising consultants in your community may be able to direct you to the appropriate list. Remember, you can locate them in the *Directory of Members* of the American Association of Fund Raising Counselors, described at the end of Chapter 9.

You should also know that there are a number of list brokers available in most metropolitan communities. They can either design or locate the appropriate list for you. For example, there are lists of music lovers, people who buy diet books or classical records, attorneys, business executives, psychiatric nurses, members of certain clubs, alumni of universities and colleges, and contributors to other organizations.

You may not need to go to a list broker. Your local librarian may be able to help you locate the appropriate reference book in which you will uncover lists of lists. You will recall that *Standard & Poor's Register, Dun & Bradstreet's,* or the *Directory of Directors* publish lists of companies nationwide, arranged geographically, with designations of the kinds of business they perform. Such lists can be used to locate industries that may have interests that complement those of your organization. Thomas's *Register of American Manufacturers* indicates the kinds of products produced by most manufacturing concerns in this country. Moody's *Industrial Manual* lists corporations, the names of their offices, plant locations, the names of trustees, and the names of corporations' attorneys and accountants.

Let your fingers do the walking. Consider the telephone directory or the local newspaper. Telephone directories frequently list professionals in the community by occupation in the Yellow Pages. Some cities publish a "reverse telephone directory" that can be purchased directly from the telephone company by any subscriber. In this type of directory, streets are listed alphabetically by neighborhood; house numbers are then given, and then the names of residents in each of the buildings, with their telephone numbers. This is an excellent source for a neighborhood canvassing program, and it permits you to target specific neighborhoods in the community.

Local newspapers are too often ignored. Staff members or volunteers might be assigned the task of clipping feature articles on wealthy people, those with special interests or life experiences, obituaries, birth announcements, and—as one professional fund raiser told me—"even robberies, which sometimes include the size of the home and provide a clue to the donor's interests."

BIG GIVERS

At one time or another, we have probably all had fantasies of a big giver bailing us or our organization out of a bind we may have found ourselves in. But big givers, like heroes, are made—not born. It may take a long time to cultivate a donor. A donor's gift can grow over time. In most communities and around most issues, there are some persons who will be able and willing to contribute handsomely. Some—a few—may seek you out directly or through an intermediary such as a tax attorney or a trust officer. You can locate the potential contributor through the same third parties. Or check with colleagues in the human services. They may know of someone who is not interested in their organization but who may be interested in yours.

Big givers may not be interested in any involvement with your organization beyond their financial gifts. Others will want to be involved in the campaign at a level that is commensurate with their gifts. Be careful not to move people up the leadership structure unless they have paid their dues in more than money alone; it is easy to demoralize other committee volunteers who may have worked painstakingly into positions of leadership.

THE SOLICITOR'S PITCH

The solicitor's pitch should emphasize those features in the agency's program or campaign objectives that the prospect is most likely to be interested in, those things the prospect values: religious concerns; the survival of an ethnic group, caring for needy children; fairness for the elderly; opportunities for the donor's children to attend college; the survival of a species; or the clean-up of the environment. The prospect may wish to know how the money given is to be used; what proportion of the budget raised will be allocated to one or another aspect of the program; perhaps how much is being used for the administration of the campaign.

It may be even more important to indicate who else is being solicited and, without disclosing confidences, the average size of peer contributions. If the prospective donor contributed the previous year, it may be helpful to recall the amount and to indicate the general target for upgrading contributions this year. If the solicited individual gave a minimal amount in previous years, it may be time to try to upgrade the gift to a more adequate sum.

Most fund raisers agree that it is not wise to try to move people up (increase the size of their gifts) too rapidly. A solicitor might try one of the following approaches: "Last year you gave ten dollars, this year we'd like you to put aside fifty cents a week. It's not necessary for you to give the full amount all at once, you can pay off your pledge in quarterly payments." Or, "I'd like to see you move up to what I'm giving. Last year I gave five hundred dollars, but I know it's not easy to make that jump from a hundred dollars all at once. Why not consider two hundred dollars this year, and perhaps moving to three or four hundred next year?" Or, "Your gift is so close to what our pacesetters give, why not consider jumping from seven hundred and fifty to one thousand dollars? I know it is a strain in today's economy, but your previous gifts clearly show your commitment, and you are a well-respected member of our community. You really should be among the pacesetters. You've given so much in other ways."

Quoting the tax advantage of giving is no small motivator. Make certain that donors get receipts they can use for tax purposes, but remember that tax receipts do not substitute for acknowledgments. Donors should receive thank-you letters, even if these are not personalized. On the other hand, a personal phone call or a hand-written note, in particular to a donor who has made a large initial pledge or who has made a large jump from previous years, may be essential to maintaining that level of giving or to raising it in the future.

Most solicitors do not come to a campaign ready to make the pitch successfully. They may need training and practice in reaching individual or organizational prospects. Solicitor training frequently includes the use of films, role play, and coaching by an experienced solicitor. Coaching may include going along and observing an experienced worker, or listening to a telephone solicitation conversation. Because the information can be overwhelming, you should consider providing manuals, information booklets, and question-and-answer sheets for solicitors.

Working together in teams often provides the necessary support for solicitors to keep going when the going gets rough. It also permits them to learn from each other about how to be effective and how to be realistic about their own accomplishments. Many solicitors also need periodic inspirational (or "pep") talks. They need to be recognized for their efforts. Some organizations use prizes or special inducements to maintain high solicitor motivation. They recognize successful solicitors at banquets and other end-of-campaign functions, through newsletters that go to other campaign workers, and even through press and other public relations releases.

Solicitors often go directly to people's homes or offices. They also work by telephone. The United Jewish Appeal (UJA) tends to approach pacesetters and others who give medium-sized gifts in person, but it uses telephone solicitation to reach others who are not able, ready, or willing to make larger contributions. To make life more bearable for solicitors, most UJA campaigns sponsor a "Super Sunday" in which telephone solicitors work 1½- to 2-hour shifts. Each shift is preceded by a brief training session.

Coffee is available at these sessions, and so is consultation and help when a solicitor has a particularly difficult prospect on the phone. Solicitor and donor prospects may be matched by organizational membership, previous associations, professional identity, neighborhoods, and so on. Telephone solicitors get support from each other. A snack or lunch may be served by other volunteers. Those solicitors who have gotten donors to make significant increases in their pledges may get special recognition, a novelty prize, or the like.

LETTERS

Everyone likes to get fan mail, but no one likes junk mail. People also like to learn something new and most have a need to belong, in the sense of being part of something larger than themselves. Letter campaigns build on just such insights—this is what makes the first impression in any fund raising letter so important. Let us start with the way in which the reader is to be greeted. Wherever possible, the reader should be addressed by name, so that it seems that at least someone was interested enough to locate him or her. With word-processing equipment, it is relatively easy to insert a recipient's name on an otherwise printed letter. If that is not possible, the reader should be identified as a member of a group or collectivity with which you know he or she is identified. Typical openings are Dear "Colleague," "Congregant," "Community Elder," and "Fellow Alumnus."

The *opener,* the first sentence, counts for more than almost any other part of the letter. It should be just what its title implies, an eye "opener," an interest "opener," and a commitment "opener." Successful political campaign managers know that the first ten seconds after a letter has been opened are the most important. If the reader's interest has not been aroused in those ten seconds, the letter is likely to wind up in the wastebasket. That interest can best be aroused if it focuses on "you, the reader" instead of "me, the writer." Consider the following openings:

"You, as a mother, will . . ."

"Because you are an adoptive parent . . ."

"Whenever you see an elderly person, do you . . ."

Instead of beginning with information about your organization, speak to the person's interests, so that when you begin to talk about what your organization does or how its clients and others might be helped, it will strike a responsive chord. For example, if the list you use for one batch of letters is composed of people who have received services at the county hospital, the opener might begin, "When you recently used the services of the county hospital, . . ." A list generated from the local newspaper might begin, "When your children were married at . . ." The point is to begin with who the person is.

If you are not sure about the person or if your list is of a more general nature, you might begin with a personal interest story. For example, "A little girl cried last night. She was hungry. Her father, too let down from months of unemployment, never came home to say good night." The letter could then go on to indicate that the little girl will get less than one-third of the nutrients required for her to grow into a healthy adult.

I recently received a letter that began, "Did anyone help you through school when you needed a helping hand? Why not take advantage of a tax break while ensuring that a needy student will be able to earn the same degree you did from XWZ University?" That second sentence was a beauty. It identified me, it stroked my guilt while assuming I was sure to be helpful, and it offered me a tax break to boot!

The rest of the letter should focus on that part of your organization's services most likely to generate the greatest human interest. Whatever you write, it should be accurate, true to the facts. Just as important, it should project a feeling of authenticity. It has to be believable and sincere. It should speak about concrete services, not about abstracts.

The closing sentence or paragraph should be punchy, straightforward, and forthright. It should spell out what is expected from the reader, but it should never apologize for asking. Be clear about what you are asking, and provide the prospective donor with a number of guidelines for the choices he or she might make. For example, you might want to spell out the range or size of gifts. You might even include a checklist. It is not unusual to include a list of specific sums, with boxes that donors can check. You should tell the potential giver how to give—through a check, through Visa or Master Card, or through later billing.

Whatever you write, use plain English, simple words, short sentences, and, especially, short paragraphs. Indent those paragraphs that you want to single out for special attention, or have them printed in a different typeface or color. Tell your story in all the detail that you think it needs, but get to the bottom line relatively early. Nothing is as annoying as waiting to find out what the writer is asking of you and scanning ahead to find the bottom line, only to discover that it is obscured by detail. Sometimes the *bottom line* can be located on a separate enclosure, a brochure, a gift list, or a return mailing card or envelope.

HONEST ABE

How long should the letter be? I have a preference for short letters with long enclosures, rather than long letters with short enclosures. But this is a matter of judgment-based trial and error, and also, to a certain extent, a matter of personal taste. When Lincoln was asked how long a lecture should be, his answer was informative, although today we might call it sexist. "Like a woman's skirt," he said, "it should be long enough to cover the ground, but short enough to be interesting."

One of the more interesting and convincing parts of a letter is the signature. I do not know about you, but I am more likely to give if someone I respect, or if someone I want to be associated with, has asked me to give. And I always look for names of other persons who have given or who are supporting the campaign. The promise of being affiliated with a group that I want to belong to or with people whom I respect is an important inducement. These names are often found on the letterhead or on a list of sponsors.

Although what the copy (the content) of the letter says and how it is conveyed are most important, the style and format are also of great consequence. An organization struggling for survival and appealing to moderate-income publics would do well not to use a "slick" typeface or expensive paper. Nevertheless, there are advantages to using a distinctive style. The stationery, properly designed, will convey the type of program or service you are promoting. It may include a photograph, a recognizable logo, or a sketch of the program or the clients it aims to serve. Color, changes in the typeface or typewriter element, indentations, and checklists help to relieve the monotony of a long letter.

Consider also the envelope. Properly designed, it may wind up on the desk or the kitchen table instead of in the wastebasket. It may even be opened!

Just as important as format and content, I have found, is conveying a respect for the reader's judgment. Remember, the reader is being asked to make a contribution. The reader should also have the opportunity to make a choice; to give or not to give is the simplest choice. Other choices should include more than the size of the gift or its timing. They can also include what the gift should be used for. Some readers will prefer to make their gifts for a summer camp, whereas others might prefer theirs to be used for a family life education program or a scholarship fund. Provide choices wherever possible.

USING ANNUAL REPORTS IN THE CAMPAIGN

In addition to letters, many of which include pledge or solicitation cards, your organization may also wish to mail annual reports to prospective donors, to other persons important to the organization, and, of course, to people who have already contributed. Whatever else it contains, make sure the annual report clearly specifies the organization's name and address, its board members, and the period covered.

Include information on the source of support, the purpose of the work the organization does and how long it has been involved in that kind of work. Indicate who does the work (if professionals, what type, and if volunteers, who). If the organization raised funds from a variety of sources during the previous years, what were the sources and how much was raised from each? On what was the money spent? How has the program been modified to meet current needs? What are the future directions the organization is considering or has chosen to take? Who currently uses the organization's services and who will use those services if the plan for future directions is put into effect because of successful fund raising efforts? Finally, how will the average citizen (presumably, there are many of these among the readers of the report) benefit from these programs and services?

Annual reports, like letters, can be used to awaken interest. They should be written in tangible, human terms. They should be graphic, not only in design, but in the imagery that the words evoke.

Some organizations use more than one version of the annual report. Although each covers roughly the same material, each is targeted to a specific audience. If a single annual report is used, but mailed out to a number of different audiences, different cover letters might tailor it to each of those publics. For some publics, a summary report with the information about where to obtain a longer report may be all that is necessary.

SOME ADDITIONAL TIPS ABOUT
SPECIFIC TYPES OF CAMPAIGNS

Brick-and-mortar experts suggest that the campaign should not start until 25 percent of the needed funds are already "in the bank" or on pledge cards. This means reaching the pace-setters and generating the special gifts early. They also suggest that the campaign not assume an average gift from each of the prospective donors. The prospects should be divided into pace-

---

EXERCISE 10.1
DESIGNING A CAMPAIGN

(1) Review your reading notes. Go over all the practice principles in this chapter and in the previous five. Examine the matrix you completed for Chapter 9. Go over your preliminary considerations, those you thought through before moving on to the sections of this chapter dealing with building a campaign structure. You are now ready to sketch out the outline of your campaign.

(2) In six pages or less, outline a campaign. Indicate if it is to be a general solicitation, bricks-and-mortar, a development fund, or a bequest program. Include the following:
>   overall goals
>   target objectives
>   organization structure needed
>   composition of the teams that will be managing or conducting the activities
>   special instructional needs the fund raisers may have and how they will be met
>   overall promotional activities
>   the timetable

(3) With whom should this preliminary plan be discussed? What are the next steps for you and others in the organization? From where might you seek outside help (books, consultants)?

(4) What are the dangers involved if you do not meet your dollar goal? Are there other benefits, besides dollars, that may overshadow a poor financial showing?

---

setters, second-level gift givers, third-level gift givers, and perhaps even fourth-level givers.

Roughly a fourth of the total should be raised from the pacesetters, most of it before the campaign is officially kicked off. These may make up only 5 to 10 percent of all donors. About a third should be raised from the second-level givers, who generally make up almost half of those who contribute. The rest should be raised from third-level givers, who will make up as much as 40 or 45 percent of those who contribute. Fourth-level givers, if you decide to try to reach them, may be persons who have not previously been actively involved in the organization, or who are not members of it, but who may be committed to the idea of an expanded service facility.

Are there other ways of dividing up your prospects list? Should heavy users of certain programs or facilities by approached by other users—men approached by other men, and women approached by women? Remember that capital campaigns are special. They occur rarely, sometimes only once in an organization's lifetime. And they require special gifts, above and beyond those that donors may make on a regular basis.

Bequest campaigns also require special approaches. Typically, the bequest program will include the following ingredients: (1) a bequest committee or task group that plans and manages the program; (2) a booklet or other descriptive material that spells out details of the bequest program—how it will be used and for what purpose, the types of gifts that might be given, how the gift will be built upon, how taxes favor the individual who gives, or his or her trust or other beneficiaries, and other useful information. It also requires development of (3) a list of prospective givers and others who might be appropriate solicitors. Finally, it requires (4) a set of procedures used to canvas that list and to target certain individuals at the appropriate time.

Development funds are generally earmarked for new or special programs the agency hopes to establish in the future, or for ongoing programs that require expansion or modification. All but special events require lists of actual and prospective donors. They may also require door-to-door interactions, letters, the targeted use of annual reports, and related public relations activities. In lieu of a campaign cabinet, it may have a *development council* made up of staff, board of trustees members, and others. In some organizations, the council coordinates and manages all of the organization's fund raising activities, seeing to it that grantseeking, campaigns, and other events all do their share in the resource development process.

REVIEW

Campaigns tend to have their own structures, often composed of a cabinet, a steering committee, and a number of working groups or task forces. Solicitors often train or work in groups under the leadership of a team captain. Campaign leaders and workers both need ongoing training and support. Campaigns may target certain individuals for large gifts, or otherwise segment the populations at which they aim—for example, by occupational groups or by services received.

SUGGESTIONS FOR FURTHER READING

Review the suggestions in Chapter 9 for useful references and annotations. The following books complement them and deal somewhat more extensively with organizational methods and techniques of fund raising.

Blanchard, Paul, Jr. (1981). *The KRC fund raiser's manual.* New Canaan, CT: KRC Development Council. (The KRC Development Council is a good source for many materials on fund raising, some published by KRC, some distributed by the Council for other publishers. For a list of publications and services, write to KRC, 212 Elm Street, New Canaan, CT 06840.)

Brakeley, George A. (1982). *Tested ways to successful fund raising.* Hartsdale, NY: Public Service Materials Center.

Dermer, Joseph (Ed.). (n.d.). *America's most successful fund raising letters.* Hartsdale, NY: Public Service Materials Center.

Drotning, Phillip T. (n.d.) *500 ways for small charities to raise money.* New Canaan, CT: KRC Development Council.

Fisher, John (1978). *How to manage a nonprofit organization.* Toronto: Management and Fun Raising Centre.

Friant, Ray J., Jr. (1971). *Preparing effective presentations.* New York: Pilot Industries (347 Fifth Avenue, New York, NY 10016).

Keller, Mitchell (Ed.). (1979). *The KRC guide to direct mail fund raising.* New Canaan, CT: KRC Development Council.

KRC Development Center (1981). *The KRC aide and advisor to fund raising copy writers.* New Canaan, CT: Author.

Mercer, Florence (1978). *Getting started: Funds for community based economic development.* Cambridge, MA: Center for Community Economic Development (639 Massachusetts Avenue, Cambridge, MA).

Seymour, Harold J. (1966) *Designs for fund raising: Principles, patterns and techniques.* New York: McGraw-Hill.

Stein, Louis (Ed.). (1979). *Building a successful campaign.* New York: Council of Jewish Welfare Federations.

Tatum, Liston (1978). *The KRC computer book for fund raisers.* New Canaan, CT: KRC Development Council.

CHAPTER *11*

Writing the
Project Proposal:
A Blueprint for Action

VIGNETTE 11: A PLAN FOR ACTION

I represent the school of thought that espouses clarity and precise statements of intentions in proposals, I do not view a proposal as a precursor to a design or to a plan for action. A proposal should be a plan for action. It should be written in operational terms. It should offer clear and precise projections about strategies, activities, and schedules, end results, and so on. If a project is intended to have a specific impact, that impact should be detailed in the proposal. Impact should be measurable, and the writer should indicate how it is to be measured.

The way I look at it, if funds are granted, planners should not then sit back and ask themselves what to do next. The next step should be clear from the proposal. I can't repeat too often that a proposal should be a "plan for action." It's a deliberate, rational design for social intervention.

I've been around long enough to know many planners who regard proposal writing with utter cynicism. "Give the funders what they want," they figure, "and they'll give you what you want." While there may be some validity to their position, I'm not willing to let this perspective govern my actions. I never promise more than I know I can produce. I think I've developed a reputation for integrity. We're not in the fast buck business. We're in it for the long haul. Intent, integrity, and successful grantseeking go hand in hand.

PUTTING IT DOWN ON PAPER

I could not agree more. In this chapter we will examine what goes into successful proposals. It is not just what you put into a proposal, however, or how you write it. The clarity and sincerity of the intent will also be evaluated against the funder's own interests and priorities. Proposals are statements of intent; they are intended to serve as a beginning blueprint for action. If you have checked out your environment, identified the appropriate funding source or sources, examined your own organization's capability, and followed our other suggestions for "getting organized," you are ready to commit the proposal to paper. There is, of course, no perfect pattern to recommend for all grant applications. If I were to suggest any single hard-and-fast rule, it is this: Follow exactly whatever instructions are spelled out by the prospective funder.

Each funding source will have its own special requirements. In some cases, instructions on format and length will be quite detailed. In other cases the funder will permit you considerable latitude. This will vary not only with different funders, but with the kinds of projects they are likely to support. For example, research proposals are likely to require a significant review of the literature, a rigorous methodology section, and some attention paid to the significance of this particular project in light of previous findings or the problem examined.

Those oriented toward the provision of services will require documentation on the needs of those to be served or problems to be addressed. You may have to justify your proposal in terms of the lack of other available or efficient services, the anticipated impact of your project, and the potential for its replication elsewhere. If you are designing a training proposal, you will probably be asked to show the connections between training and service delivery and may be required to justify your project in terms of reduction in costs or increase in effectiveness of service programs.

THE ANATOMY OF A PROPOSAL

Keeping these differences in mind, it is nevertheless possible to examine the anatomy of a typical proposal. Generally it includes the following components:

(1) the title and cover pages;

(2) the project narrative;

(3) the capacities of your agency or organization;

(4) the budget; and

(5) an appendix.

Before examining each of these components, I want to share a few suggestions with you. First, try to keep your narrative down to a reasonable length. Reviewers have a hard time dealing with more than fifteen pages and usually prefer a document that is no more than twelve pages long. Some foundations and businesses may limit you to five or six pages. This may not give you sufficient space to detail the scope of the problem you are addressing, to describe your organization's capacity, or to explain your budget properly. That's what the appendix is for.

If the reviewer wants more information, refer him or her to the appendix. Here, you can be as detailed as you wish. I often set off the appendix so as not to overwhelm the reader. For example, I use white for the cover pages, the narrative, and the information about the organization and budget, but I find it useful to duplicate the appendix in a different color. This is especially true when the appendix is three or four times as thick as the rest of the document. Don't minimize the problems that the reviewer may have in going over your proposal. The easier you make it, the more attention will be paid to the substance of your proposal rather than to its form.

For that reason, I recommend you use simple, concise language, presenting the facts of the case in a straightforward manner. Avoid the eloquence of professional jargon. Many of the best administrators and program developers I know have writing hangups. If you find yourself in this position, get some help. You don't have to go to a professional writer. You may need an editor to go over your first draft. Or you may need someone to put it down on paper the first time around. That won't absolve you of the hard work of making detailed notes for each component. Effective collaboration on any writing project takes some time to develop. The first joint writing effort may be a bit rough or may take longer than you anticipate. Give yourself enough time. It will pay off in the final document.

PREPARING THE COVER AND TITLE PAGES

Most governmental funding agencies include forms for the title page or pages. Make certain you leave none of the required information incomplete. Follow the instructions given, to the letter. Proposals with incomplete title pages may not be accepted.

If no standard form is required, include the following information on the title page of your own design:

(1) title of the project;

(2) name and address of your agency or organization;

(3) submitted to (name of funding source);

(4) proposed project dates;

(5) the amount of money requested for this fiscal year and over the life of the project;

(6) date of submission;

(7) the name and signature of the project director and/or official who will be legally responsible for the project; and

(8) a one-paragraph abstract.

Your cover page or pages may also differ from the others in color or weight of paper. But they should not be elaborate or slick. Even when an abstract is not required by the funding agency, it is a good idea to include one. The abstract can be used by the reviewer to get a quick overview of what the proposal is all about. It can be used by the funder to code the types or nature of projects under consideration and for dissemination of information about projects reviewed or funded.

Typically, an abstract is no longer than 200 words. It summarizes the objectives and significance of the project, the procedures to be followed in carrying it out, and the plans for evaluating the results or making the results available to others. Facts given elsewhere on the title page need not be repeated in the abstract unless specifically required by the funder.

THE PROJECT NARRATIVE

The narrative should include all or most of the following information: (1) need or problem addressed; (2) objectives to be reached; (3) specification of the problem; (4) populations to be served, or systems to be targeted; (5) alternative approaches to dealing with the problem or serving the population; (6) procedures to be followed; (7) schedule or timetable; (8) administration and staffing; (9) evaluation; (10) dissemination and special features; and (11) continuation.
It is not unusual for the funder to request this information in a different order. For example, most federal agencies require information about your organization to appear first in the narrative. The schedule or timetable is often a separate item appearing after the narrative or somewhere between the narrative and the budget or appendixes. Research proposals may follow a different format. So may training proposals. Proposals for capital expenditures certainly will. A number of the suggested categories can be collapsed. Remember to follow the instructions given by the funding source. The funder may not need all this information. Alternatively, the funder may have other questions it wants addressed.

The instructions that follow presume you are working on an action or service delivery proposal. I have found it useful to draw up a brief statement of the problem or need (about a half-page) and to locate it at the start of the narrative. Answer the following questions:

What   is the situation that concerns the planner?
            makes this a problem?

Who   is directly affected?

             is indirectly affected?

Where   is the problem located with reference to this program?

Follow this up with a statement of the goals and objectives to be reached. These might also be written to take no more than a half-page. The goals and objective statement should be in vivid contrast to the statement of the problem. Review the discussion of goals and objectives and your completed exercise material in Chapter 4. Remember that while goals are stated in general terms, objectives are stated in performance terms. They specify

- what is to be done (operations or activities), and/or the outcome expected;
- and within what time frame.

Some objectives also include the

- conditions under which performance is to take place, or the
- criteria by which you will know whether or not the objective(s) has (have) been reached.

If there are too many objectives to include in this brief section, consider writing only the goal statement and relocate the objectives in the section on approaches to be followed.

Wherever it appears, a properly designed statement of objectives will do several things for you. It will establish the criteria against which your project can be evaluated. It will provide you with a base from which you will design your intervention approaches, your training strategy, or your research methods. You may now want to go back to specification of the problem you outlined earlier. Your other statement may be too brief to provide an adequate basis for action. This section should include both conceptual and empirical material.

On the empirical side, you should describe the problem as concretely as possible. Determine whether the focus of attention is to be on (1) populations, groups, and individuals (e.g., skill, knowledge, and attitudes); (2) services (e.g., availability, accessibility, effectiveness, efficiency, and accountability); or (3) management (e.g., internal—productivity, relationship, authority, innovation—or external—continuity and comprehensiveness).

Don't let your knowledge run away with you. Include only information on those aspects of the problem or need that you will be addressing in your project. Everything else is extraneous. If you include it, the reviewer will wonder why your project does not address a broader need or problem. You may refer to a preliminary study you have conducted or to other available data found in census reports, surveys, or agency reports. If these data are extensive, refer to them in the narrative, but locate the bulk of the information in the appendix.

Information is often trivial unless it is accompanied by some conceptualization or explanation. You may wish to explain how you perceive the cause of the problem and the conditions that accompany the problem. There are many ways to do this. I've never found a grants writer as eloquent in describing problem conceptualization as the person in Vignette 12.

VIGNETTE 12: USING CONCEPTS

I draw on the literature to put the problem in a more conceptual framework. It's not that I think there are many theories of causation in the social sciences leading directly to intervention strategies. But I do think that isolated facts are meaningless. They have to be ordered through some concepts, or else one's rationale for action stands on very tenuous grounds.

What I do is search the literature for concepts that help me to understand the problem. If my concern is with the alienation of older people, I'll go through the literature on alienation and identity to find some appropriate intervention strategy. If my concern is with powerlessness and lack of participation, I'll look for concepts to help me understand participatory action better.

There are times when I just don't know where to look in the literature. I may ask a colleague or a friend who is familiar with the problem. Or I may just fall back on a sort of trick I've developed

*that helps me get alternative insights into the causes of a problem. I
borrowed it from a sociologist friend of mine.*

*Suppose I'm concerned with getting more elderly people to take ad-
vantage of a particular service agency's program. I might begin by
jotting down on one piece of paper all the reasons why older people
might not be taking advantage of the program. Is it because they
don't know of its existence? Is it because the agency is located in-
conveniently or the hours make it impossible for potential clients to
take advantage of the service? Do clients feel the agency staff is con-
descending or unresponsive to their interests? Do they distrust that
agency or the kind of service it gives because of previous experience? Are the costs—financial or psychic—too great? Then I make a
similar inventory of possible reasons that the agency is not able to
serve that particular population. Is it because agency staff don't understand the needs of older people or of a particular ethnic minority
among the aged? Is the technology they're using inappropriate to
this population? Are there insufficient numbers of staff people
available?*

*Next I try to match one of the problems on the agency side with one
of the problems on the consumer or client side. I'll draw up a 2 × 2
table:*

Client's Mistrust or Fear of

Agency's Technology

	+ (No Fear)	− (Fear)
+ (Appropriate)	(1) ++	(2) +-
− (Not Appropriate)	(3) -+	(4) −

(Row label, rotated: Agency's Technology)

*If, on analysis, I find that the agency's technology is appropriate and
the clients neither mistrust nor fear it, as indicated in Box 1, above,*

then I know that's not the reason they're not making use of the service. On the other hand, the technology may be appropriate but the clients may fear it (Box 2). In this case, I know that part of the solution is related to consumer education or more effective outreach by the agency. What if the facts show that there is no consumer anxiety, but the agency's services are nevertheless inappropriate (Box 3)? In this case, the appropriate action might be to get consumers to help educate the agency staff about what a particular client group really needs, or to put some pressure on that agency to change its procedures. It may also be important to create some staff training or development activities. But what if the agency's technology is bad and clients mistrust the agency (Box 4)? Some planners make the mistake of trying to move directly from Box 4 to Box 1. That seems to me to be a giant step. It may be more appropriate to move from Box 4 to Box 2 and then to Box 1.

Generally, I try to create the same 2 × 2 boxes for every logical combination of service blockages from both the agency perspective and the client perspective. Sometimes I find it useful to combine them all into a single larger table. When that's done, I suggest a strategy or set of strategies for dealing with the problem. I can now define the problem in operational terms. It's possible for me to list alternative intervention strategies and then select the best course of action. In my proposal, I give reasons for my selection. More than likely, the reasons will have to do with feasibility—that is, with what can be accomplished in view of available resources, support at the community level, the time available, and the political or sociological constraints limiting our possible interventions.

The grant writer has moved us to the next section of the narrative: that which examines alternative intervention approaches and describes which ones are to be pursued. Before we move on as well, let us make sure we have said all that needs saying about the populations to be served or targets of intervention. In designing a new service delivery program, for example, your objective may have specified that you want to serve the elderly in a low-income neighborhood. Which elderly? Where are they located? How many are there? What are their specific characteristics, and how do these differ from the general population or from the elderly in other communities? Segment the population according to geography, function, demography, and/or psychography.

Some proposals will be aimed at effecting changes in target populations as well as in target organizations. For example, your projected intervention may be targeted on foster care workers and supervisors whose knowledge, attitudes, or skills require changing. It may also target the agency itself, its procedures, its policies, and its patterns of resource allocation. What changes in each are required so that changes in one are not cancelled out by lack of change in the other?

Let's turn our attention now to the selection of an appropriate intervention approach or approaches from among several alternatives. These approaches may be based on your conceptualization of the problem. They may also come from an "idea inventory" you participated in with others, perhaps using the "branching tree" technique discussed in Chapter 4. The approach selected may also be drawn from your knowledge of how other agencies or projects have dealt with the problem. If you are replicating something that has been done elsewhere, or if it is somewhat different, indicate *why* and *how*. Your selection from among alternative approaches may be based on one or more of the following factors: the way you have conceptualized the problem; cost; the capacity of your agency and your staff; the novelty of your approach; your assessment of its effectiveness; the probability that it can be institutionalized within your organization; and/or the likelihood that it can be replicated elsewhere.

The section on "procedures" is sometimes referred to by funding agencies as "program implementation" or "methodology." It should be prepared with great care. This is a place where you map out the specific techniques or approaches you will use for delivering the proposed service or conducting the research. You may include how the staff will be recruited and trained, the way in which service recipients will be engaged or served, and what, if any, follow-up steps are to be taken.

This is the place that often receives the greatest scrutiny by the reviewer or reviewing panel. Reviewers may think you have done a good job in describing and analyzing the problem and in specifying your objectives. But if they don't think that you know how to conduct research or training or how to manage a service project properly, they are not likely to fund the project.

It often helps to divide this section into subsections, particularly if you can group the project's tasks into specific categories. A training project, for example, might include consultation, the design and testing of training materials, the development of a curriculum plan, and the training of specified populations. The procedures used in each of these subsections should be described separately.

It sometimes makes sense to describe these activities chronologically. This is especially true when one activity or subtask must be accomplished before another begins.

The inclusion of a time chart in the proposal gives evidence of serious planning on the part of the applicant agency. In its simplest form, the chart might include a column for the target date or dates or for the months of the year. Another column might include the corresponding activities to be conducted during those periods. The following example of a timetable for proposal development can serve as a review of some of the things covered earlier and as an example of the kind of timetable that funders often request.

TIMETABLE FOR PROPOSAL DEVELOPMENT	
MONTH	**ACTIVITY**
March	Idea identified. Preliminary discussions held with colleagues in local agency to determine their interest; contact made with colleagues in other communities or states to determine the regional or national significance of the idea. Preliminary discussion held with agency administrators.

April	Needs assessment instituted. Inquiries submitted to national information systems [see Chapter 2] to determine if similar idea has already been tried, to get names of communities or agencies with related experience and to identify related research. Statistical data collected to support statement of need.
May	Various approaches to implement idea discussed. Best approach chosen after contacts made with other local agencies, state agencies, etc. Approval to proceed with development of project obtained from administrators. Project director or program developer selected and other staff to be involved in proposal preparation. First draft of ideas in project form developed and discussed with agency administrators, potential population to be served, and other groups necessary to local support.
June	Potential funding sources identified and preliminary outline sent to determine their interest in the project and to acquire necessary application information [see Chapter 3].
July	Project idea modified by input received during previous months. Another inquiry to potential funding sources may be warrented. Second draft completed and circulated for review to agency administrators and any local or state group involved in a clearance procedure.
August	Funding source chosen. Final draft prepared based on source's forms or requirements. Official clearance received from local administrators. Review and clearance sought as necessary from any local or state agencies.
September	Proposal submitted to funding source. Receipt card with processing number received in return.
December to February	Approval or rejection received. In either case comments of reviewers should be sought.
March	Authorization for expenditure received.
April	Recruitment of personnel. Modifications started on facilities, if necessary.
May-June	Plans developed for staff training. Materials prepared.
July	Personnel salaried and project started. Staff training initiated. Detailed management plan outlined. Assignments and responsibilities clarified.
October	Refunding application prepared and submitted.

SOURCE: Mary Hall, *Developing Skills in Proposal Writing*. Eugene: University of Oregon Continuing Education Publications, 1979.

Some funders and some proposal writers prefer to use what is sometimes referred to as a Gantt Chart. Henry Gantt, a turn-of-the-century industrialist, was one of the early pioneers of scientific management. He found it helpful to both managers and workers to use bars or lines as a way of spelling out when something should be worked on and by what time it should be completed. It is little more than a set of dates posted at the top of the page (in weeks, months, quarters). In the left-hand column, the major tasks to be accomplished are listed. Lines are then drawn on the chart to indicate start and finish dates for a task or activity complex.

Sample Gantt Chart

	1st Quarter	2nd Quarter	3rd Quarter	4th Quarter
Staff				
Recruitment and Selection	—			
Training	—	—		
Advising Committee				
Appointed	—			
Meetings	—	—	—	—
Assessment				
Instrument Designed	—			
Survey Conducted		—		
Report Issues			—	
Block Checks				
Organizations				
Activities	——	—		
Meetings		— —	— —	—
Association Formed			—	
Conference				—
Evaluation				
Ongoing Monitoring	————————————————			
Evaluation Designed		—		
Evaluation Conducted			——	
Report Issued				—

Program Evaluation and Review Technique (PERT) can be used to chart a more complex system of events and activities than is possible on a Gantt Chart. It is, in effect, a map of the activities that must be performed over time to achieve predetermined end points known as "events." Most events are depicted as circles on the chart, whereas "milestone" events (completion of a project, a turning point, or the like) are sometimes shown as squares or circles within squares. The lines between circles and squares represent the time it takes to perform those activities leading up to an event.

For example, on the following chart, 1, 2, 3, 4, and 5 are events, and 5 is a milestone event—the final event in the process. It is at the right side of the PERT network because it follows the international charting convention of moving from left to right. Events that follow others are called "successor" events, whereas those that precede others are "predecessor" events. On the chart below, 3 is a successor to 1 and a predecessor of 5, which means that it cannot occur until 1 is completed, nor can 5 occur prior to the completion of 3 (or, for that matter, 2 and 4 on the chart).

Sample PERT Network

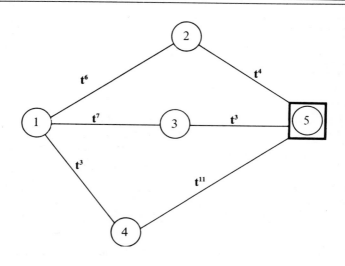

The t with a number next to it on each line of the chart refers to the time needed to complete the activities between events. Assuming the time is measured in weeks, it would take six weeks of activity to get from the starting point to event 2 and another four weeks to get to completion (event 5). The entire chain of events and activities takes ten weeks—the same as from event 1 to event 3 and then to 5. But notice that it takes three weeks to get to event 4 and then eleven weeks of activities to get to the final event. Clearly, the entire project cannot be completed in less than fourteen weeks, even though some activity chains require less time. This longest chain is called the "critical path," which is why PERT is sometimes referred to as the Critical Path Method (CPM).

PERT (or CPM) is an excellent tool for charting complex chains of events. The process, however, is a bit more complex than that described above. Moreover, in a relatively simple proposal, such a method is likely to provide the reader with an information overload.

In addition to its uses for impressing the funder with your capability, you might find the time chart helpful in planning your activity, anticipating those peak times in which human resources and facilities will be needed, and monitoring your progress once the project is under way.

The next section of your narrative focuses on the project's administrative location within the overall agency. In which department or subunit will it be lodged? To whom is the project director administratively and programmatically responsible? Will the project have an advisory committee or a policy board? Is it to be made up of agency staff or staff from other agencies, of agency consumers, and/or of a panel of experts drawn from a local or national pool? How are the membrs of the advisory or policy group to be selected? What are their specific responsibilities to be? You will also need to spell out the internal administrative arrangements within the project, the lines of authority and supervision, and the management procedures to be used.

This is also a good place to describe the staffing of the project. You will want to give brief job descriptions for all the key professional staff. If you are to use consultants, indicate for what purposes and to what extent they will be involved in the project. If you know who the persons will be who will perform each of the staff roles (such as the project director, associate director, assistant director, administrative assistant, senior researcher), indicate their names. Discuss their specific qualifications briefly. This may include previous work done or their other supportive or complementary roles within your organization or agency. More detailed information on the staff should be located in the appendix. It might include either abbreviated or complete resumes on all professional staff persons to be involved in some significant fashion.

There are several issues to consider in setting up the project's evaluation procedures. Both the project's operations and its outcomes should be evaluated.[1] The evaluation of outcomes relates directly to the objectives you established for the project. Did you accomplish what you set out to? Were you able to serve the number of people you anticipated at the planned level of service? Did the behavior of staff change in terms of increasing permanence for children? What were your measures of attitude change?

The second focus of evaluation is on the project itself and the procedures used. Did you follow your time line? Were intra-agency supports adequate? Was staff orientation sufficient? If the original plan was not followed, on what basis were changes made? This aspect of evaluation should occur throughout the project. It will permit you to monitor your progress according to plan and to make shifts in procedures or even in objectives if circumstances warrant.

Finally, your evaluation should indicate the connections between the procedures followed and the project outcomes.

At this point, you will want to make some statements about special features, replication, or dissemination. What distinguishes this approach from others? How does it articulate with the interests of the funder or those of other publics? How can successes be replicated elsewhere? How will the results be reported? How can others be alerted not to make the same mistakes or repeat the same errors that your staff may commit?

---

1. Review the discussions on the "focus of attention" and "types of objectives" in the section on Goals in Chapter 7.

Consider the kinds of project report or reports that will be prepared. To whom will they be distributed? Will there be any publications? Will dissemination occur only locally through news items or TV documentaries? Will staff share their experiences with representatives of other agencies in your locale? At regional and national meetings of professional associations?

In many instances, funders provide money to initiate a new program or service on the assumption that the recipient agency intends to continue the program beyond the initial grant. Is the project to be absorbed within the ongoing operation of your organization? If new financial resources are needed, from where will they come? From outside sources such as fees for service or other grants? From reallocation of the agency's internal budget? Even when a commitment to continuation is not specifically required, it is often helpful if the proposal demonstrates the applicant's concern for the future. This is particularly true when the absence of continued funding might jeopardize the client population through sudden termination of services.

ABOUT YOUR AGENCY AND ITS CAPACITIES

Having made your case for the need or the importance of the problem to be addressed, the relevance of your objectives, and the feasibility of your intervention plan, you must now provide convincing evidence that your organization has the competence to conduct the project successfully. If your agency has a good track record of conducting training programs, of managing research of national significance, or of innovative service, describe that record. This is no place to be modest.

If you already have established relationships with the population to be served and have demonstrated an ability to make proper use of community resources, review the history of those relationships and your use of resources. Extensive information might be lodged in the appendix. Letters of endorsement from prominent people who are well acquainted with the funding agency as well as with your program are sometimes of value. These also belong in the appendix.

Some experienced proposal writers prefer including information about the project staff in this section rather than in the program narrative as suggested here; I have no particular preference for one approach or another. Just remember to include detailed resumes in the appendix for the director and other key professionals who will be involved in the project.

THE BUDGET

The best-laid plans must now be translated into dollars. It is the grantseeking process, after all, that motivated you to write the proposal in the first place. I have known some awfully good project designers and proposal writers who turn over the responsibility for budget preparation to others who may be better with figures. This is a mistake. Only those who are thoroughly familiar with the objectives of the project and the procedures that will be used to accomplish those objectives should make the decisions about how much money will be sought and for which categories of expenditure. You may want to involve people who are knowledgeable about costs, but you won't turn over the decision on how to allocate money and for what to people who are not programmatically knowledgeable or administratively responsible.

Most funding agencies have set procedures for the budget description section in the proposal. Forms may be provided for inclusion in the cover pages. Additional explanations and justifications, however, may be requested. In general, most funders require a line budget itemization. Line-item budgets reflect expenditures. They show exactly what money will be used for.

The construction of a line-item budget is detailed in the next chapter. It is compared with functional budgets—those known as performance and program budgets, which can be used to cost out major activity complexes and the achievement of program objectives. You might want to read that chapter before completing your project narrative. Some proposal writers use the budget as a planning document. They design it first, before completing the rest of the project design or committing it to paper.

If you have completed the other parts of a proposal, you know pretty much what should go into the appendix. Consider including (1) greater specification of the problem and the needs being addressed; (2) a review of the literature or of other service programs similar to the one you have projected; (3) information on both the agency and staff involved, including resumes; (4) more fully spelled-out time projections; (5) full budget justifications; (6) letters of endorsement; and (7) any other items you feel are relevant but not important enough to appear in the narrative itself.

THE FINISHING TOUCHES

You are not finished yet. After all parts of the proposal are committed to paper, a few steps remain. The first of these is to have the entire document reviewed from at least three viewpoints. The writer must check detail by detail to make sure all aspects of the project have been covered. Another person familiar with the project and your agency should determine whether the plan is accurately described. And someone without previous knowledge of the project should be asked to make sure that every section of the proposal is understandable.

You may find this brief checklist helpful in your final review:

- Are the important points easily discovered in skimming the proposal?

- Has the applicant made a convincing case for a specific local need, outlined a realistic plan for meeting that need, and demonstrated that it is the agency best positioned to carry out the plan?

- Are the stated objectives clearly reflected in the sections on procedures, personnel, and budget?

- Does the proposal present an honest, factual picture of the applicant agency and of the resources and personnel available for the project? Are the "plus" factors emphasized, but without exaggeration?

- Is the presentation grammatical, clear, and concise, avoiding jargon, overblown phraseology, and unexplained abbreviations?

- Have all requirements of the funding agency been met?

THE LETTER PROPOSAL:
A SPECIAL CASE

Throughout the chapter we have been assuming that you will be writing a full-length proposal.

Under certain circumstances, however, it may be appropriate to write a letter proposal. This is sometimes all that is required (or even allowed) by some foundations, civic associations, or business companies. Letter proposals need not exceed two pages of perhaps six or seven paragraphs. The emphasis is generally on the problem to be addressed or the need of a consumer population. Letter proposals should be tailored to the expressed interests of the funding source. The Outline for a Letter Proposal is adapted from suggestions made by the Public Management Institute.

EXERCISE 11.1
WRITING YOUR OWN PROPOSAL

(1) Decide whether you wish to work on a full-length or a letter proposal. Go to your reading notes on Chapters 4 and 5, or reexamine the chapters themselves and the exercises you completed for Chapter 4.

(2) Write a proposal using the categories suggested under Anatomy of a Proposal, or the Outline of a Letter Proposal, suggested in this chapter; or follow a funder's guidelines. If you are writing a budget, follow the instructions in Chapter 12.

(3) Review the proposal using the funder's review criteria or those suggested in Chapter 13.

REVIEW

Full-length proposals are generally divided into the following sections: (1) the title and cover pages, (2) the project narrative, (3) the organization's capacities to do the job, (4) the budget, and (5) the appendix. The narrative is further subdivided into problem description, goals and objectives, populations to be

Outline for a Letter Proposal

First Paragraph	**(1)**	*Addressee* — the person requesting the proposal or the official contact person at the funding source, to the address of the funding source.
	(2)	*Introduction* — the reason for writing, and in particular, to this funding source. For example: "Robin Martenns suggested that our interests and those of the foundation are closely related. I am writing about . . . "
Second Paragraph	**(3)**	*The Problem of the Need* — in one or two sentences state the problem, the need, or the desired state of affairs your project addresses. Examples: "Last year 87 people committed suicide in Midtown and 430 attempts were reported. We think there may have been twice that many." Or, "Books don't reach children in the west end."
Third Paragraph	**(4)**	*Your Proposed Action* — an outline of the project in 4 to 6 short sentences presented as a solution to the problem or need just described; include the timetable.
Fourth Paragraph	**(5)**	*Benefits* — how clients or the community will benefit from the intervention directly and indirectly; who else cares.
	(6)	*Unique Features* — how this project differs from others, the sponsors of the project (i.e., who was involved or who cares), complementarity with the funding source's interests.
Fifth Paragraph	**(7)**	*Budget* — brief summary, perhaps broken down into broad performance or program expenditures.
	(8)	*The Amount Requested* — dollars sought for this year or for entire project period, and amounts to be donated from other sources.

served, alternative approaches to dealing with the problem or serving the population, approach to be taken and procedures to be followed, timetable, administration and staffing, evaluation, dissemination and special features, and continuation. Letter proposals are abridged versions of the above.

SUGGESTIONS FOR FURTHER READING

Borden, Karl (1978). *Dear uncle, please send money—A guide for proposal writers.* Pocatello, ID: Auger Associates.

Citizen Information Service of Illinois (1976). *Steps in writing a proposal.* Chicago: Author.

Dermer, Joseph (n.d.). *How to write successful foundation presentations.*
A manual on proposal writing. Includes approaches to use for hard-to-fund programs; largely for social action programs.

Ezell, Susan (Ed.). (n.d.) *The proposal writer's swipe file.* Washington, DC: Taft Corporation.
Includes fifteen professionally written proposals that can serve as models for writing and design.

Hall, Mary (1981). *Developing skills in proposal writing.* Portland, OR: Continuing Education Publications.
Particularly geared to proposals dealing with training, demonstration, and service programs rather than research activities. Special emphasis on forms involved in government funding.

Jacquette, F. Lee, & Jacquette, Barbara I. (1973, January). What makes a good proposal. *Foundation News.*

Kiritz, Norton J. (1980). *Program planning and proposal writing.* Los Angeles: Grantsmanship Center.

Krathwohl, David R. (n.d.) *How to prepare a successful research proposal.* Syracuse, NY: Syracuse University Bookstore.

Lefferts, Robert. (1982). *Getting a grant: How to write successful grant proposals.* Englewood Cliffs, NJ: Prentice-Hall.
Strong on the basics; easy-to-follow step-by-step procedures.

Orlich, Donald C., & Orlich, Patricia R. (1977). *The art of successful R&D proposals.* Pleasantville, NY: Redgrave.

Public Management Institute (1978). *The grant writer's handbook* (Vol. 1). San Francisco: Author.
Both volumes of this handbook are loaded with how-to tips, outlines, and checklists.

Public Management Institute (1980). *The grant writer's handbook* (Vol. 2). San Francisco: Author.

Public Management Institute (n.d.). *Evaluation handbook.* San Francisco: Author.

Public Management Institute (n.d.). *Needs assessment handbook.* San Francisco: Author.

Smith, Craig (1980). *Getting grants.* New York: Harper & Row.
A creative guide to the grants system: how to find funders, write convincing proposals, and make your grants work.

White, Virginia (1975). *Grants: How to find out about them and what to do next.* New York: Plenum.

CHAPTER 12

Drawing Up the
Budget

When I got to the budget part of my proposal, I thought I was over the hump. Was I ever wrong! By the time I had costed out what we intended to do, it totaled $256,000. The funder's average grant for last year was under $80,000. Not much chance that we could get what we needed for the project.

And there was just no way we could trim what we were planning to do without so emasculating the program as to make it relatively worthless. I should have started with the budget, then figured out what we could do with the limitations imposed. We would probably have designed a different project, or looked for alternative sources, maybe even more than one source of support.

The program planner quoted learned the lesson too late. There was no longer sufficient time to go back to the drawing board and redesign prior to the funder's application deadline. You can do better, but it will take some understanding of the budget-making process.

Author's Note: Much of this chapter is adapted from Chapter 12 of *Doing Continuing Education and Staff Development,* by Armand Lauffer with Celeste Sturdevant (New York: McGraw-Hill, 1978). A more detailed discussion of the budgeting process may be found in Chapter 11 of *Strategic Marketing,* by Armand Lauffer (New York: Free Press, 1984).

The budget is both a program and a fiscal document. Think of it as a plan expressed in financial terms. It details how much you intend to spend (in dollars) for what (personnel and materials, activities, or end results) over a designated period of time. Because the budget permits you to put what you propose to do and spend down on paper, it provides you with an instrument to monitor your activities in both programmatic and fiscal terms. Budgets are generally presented in tabular form, the budget table being explained in a narrative "budget justification."

THREE KINDS OF BUDGETS

There are different kinds of budgets. Each has its own advantages and disadvantages. The *line-item budget* is probably the one with which most administrators are familiar. It is the most commonly used. Budget lines list expenses just the way they are paid out. Typically, line items for continuing education programs include personnel, consultants and instructors, facilities, equipment, consumable supplies, and travel.

The *performance budget* projects the cost of performing a certain unit of work—for example, conducting a workshop, counseling clients, managing a project. It reflects the work to be done and anticipates the cost of doing any given number of units of work. A properly designed performance budget might even show the relative savings of increasing the number of units of work. For example, because overhead expenses remain fairly stable, it may cost $160,000 to retrain forty unemployed workers, and only half that much to train forty more. The cost may get progressively lower until it levels off at about $1500 per trainee when the project contracts to train 150 or more.

A *program budget* goes one step further. It categorizes expenditures in relationship to the agency objectives or the objectives of a particular project. Administrative and maintenance costs are allocated to specific objectives, such as placing retrained workers on the job, getting a hard-to-place child adopted, completing a plan for staff and organizational devel-

TABLE 12.1 Simplified Line-Item, Performance, and Program Budgets Compared

Line-Item Budget		Performance Budget		Program Budget	
Personnel	$20,000	Consultation on program design and development of plan	$6,500	Plan for staff develop-ment	$11,500
Consultants	6,000				
Facilities	2,000				
Equipment	1,000				
Supplies	2,000	Staffing of planning committee	3,000	Instruc-tional materials	20,500
Travel	1,000	Design of instructional materials	18,000		
		Printing	1,500		
		Administra-tion	3,000		
Total	$32,000		$32,000		$32,000

opment, or producing instructional materials. The examples in Table 12.1 may help you visualize the differences among these budgets.

You'll notice that the line-item budget tells you exactly what you expect to spend money on. For that reason, it makes it easy to monitor your expenditures. It is a good device for tracking the outflow of funds, but it has several disadvantages. First, by focusing on the expenditure of resources rather than on accomplishment, it does little to reflect the purpose of those expenditures. The budget is considered merely an accounting device. It is not very helpful in designing your program. The program or project, in fact, has to be designed fully before its objectives or activities are translated into budgetary terms. Because line-item budgets don't say enough about *why* each item is included, they generally require explanations that appear in a budget narrative following the budget summary. These explanations or justifications are sometimes given in performance or program terms.

The performance budget describes the work authorized or projected. It aggregates the items found in the line budget. Thus the category of consultation and program design in the performance budget includes personnel, consultants, supplies, and travel expenditures from the line-item budget. The program budget, focusing on outputs, aggregates further. In Table 12.1, the two products are a plan and instructional materials. Expenditures under each include those categories found in both the line-item and the performance budgets. For example, the plan will require consultation on program design, staffing of planning committees, and some of the funds allocated to general administration found in the performance budget. It can also be broken down into line items.

THE LINE-ITEM BUDGET:
A CLOSER LOOK

Because line-item budgets are most common, it might be helpful to describe what goes into each item and then make a number of suggestions about what to consider in assigning a dollar value to each line item.

Personnel. Includes estimates of the salaries (including raises) and fringe benefits that will be paid to all personnel employed by the agency or project. Fringe benefits and employee pay are generally posted separately as two items on the budget document, but may be combined as a single item. Personnel includes full- and part-time staff who perform professional, clerical, maintenance, and other supportive tasks. Indicate on your budget if personnel are to be full or part time. One way of doing this is to specify the full-time equivalent (FTE). For example, 5 FTE would indicate that salaries sought cover the equivalent of five full-time employees in a particular category. In point of fact, these might be for ten half-time employees. A note of 0.5 FTE would indicate a single person working half time or several persons sharing the equivalent of a half-time person. In your narrative you may have to justify the number or categories of personnel and explain your use of several people to equal one FTE.

Consultation and Contract Services. These include services required by the project that its staff are unable to provide. Consultation services are performed by individual consultants or organizations with whom you contract. Anticipated fees as well as expenses incurred by consultants in providing service (for example, travel and per diem) may be posted as a single item on the budget document or broken down into several cost estimates. Your narrative can be used to justify costs.

Facilities. Includes space required by the project to administer and perform its activities. Space may be leased, rented, purchased, or donated as an in-kind contribution. If space requires remodeling or renovation, these costs should also be distinguished as a line item on the budget document and the rationale for altering the site should be outlined in the budget justification. Remember that few funders are likely to cover renovation or purchase costs for projects that are not expected to last beyond one or two years.

Equipment. Includes both office and program equipment such as furnishing, typewriters, and audiovisual (AV) equipment that staff use in administering or carrying out activities. Costs appearing in the category of equipment may represent items purchased or rented. An explanation of the need for special or costly pieces of equipment should appear in the budget justification. Note that it may be possible to lease equipment that the agency can purchase for $1 or some minimal sum on completion of the project.

Consumable Supplies. Includes office supplies such as typing materials and stationery, lavatory supplies, and other commonly used and less expensive office implements, such as staplers and in-baskets. It also includes paper, film, books, and other supplies used in your service programs. Communication and telephone costs may also be included, although if they are expected to be high, they may require a separate category. Include estimates of the costs of monthly rental, or charges for long-distance telephone calls, and fees that might be charged for radio, television, and newspaper announcements. Printing and reproduction costs may be included here or may go into a special program or publications category. Cost estimates might include the rental of equipment required to print or copy materials as well as the costs of purchasing reproduction machinery or having the work performed by an outside contractor.

Travel and Per Diem. This item includes estimates of the travel expenses that will be incurred by staff and volunteers within the local area, when leaving the local area to carry out agency business, and, occasionally, travel expenses incurred by consumers participating in agency activities. Per diem costs include expenses for room and board incurred when staff or clientele must leave the local area to participate in activities or perform business meaningful to the operation of the program. Expenses for consultant travel and per diem may be included in either the consultant or the travel category of the budget document.

You'll find that most funders—your host organization, a foundation supporting a project, another agency contracting for your services, or a federal bureau with a grants program— have their own instructions for designing a line-item budget. Be sure to follow their instructions or guidelines. If you've never put a line-item budget together, you might find the format on the sample budget in Table 12.2 helpful.

DESIGNING THE LINE-ITEM BUDGET

Line-item budgets are generally divided into two major categories: personnel and nonpersonnel items. The "tabular" budget is usually followed by the "budget justification." Budgets should be designed to communicate all necessary details to relevant audiences. If you are using a funder's guidelines, make

TABLE 12.2 Sample Line-Item Budget for a Training and Materials Development Project*

Line	Requested	Donated	Total
1. Personnel			
a. Professional (percentage of appointments/length of appointment)			
(1) Director at $24,000 (.125 FTE)**		$3,000	$3,000
(2) Associate Director for Materials Development at $20,000 (.25 FTE)	$5,000		$5,000
(3) Trainer/Evaluator at $18,000 (.5 FTE)	$9,000		$9,000
b. Nonprofessional			
(1) Secretary at $10,000 (.25 FTE)		2,500	2,500
(2) Bookkeeper at $20,000 (.05 FTE)		1,000	1,000
(3) Maintenance people at $10,000 (.05 FTE)		500	500
c. Fringe benefits (22% of above)	3,080	1,540	4,620
2. Consultants			
a. Six consultants @ $200/day for 5 days each	6,000		
b. Travel and per diem (one trip per consultant)	3,000		9,000
3. Nonpersonnel			
a. Equipment			
(1) 50% purchase price of typewriter and desk	1,000		
(2) Rental of audiovisual equipment as needed	500		1,500
b. Consumable supplies			
(1) Office consumables (paper, typewriter ribbons, etc).		600	
(2) Telephone (monthly charges plus long-distance costs)		400	
(3) Consumable instructional materials		1,200	2,200
c. Staff travel			
(1) Mileage at reimbursable rate of 24 cents per mile for 2000 miles		480	
(2) Four out-of-town trips @ $200 each		800	1,280
d. Facilities			
(1) Rental of office space	1,200		
(2) Rental of conference facilities		800	2,000
TOTAL***	$28,780	$12,820	$41,600

  *   This budget does not include indirect costs. Most host organizations charge indirect costs on the basis of either total direct costs (TDC) or a percentage of the personnel costs.

  ** In the budget justication, this is described as 25% time for six months.

  *** In this budget, the applicant is contributing almost 45% of the amount needed for the project in both out-of-pocket and in-kind donations. Which are the in-kind donations?

sure that you follow those guidelines to the letter. If you are following the procedures generally used in your own organization, make sure you understand those procedures and that you use the categories considered standard for other programs and departments.

Referring to Table 12.2, let's look at the anatomy of a fairly standard line-item presentation. Notice that there are three columns: one for the *total* budget, one for the *requested* amount, and another for the *donated* amount.

The *total* budget projects what the program will actually cost, regardless of sources of income. The *requested* column specifies the amount you are requesting from a particular source, say, the United Foundation, the Community Mental Health Board, the City Council, the Federal Office of Human Development, the local Kiwanis organization, or Litton Industries. The *donated* column refers to all other sources.

For different audiences you may wish to use different categories. Instead of the *requested* and *donated* categories, for example, you might prefer designations such as *sponsor,* or *cost sharing.* If you have several sponsors, you might wish to divide the *requested* column further for each of the sponsors to whom you are submitting a proposal. If other suppliers have already committed funds, include a "committed" column. In this case the *donated* column would reflect only your own organization's contributions. Should you be seeking funds primarily from the organization's *general fund* or other internal source, the columns might include "general fund allocation," "fees from clients," and "parents appeal campaign." Clearly, there are many possibilities. Budgets are flexible tools. Design yours to communicate what is significant in your circumstances. The categories you decide to use should be determined by what you hope to convey to the publics you are addressing.

The tabular budget must include as much information as possible, but no more than is needed. This may become clear when we examine each of the line items. Let us begin with personnel. The section on personnel generally includes three subsections: (1) salaries and wages, (2) fringe benefits, and (3) consultants and contract services. You might wish to subdivide salaries and wages further into "professional personnel" and "support staff."

Indicating the specific salary allocated to a given staff member may be insufficient without designating the number of months that person will be working on the project or the percentage of work time allocated to that project. Assume that the project director's annual salary is $24,000, but he or she is assigned only quarter time to the project. Assume further that you are asking the funding source to cover the full 25 percent of his or her time allocated to the project for the entire twelve months. Here is how you could communicate this as a line item:

	Requested	Donated
Project Director: .25 FTE at $24,000	$6000	—

Suppose your project includes five caseworkers. The next line item might then read as follows:

	Requested	Donated
Caseworkers: 5 FTE at $20,000	$80,000	$20,000

In this case the agency or some other donor is contributing 20 percent of the salaries from some other source. If one of those workers is already on staff, this might be the agency's *in-kind* contribution. You may wish to explain this in the budget justification. If you expect to be refunded the next year, that explanation may be crucial. Some budget writers prefer to designate each item that is to be subsequently explained with an asterisk (*) or some other symbol; others prefer to use superscript numbers much as they might footnote in a professional article; still others prefer none of these designations, trusting that the reader will understand what is being communicated when reading the justification section.

If you expect salaries to change due to union contracts or annual merit increments during a given fiscal year, you will want to show this in the budget as well. Do so by designating that the project director will be paid for three months at $24,000, and nine months at $26,000. If you decide not to use FTEs this is how you might show it on your line-item budget:

	Requested	Donated
Project Director at 25 percent of $24,000 for 3 months and 25 percent of $26,000 for 9 months	$6250	—

In FTE's this would still amount to .25. It might be written as 0.25 FTE $[(24,000 \div 4) + 3(26,000 \div 4)]$. A similar procedure would be used for each of your professional and support staff: the secretaries, clerical assistance, bus drivers, maintenance personnel, accountants, and others.

Let us assume you have decided what work needs to be done, and how many people it will take to do the job. Each job is given a title. So far, so good; the trouble is, you are not sure how much each person should be paid. What to do? The first step is to find out what comparable programs, within your organization and outside, pay staff who have similar responsibilities. Is there a going rate in your agency and in your community for certain jobs? Pay rates on newly funded projects should neither exceed nor fall below pay rates for comparable positions elsewhere in your agency. The same holds true for pay raises and fringe benefits.

If some or all of the staff to be assigned to the project are new, you will have to make some guesses about where, on a range of possible salaries, each might be placed. Assume for a moment that the salary for a caseworker ranges from $18,000 at entry level to $28,000 per year for those at the upper end of the scale. If you estimate too low, say, close to the $18,000 beginning level, you will not be able to attract more experienced or expert staff persons. If you start too high, your funders are likely to be suspicious, fearing that you are padding the budget. As a rule of thumb, it is helpful to divide the salary range into six segments. In this case, it would be $18,000, $20,000, $22,000, $24,000, and $26,000, the upper limit being $28,000. You would not want to hire all the staff at the upper level, with no hope of advancement. Pick the anticipated salary level for the new employees somewhere at the middle or just above the middle range, say $23,000 or $24,000. This is the figure you will use in your line-item budget. In the sample line-item budget we assumed a narrower range of $18,000 to $22,000 for the associate director, with a midpoint upon which the request was made of $20,000.

FRINGE BENEFITS

Fringe benefits are generally calculated as a percentage of all salaries and wages. If you work for an established organization, chances are that these average about 22 percent to 26 percent of total salaries and wages for all professional and support staff. However, there may be separate fringe packages for different categories of staff, with differential agency contributions to health, life insurance, or retirement benefits for various categories of staff. All will include mandatory workers' compensation and FICA (social security), which accounts for 10 percent or more of salaries and wages.

The fringe package may also include voluntary contributions to (1) health, mental health, and dental health insurance programs; (2) an annuity or retirement fund; (3) life insurance; or (4) some other benefit program. Some organizations also provide what have come to be known as "perks." These may include payment to attend training programs, memberships in professional associations, access to agency services and facilities, subsidized rent, use of an agency vehicle, and so on.

If your organization has already developed a fringe package, use the percentage allocation in your budget; otherwise you will have to design a new one and justify it.

CONSULTANT AND CONTRACT SERVICES

Remember: These are services your staff does not have the competence to perform and that it is cheaper to contract for. Be especially careful to detail consultant and contract costs. Funders are likely to be suspicious if the fees you pay are high. Here again, you will have to check on the going rate. Recognizing that some consultants demand much higher fees than others, your agency may have to establish an upper limit beyond which it will not go in paying consultants. The reason consultants are not listed as professional staff under the "salary and wages" category is that they do not receive fringe benefits.

NONPERSONNEL ITEMS

Look over the sample line-item budget. Most items are self-explanatory. Remember that unusual items or costs must be explained in the budget justification. Let me take up a few that might cause you some grief if they are not properly addressed.

Whatever is requested for travel must be reflected in the program narrative. If part of that program includes a transportation service for the elderly or for other clients, in contrast with the travel costs anticipated for staff, you would not include those costs on this line. Develop a separate line item called "transportation service" in the "program expenditure" column. That line might even include several sublines dealing with maintenance and repair, parking and garaging, and so on.

Trainee travel costs and appropriate per diem expenses may be allowed. Check this item and any restrictions. No sense in having a whole project rejected because you were unaware of the funder's limits.

Out-of-town travel for staff is probably one of the most vulnerable sections of the budget. If you have a regional or statewide project, and that project requires that your staff travel to sites throughout the area, that travel will generally be considered local in nature because it deals with your program's locality. "Out-of-town" travel refers only to the trips outside of the locality in which the organization provides its services. The reasons for such travel might include participating in professional conferences, meeting with staff of comparable or sister projects in other parts of the country, attending staff training programs, and so on.

The designation "other costs" can be used as a catchall for a variety of items, such as fire, theft, and liability insurance; dues to professional organizations; and items that do not seem to fit anywhere else. If, however, they are of central importance to the project, they should have their own category. Suppose you intend to design a series of how-to guides (or videotapes) for use in community education. This probably should have its own line, with a number of subitems such as typesetting, printing, binding, addressing, and mailing.

INDIRECT COSTS

Now let's talk a little bit about one of the least understood aspects of the budgeting process: the request for indirect costs. Although the direct costs (those we have been discussing so far), may be easy to identify, they may not be so easy to specify. For example, if the project in question is located in an existing agency, new office space and equipment may not be necessary. Accordingly, there is no need to request line-item funds for space leasing, utilities, maintenance, and the like. These are costs typically incurred for common purposes in the operation of the total organization. The project does, however, use agency office space and equipment and the maintenance that goes with them. Such items can be legitimately charged to the project, but the exact costs involved may be difficult to ascertain. To reflect these real costs, you may be permitted to charge a percentage of all salaries and wages or of the total expenses as indirect costs. In this case you would not also list them elsewhere as line items.

Check with the funder about what is allowable. Do not overlook indirect costs. Without them a project can end up costing the agency a great deal. Note that, in many cases, a funder will not pay indirect costs but will permit the agency to use these as a required match. In this case, they would go in the "donated" column.

COST SHARING

When used this way, indirect costs become part of the applicant organization's *cost-sharing* effort. Many government and foundation awards require some form of cost sharing or *local match*. Any real cost to a project, whether direct or indirect, may be counted in cost sharing. Examples include fees paid by consumers, staff effort devoted to a project at no cost to the sponsor, and services (such as maintenance). In some cases the time contributed to a project by volunteers can be used for cost-sharing purposes. However, this is a bit tricky. You will have to check with your sponsor to find out if this is, in fact, permissible. When volunteer time is used, you will have to spell out the actual dollar value of the time contributed before you can locate it in your "donated" column. There are generally two accepted ways of doing this. The first is to find out what the going rate would be for a comparable service if purchased in the open market. The second is to determine what the volunteer would be earning if employed for money elsewhere.

Other contributions may include consumer fees; third-party payments (for example, insurance company payments); the income from a fund raising campaign or endowment; or funds contributed by another funding source—a local foundation, business corporation, civic association, or the United Way.

It is not enough to claim that costs are shared. Anything in the "donated" column is as subject to audit as are requested funds. You may be asked to document staff and volunteer time actually allocated to the project.

BUDGETS ARE STATEMENTS OF INTENT; INTENTS CHANGE

Budgets are plans written in tabular form. As with other plans, they are subject to review and modification if original projections prove to be infeasible. Most funders will permit you to make minor adaptations in the budget without demanding prior approval. Permission is rarely required to make adaptations of 10 percent, more or less, on any given line item, or any line-item category (such as professional personnel). Thus, if the project director's salary turns out to be lower than you anticipated, but a caseworker's salary turns out to be somewhat higher, and all this does not exceed the 10 percent limit, it will not be necessary for you to ask permission prior to hiring the person in question. A 3 or 4 percent reduction in personnal expenses, if those funds are shifted to consumable supplies, may result in the 25 or 30 percent raise in the amount of money allocated toward supplies. You will need permission from the sponsor before making that change.

GETTING AUDITED

The nice thing about "donated" and "requested" columns is that they show the funder what the money requested is to be spent on. This is what will be examined should your project be audited during or subsequent to its completion. To prepare for an audit, you will have to do an accurate job of accounting. "Accounting" refers to those ongoing activities involved in maintaining an updated and accurate record of the flow of income and expenses related to a project. Accounting is used to ascertain that income and expenses are in line with projections in the budget. The idea behind accounting is to make sure that money is not only spent as prescribed, but also at a rate of expected or available income. Unless the rates of expenditure and income are in balance, or in favor of income rather than expenditure, the program may find itself in considerable trouble.

Audits are periodic examinations of the fiscal records involved to see whether or not income and expenditures go according to plan (the budget). The auditor considers whether or not the amounts expended on specified items were proper, whether the sources from which money was drawn were proper, whether the timing was appropriate, and whether documentation of each of these was correct. Audits may be conducted internally or externally.

Internal audits are generally conducted by an accountant or other staff member within the organization itself. External audits may be conducted by the sponsor or funder or by an outside agent acting on behalf of the sponsor. Audits are sometimes conducted two or three years after a project has concluded its activities. Thus it is important not only to maintain good records, but to keep them for a minimum of three to five years.

WHAT FUNDERS LOOK FOR
IN BUDGET REQUESTS
AND SUBSEQUENT AUDITS

Funders are going to scrutinize your budgets carefully. Exercise 12.1 is followed by a checklist of issues they are likely to concentrate on. Use them to go over your own budget prior to submitting it to agency administration or to a potential funding source.

REVIEW

The budget is a program and fiscal document. It can be used to plan programs and services, anticipate cash income and outflow, and hold the organization accountable for what it sets out to do. It is not an immutable document, however, and should be changed in relation to changed circumstances or modified program objectives.

The most common budget categorizes all of its expenditures into line items. These items are generally divided into two major sections: personnel and nonpersonnel. Personnel items may include salaries and wages for professional and other personnel, the fringe benefits they receive, and fees for service from consultants and outside contractors. Nonpersonnel items include rental, leasing, and related expenses; disposable office supplies; program supplies; and equipment. A number of programs or projects may also include travel and per diem expenses for staff, board members, trainees, and so on.

All line items must be consistent with the program narrative in a project plan or proposal (as when a project application is

EXERCISE 12.1
DESIGNING YOUR OWN BUDGET

Now it is time for you to try your hand at budget design.

(1) Pick a program or project that requires a new or revised budget. It might be the program you began planning as you worked on the exercise in the previous chapter, a current agency program that is expected to expand or to be cut back next year, or a fund raising drive (these also require financial outlays and require their own budgets).

(2) Design a tabular line-item budget. Make certain that all anticipated expenses are included. Decide which are to be requested and which are to be donated. If your organization has a salary scale, travel reimbursement policies, a regular fringe benefit package, and so on, use the figures and percentages recommended by the agency's fiscal manager. If it does not, find out what other organizations in your community do, or what the funder will permit. As your guide, use the outline in Table 12.2, a budget previously submitted by your organization for this or another program, or the budget format suggested by the funder. If you intend to use your budget to submit to a funding agency, be certain that the funder's instructions are followed.

(3) Write up the budget justification of the line-item tabular budget, explaining any items that might be questioned or that may seem out of line, or that are not clear from the program narrative you may have written for the exercise in Chapter 11. Justify your projected expenditues in program and/or performance terms.

(4) Now translate the line-item budget into either a program budget or a performance budget, or, for additional experience, do both. For example, should you be designing a budget for a fund raising campaign, the performance budget might aggregate expenses under the following categories: brochures, letter campaign to general audience, dinners and banquets, solicitor recruitment and training, administrative costs, and so on. The program budget might focus on the achievement of campaign goals, and these might be divided into such categories as pacesetters, medium-sized givers, general public. For each you would have a target goal in terms of funds raised, and a breakdown or expenses needed to raise those funds. How might you break down the Sample Line-Item Budget in Table 12.2 into program and performance terms? Look for clues in Table 12.1.

(5) On completion of your budget table and narrative, review it the way a funder might. Use the Funder's Checklist.

FUNDER'S CHECKLIST

(1) All budget items are justified in the text of the proposal, the narrative, and the budget justification. No important items have been left out of the budget.

(2) Each figure is properly explained unless it is clearly self-explanatory.

(3) The budget designates *requested* and *donated* sums or uses some other designation to convey what is required of the funder and of the recipient.

(4) The budget is broken down into logical segments: personnel, nonpersonnel items, indirect costs, and so forth.

(5) Budget figures are realistic. For example, fringe benefits are not out of line, salaries are compatible with local standards. The costs are reasonable and made in relationship to concerns for efficiency.

(6) Out of the ordinary costs (high telephone or travel costs) are fully explained in the budget justification.

(7) The total size of the budget is appropriate to the project itself.

(8) Line items represent not only reasonable estimates of current cost, but include estimates of future costs, taking into account inflation or changes in salary rates.

(9) The proposal is tailored to the funder, and follows the guidelines or procedures and forms required by the funder.

(10) Figures total properly. The writers know their arithmetic.

---

submitted to an outside funding source). Items may need to be explained further in a "budget justification" section that generally follows the "tabular" budget. This justification is generally couched in program or performance terms. Performance budgets describe the cost of performing certain program activities and generally relate to the functions or work of distinct operational units. They are most useful in describing the work planned or authorized and are useful management devices. Program budgets focus more directly on the purposes of an operation and the goals and objectives to be reached.

The accounting process is aimed at tracking funds into and out of an organization or program, and checking on whether the rate of income is adequate to cover the rate of expenditures. The auditing process is used periodically to determine whether the expenditures are proper and according to plan.

SUGGESTIONS FOR FURTHER READING

Fortunately, there is a growing literature on budget development and design. If there is a budget officer in your organization, it may not be necessary for you to design the budget on your own. In many cases the funding organization will provide you with all the guidelines you need in order to design the budget according to acceptable standards. If you wish to read further, however, the following two items should prove most helpful:

Vinter, Robert, & Kish, Rea (1984) *Budgeting for not-for-profit organizations.* New York: Free Press.
   A thorough account of the budgeting process; no better document is available to nonprofit organizations.
Lohman, Roger (1980). *Breaking even: Financial management in human service organizations.* Philadelphia: Temple University Press.
   Goes beyond budgeting to examine ways of accounting for and pricing services to reduce the likelihood of deficits.

In addition, the national association with which your organization may be directly or indirectly affiliated should also have materials available for you. The following are excellent examples:

Family Service Association of America (1969). *Budget presentation: Some guides for family service agencies.* New York: Author.
United Way of America (1975). *Budgeting: A guide for United Ways and not-for-profit human service organizations.* Rosslyn, VA: Author.

Other useful documents include the following:

Carter, Reginald (1984). *The accountable agency: Everybody cares but nobody knows.* Beverly Hills, CA: Sage.
Gross, Melvin J., & Warshauer, W., Jr. (1974). *Financial and accounting guide for non-profit organizations.* New York: Ronald.
Hall, Mary (1981). *Developing skills in proposal writing.* Portland, OR: Continuing Education Publications.
Jones, Reginald, & Trentin, George (1971). *Budgeting: Key to planning and control.* Washington, DC: American Management Association.
Lauffer, Armand (1984). *Strategic marketing.* New York: Free Press.
National Health Council (1975). *Standards of accounting and financial reporting for voluntary health and welfare organizations.* New York: Author.
Public Management Institute (n.d.). *Budgeting for nonprofits.* San Francisco: Author.

CHAPTER 13

What to Do If You Don't Get Funded:

And What to Do If You Do or While You're Waiting to Find Out

VIGNETTE 13:
TWO VIEWS OF REVIEWS

WHAT TO LOOK OUT FOR
(View 1)

Things went according to clockwork. The NIMH panel did a preliminary review of our proposal. We passed the first hurdle. Dr. Milton, one of the project officers, called and arranged to make a site visit with one of the members of the external review panel. A visit was scheduled for mid-April. I had five weeks to arrange our end.

I called representatives of the other agencies with whom we would have to collaborate if we got funded, sent them copies of the proposal, and invited them to one of the sessions during the site visit. One of NIMH's evaluative criteria was the extent to which there was involvement and commitment by other service providers.

The site visit went beautifully (although one of the secretaries was a little nervous and went overboard in preparing coffee and cake);

beautiful until we got to the afternoon meeting with the other agency people.

One of them was very supportive, although she had obviously not thought through all of the ramifications for her agency. Sondra Kravel of the Child Guidance Clinic sat through the first half of the session reading the proposal; then she started asking questions, even suggesting changes in the proposal. Well, that opened things up. Dr. Sussman tried to cue her in. These were not issues to discuss before the site visitors. But the cat was out of the bag, and some of the other agency representatives joined in, each trying to improve the proposal.

You guessed it. We did not get funded. The reasons: Agency collaborators had not adequately been involved in project design and improvements were still possible. We could, if we wished, resubmit during the next funding cycle. Problem was, we would have to wait six months, and the staff we wanted to assign to the new project would not be able to wait that long to find out if they had jobs or not. What a bummer!

WHAT TO LOOK FOR
(View 2)

Given a choice, I would award a grant to the person whose proposal is loosely written, but who I know from experience will do a thorough and honest job. I would be less likely to award a grant to a person whose proposal is beautifully and concretely written, but whose reputation for producing leaves something to be desired. Still, there are other considerations. It's not easy to be a reviewer.

Sometimes even the best-written proposal from the most reputable source gets turned down. I've sometimes recommended funding for projects coming from what I consider to be lousy agencies. The reason is simple. They're in a neighborhood that needs service, and they won't be able to offer the service without the project and the funds it will bring. If it means pouring good money into a second-rate agency that's going to provide at least some useful services to a minority community, that gets almost nothing from anybody, I'll vote to put the money over there. I see it as being part of my responsibility as a public official to contribute to the redistribution and relocation of resources where they are needed the most.

Now that's my bias, and I'm honest about it. But I'm professional enough to know that I can't act on that bias alone. Making effective decisions on proposals requires being clear about the overall priorities of your own agency. Even though we've got a set of regulations that spells out many of these priorities, each proposal forces us to reexamine our values.

Our regulations, for example, include clear statements about the "right to service" and the "universality" of those services. The "regs" make it clear that social services should be available to all people as a matter of right, and that eligibility for a service is to be based on need relative to the purpose and function of that service, without regard to a person's ability to pay. The plan also makes it clear that services should be accessible to everybody at whatever point they may choose to enter.

But we've got another statement in our "regs" that says that the resources should be allocated where they're needed most. It specifically identifies low-income neighborhoods and ethnic minorities that do not currently have easy access or entry into the service system. When a proposal comes in that talks about establishing a multipurpose center for Cuban refugees, we've got a hard decision to make. The proposal clearly meets the criterion for putting resources where the need is greatest, but are we negating our principle of universal right to service? No people other than Cuban refugees would be using the center.

We have a couple of other policy statements, too. One is that social services should permit consumer choice and should allow for the protection of individuality and consumer participation in policymaking. Now those are nice principles, but they're not always operable. If a good proposal comes in that doesn't include consumer participation in policymaking, but does protect the consumers by providing them with a variety of grievance mechanisms, we're likely to fund it. Another project might come in that doesn't allow for grievance machinery and in fact threatens the principle of confidentiality simply because clients are involved in policymaking. How do we choose?

Reviewers do not always find it easy to make the right choice. If the criteria for the review process create dilemmas for panelists, how can the proposal writer be sure that the right issues have been stressed and the right form used? There are no hard-and-fast rules. But there are some things you can do to increase the likelihood of success.

In this chapter we will begin by examining how proposals are reviewed and by whom. Careful attention to a number of critical issues will increase your organization's likelihood of getting funded. But the processes involved in grantsmanship are not completed when you have satisfied yourself that the proposal is the best you are capable of. There are things to do even after the proposal has been posted in the mail. We will therefore also consider what you should do while you are waiting to get the results of the grant or contract review process, what to do if you do not get funded, and what to do if you do. Then we will discuss what you can do if your grantseeking efforts yield results beyond your expectations. We will also examine what happens if other fund raising efforts are successful, and what happens if they are unsuccessful. But first, we will examine the criteria by which proposals are reviewed, and what happens to the proposal after you send it off.

GETTING REVIEWED

All grantseekers should know something about how proposals are reviewed and by whom. If the information is not available in the proposal kit or other information you receive from the funder, you may have to do some investigating. The best way to find out is by asking the funding source itself.

Federal agencies generally use external panelists to review research, training, or service-oriented proposals. Panelists who are considered to be expert in their fields are often brought to Washington for one day to a week to review proposals that have first been screened by staffers for appropriateness (Was it submitted to the right agency?) or for correctness of form. Be aware that if the proposal arrives after the deadline for submission, is prepared in the wrong form, or is incomplete, it will not generally pass the initial screening. Panelists will be given a *proposal rating sheet* for the proposals that pass. Typically, the sheet will instruct reviewers to score each proposal on a five-point scale on the basis of the following criteria:

- *Significance:* importance of objectives, generalizability of impact
- *Procedures or program description:* completeness, precision and detail, compatibility with stated objectives, knowledge of related work, overall design or organization, realistic timetable, and so on
- *Personnel and facilities:* qualifications, organizational structure, availability of nonfiscal resources
- *Economic efficiency:* how expected results relate to relative costs
- *Feasibility:* whether or not the work can be done as described

Proposals that score the highest are put in one pile, those that are clear rejects go into another, and those in between go into a central pile.

If all panelists agree that a proposal should be funded, there is a strong likelihood (assuming funding levels are adequate), that it will be approved. If everyone agrees that other proposals should not be funded, they will not be. The panelists may be convened as a group to examine the middle pile, or to discuss their reasons for differences of opinion on the others. For example, if five panelists feel a proposal should be funded but two are not sure and one feels that it should not, a resolution will be arrived at through discussion intended to yield consensus.

Recent efforts to cut the cost of government spending have led federal agencies to eliminate Washington-based reviews. Panelists may be asked to rate proposals at home. Discrepancies in judgment may also be resolved through correspondence or through telephone conference calls. The site visit, described in the vignette with which I opened this chapter, may become a thing of the past except in the more costly or high-priority federal programs. In some cases, particularly when sole-source contracts are at issue, or when funds to be allocated are discretionary, the review may be made by a single federal official or by a panel of officials.

State-level funding decisions are much more variable. The procedures may change from year to year or from agency to agency. Some use external panels but most rely on staff decisions within the agency making the grants or contract awards. Often state and federal departmental decisions are subject to review by the office of the budget or the governor's budget priorities committee, which may determine that an expenditure being projected is incompatible with overall government spending priorities. The budget office can hold up, and sometimes reject, a proposal that has otherwise overcome all other hurdles.

Local government grants rarely go through an external review panel. Line staff in appropriate departments (e.g., recreation, housing) may be entrusted to issue contracts or grants. On some programs—for example, community development block grants—a citizen's review board or council may be established by the mayor or the city council to review and approve all grants and contracts. The staff may be asked to recommend action, but the discussion belongs to the board or council. This process sometimes gets extremely political.

Foundations generally rely on staff to make decisions. On small grants such decisions may be made by individual foundation staffers or department heads. Larger grants may be reviewed by the foundation's board of trustees, or by a special review panel that deals with a particular sector of the foundation's work. But the board or panel members involved will rely to a large extent on staff recommendations. This, of course, refers to the larger foundations. When it comes to the smaller family foundations, decisions may be made by the person who gave it its initial endowment, by a member of the family, or by a trustee entrusted with such responsibility. The trustee, perhaps an attorney or a banker, may know little of the subject matter or of your agency, and so may rely on someone else in the community for advice.

Corporation grants are generally made by executive officers. If the corporaton is not accustomed to making grants and has not established a procedure for making them, the review may be made by the executive officers or a community relations officer entrusted with the responsibility. Since the process of involving the private sector in human service issues is still highly idiosyncratic to the organizations and communities involved, it is too early to be able to describe prototypic patterns. You may have to help design those patterns in the community where you work.

In contrast, the United Way and other well-established fund-raising and allocating bodies in the voluntary sector tend to have highly formalized review processes. These were described in Chapter 8. Staff members work closely with applicant organizations, and guide lay committees organized into sector review panels in the decision-making process. Most of these decisions are focused on whether to increase or decrease allocations based on the previous year's experience. New applicants may be put through a particularly rough review process that examines not only the application itself but also the problem or population to which it is addressed, and the capacity of the organization making the application to do the job specified.

For civic associations the populations to be served may be the most important concern. Association members may not feel they have the capacities to make judgments about the applicant organization or how it has chosen to serve those in need. The decision may be made by an executive committee or a community services task group, but will generally have to be ratified by the board or the entire membership at an open meeting.

Understanding these differences may suggest alternative actions on your part both before and after the proposal has been submitted. These will be discussed shortly. First, I want to share with you some insights on why proposals are sometimes rejected. We will focus primarily on the federal government, because it continues to be the major source of funding for the human services and because its procedures are the most standardized and well understood.

WHY PROPOSALS ARE REJECTED

Several years ago, in a review of some 605 disapproved research grant applications, the Public Health Service determined that rejections were made on the basis of the following short-comings: the problem (58 percent), the approach (73 percent), the investigator (55 percent), and other reasons (16 percent). Note that these are not necessarily real weaknesses, only a reflection of a poorly expressed or sketchy proposal. Let us dig a bit further.

Of those proposals rejected because of the problem being investigated, more than half were determined to be of insufficient importance or unlikely to produce any useful information. Of those rejected because of the approach used, half were determined to include scientific procedures that were unsuited to the stated objective, more than a third described the approach to be used in so nebulous a manner as to preclude serious examination, and about one out of six was judged to have a poorly thought-through study design.

Investigators (project directors) were rated low especially when they appeared to have inadequate experience or training to conduct the particular research in question, because the investigator appeared to be unfamiliar with recent pertinent literature and methods, or because his or her published work in the field did not inspire confidence. Other issues related to unrealistic requests for equipment or personnel, unfavorable institutional settings, and the assumption that the project director would devote insufficient time to the project.

These reasons for rejecting research proposals are not that dissimilar from reasons given for turning down training- and service-related grant applications.

Have you heard of other reasons for rejection? Make a checklist of possible issues to look out for according to your own experiences or to the types of proposal your organization is preparing, perhaps to the funding source it will be submitting those proposals. Use the checklist for evaluating proposals being developed by colleagues and acquaintances. You may learn as much from evaluating others' efforts as you did in writing your own proposal. You may learn even more from getting others' feedback and incorporating it in a redesign effort.

Before we move on, I want to focus on two issues touched on by the persons quoted at the start of the chapter. As the applicant to NIMH learned, it is sometimes not enough to say all the right things in the proposal itself. It may be as important, or more, to get other people to corroborate your claims. A well-designed proposal was rejected because the other key players did not understand the rules of the game; they fought over the ball when they should have been passing it to each other.

The funder quoted in the second vignette spoke of the importance of fitting a proposal to the purpose of the missions of the funding agency. This is a point I have been making throughout this book. I want to reiterate it. No one is going to fund your organization because it thinks it is doing the Lord's work. Your support will come from others who are convinced that you are doing *their* work, and in the best manner possible.

WHAT TO DO WHILE YOU'RE WAITING

What should you do while you are waiting to find out if your application has been approved? Keep busy! There may be lots more work to be done.

(1) Update the proposal if necessary.
(2) Promote the proposal or the ideas behind it among relevant publics.
(3) Design a fall-back plan in case you do not get funded.
(4) Gear up for operations in case you should get funded.

We will take these one at a time.

It is not unusual, under the press of deadlines, for proposal writers to submit a less-than-perfect document. There are also times when circumstances change, and a modification in the narrative or the budget may be necessary. Funders often permit modest changes on receipt of an explanatory letter with supportive documents. This is almost always true if your materials get there before the review process takes place. For example, the results of a United Way survey may come in two weeks after you have submitted your proposal to a federal agency. If those data support your argument, summarize them and send them in with a note asking that the summary be added to the appendix. If financial support is to be forthcoming from a source mentioned as a possibility in the proposal (e.g., a gift from a foundation or from a wealthy philanthropist), inform the potential grantor to whom the application was made, and modify your budget request accordingly. If new letters of endorsement or support arrive after you have mailed the proposal, send them in and ask that they be added to your file.

Promotional activities during the period of review or just before can pay significant dividends. Not long ago, I submitted a grant application to a federal agency. The Michigan Department of Social Services was anxious that the University of Michigan get the grant. State officials informally, through telephone calls and on visits to Washington, made it clear that the project was in the state's interest. Members of the congressional staff of one of the Michigan representatives, who was himself on some pretty powerful committees, also let the word out that Michigan was interested in the project. A word of caution here: Informal influence, especially when well orchestrated, can be very effective; but it can also backfire when it is perceived as pressure or as an organized campaign.

This may be less true at the local level, particularly when citizen support is active and vocal, and when a case is made in noncontroversial terms. Local officials and citizens' task groups are going to listen to organized voters who know what they want and are willing to articulate their demands in ways that are not going to be insulting or that will not cause opposition or backlash from other quarters. When a proposal is submitted that deals with an issue that is poorly understood, press coverage of the issue (not necessarily about the proposed intervention program) is likely to help educate and sensitize decision makers in a way that even the best-phrased program design cannot.

A proposal submitted to the United Way or to a local corporation is likely to be received positively if officials in the corporation or lay leaders in the United Way are knowledgeable about your agency and the issues it intends to tackle. Their opinions may carry more weight than those of others. It may not be appropriate for you to approach them directly. It may be much more helpful if a board member from your agency or another friendly advocate does the communicating with the decision makers in question.

WHAT TO DO
IF YOU DON'T GET FUNDED

What should you do if you do not get funded? The answer will be clear if you are prepared with a fallback position. The nature of that position should depend on the centrality of the proposal to your organization's operations. If it is very central, if the organization cannot do without the grant, your fallback position should include alternative sources of funding. There is rarely any rule against support from more than a single source. Funders may ask you whether a similar proposal for support has been submitted elsewhere. You will need to so inform them. And if you do get support from several sources, you will not be able to pocket the difference or to use it for something you have not been funded for. You may have to inform the funder that you are willing to accept a smaller grant because you have gotten partial support elsewhere, or request a modification of the proposal that may expand the program or modify it to include the additional resources.

If the project is rejected, are there some ways in which you can hang on by reducing services, by using volunteers, by delaying start-up? Always find out why the proposal was rejected. If the funder does not deal with the kinds of issues you proposed, find out if there is a more appropriate source of supply. If the proposal itself is wanting, find out how it might be improved, whether you can submit again, and when.

WHAT TO DO IF YOU DO GET FUNDED

What should you do if you do get funded? You will know if you spent the time between submission and approval in gearing up. More than once I have heard from a funder, as late as August or September, that a program was approved that is to start up on October 1. Once, the word came down in mid-October (after the projected starting date), for a project that had to be completed by the end of the fiscal year—the following September 30. To avoid wasting start-up time, start seeking staff and getting needed facilities or equipment before you get final word. You may not be able to hire staff before you have the grant award, but you can start the interviewing process early; and you can negotiate with appropriate persons in your organization for the reallocation of staff from other responsibilities. You will need to make an informed judgment about the likelihood of getting funded. No sense in investing too much effort in a long shot. However, there is not much sense in being caught high and dry because of lack of preparation.

What if you get funding for an amount smaller than you requested? Your fallback plan should take this possibility into account as well. The allocation may be too small to conduct even a modified program. Other sources of funds may not be available. In this case, you may have to reject the grant. Alternatively, it may be possible to delay start-up time or to modify the objectives and the activities and yet achieve some of the goals you set forth. It may also be possible to reallocate funds from some other agency operations.

Sometimes it pays to do less than we might wish, for no reason other than to establish a relationship with a funder. This is a professional decision and it may not be an easy one to make. Remember that "a difference that makes no difference is no difference." It may not be worth the effort for the agency, the staff involved, or those the original project design was intended to help. There may already be too much going on in your organization that is of little or no benefit to anyone. Why compound the difficulties by taking on something that no one really needs?

Let us assume you do get the award, you have started the program or project, and things are looking well. Great. But it is still not time to rest or sit on your laurels. In fact, there may never be a time to sit back. Just as programs need constant attention, so do funding sources. Many funders want a careful accounting of what you are accomplishing and how close you are to your original design and to your timetable. They will want to know how the funds are being spent. Quarterly, semi-annual, and final reports may be necessary. Put as much time and effort into these as you did for your original proposal. You may know that you are doing well, but the funder will need to know this too.

Get the reports into those places where they will do most good. The local press is one place. Papers delivered at professional conferences or published in journals are other places. Send the funders copies of those articles and reports as they appear. Include testimonials from those who have been effectively served or who can honestly report on the significance of the project. Make certain that these are phrased so as to articulate with the funder's concerns and priorities.

WHAT HAPPENS IF YOUR OTHER FUND RAISING ACTIVITIES ARE SUCCESSFUL, AND IF THEY'RE NOT

How about other fund raising activities? Do we have the same obligations to donors as to funders? Yes, but they are not always worked out in the same way. Donors, because they are individuals rather than organizations, are not likely to come up with a collective set of requirements, guidelines, or performance criteria by which to monitor the use of their gifts. Nevertheless, "we can't just take the money and run," as a colleague put it to me. "We have the same kinds of obligations to our individual donors as to the larger institutional funders with which we deal. When people contribute something to this agency, they are investing in a program, an idea, a service. We have an obligation to manage that investment honestly and competently. We don't believe in defaulting on our clients. And we don't default on our investors either."

Well put—a sentiment shared by many professional fund raisers and human service agency personnel. Just as a default in business is likely to reduce confidence in a firm, a default with a provider public is likely to reduce confidence with other publics as well. But honest and competent investment of donated funds is more than a short-term tactical concern. It is also an expression of the professional values of the practitioners in the human services and of those who manage those services. The colleague quoted above explained how he fulfills what he considers his professional obligations to the public as follows.

KEEPING THE FAITH

First of all, we never just ask for money when we fund raise. We raise money for specific purposes: sending kids to camp; buying books and games for our volunteer tutors to bring to families in deprived neighborhoods; increasing the hours we can maintain a hot line. People know what they're giving for. Our door-to-door canvassers and other solicitors give prospective donors pledge cards on which they cannot only indicate how much they wish to give, but how they want their gift allocated. We make it plain on the card that 20 percent of all donations goes to general agency programs and services. That generally gives us enough flexibility to do some reallocation if all the gifts bunch up in one or another program category.

Second, we send every donor a thank you with a summary report on the campaign. A copy of his pledge card with the bill makes it possible for the donor to compare his gift with the collective gifts of others.

If we go over our target in some area, say, sending kids to camp, or if we set up a program but don't get enough takers for it, we may find money raised for a particular purpose has to be reallocated to some other program. Well, we inform the public in several ways. Donors who give over $50 or who have contributed small sums for several years get a summary quarterly report, so they know what's happening. It may sound like a lot of paperwork, but you would be surprised. Without any solicitation, we find that about 1 out of every 40 newsletters yields another contribution—enough to cover the cost of putting out the report plus some.

*We also encourage site visits—open house days—and invite donors
to special meetings with the staff or board members. This not only is
our way of saying thanks, but it nets us a big bonus in terms of
volunteers. We often recruit future solicitors, committee members,
and ultimately even board members from some of these contacts.
When people make a contribution through us, they are making a
contribution to kids and to their community, not just our agency.
What they are saying is that they have faith in our stewardship of
those funds. And we do the best we can to keep the faith.*

Successful fund raising efforts generally lead to other successes. But those successes do not always follow directly. "We
had a great bikeathon last fall," another colleague confided.
"So we decided to do a walkathon in the spring. It just didn't
go over. Our volunteers were still tired out from the effort of
the fall project. I suspect we might have had less burnout had
we tried a different fund raising approach, but long-distance
walking is just too similar to long-distance bike riding." She
was right on both counts: The events were too close to each
other and too similar. There is always a temptation to repeat
a success and that temptation need not be resisted—it just
shouldn't be succumbed to too frequently.

Sometimes fund raising efforts do not succeed. That too
might be communicated to the public. "One year we fell terribly
short of our goal for tutorial materials," the same colleague
who spoke to me about "keeping the faith" confided. "That's
not something to cover up or to blame the public about. The
fault is not theirs. We're the ones who didn't get the message
across; so we try to do it after the campaign. I was very honest
in a press release and indicated that 'despite an inadequate
information program, the public had responded generously.
Unfortunately, the sums raised would leave 80 families unserved.' That generated a few belated gifts. More important,
I used our lack of success in the following year's campaign.
'Let's not leave 80 families and 234 kids without the books they
need to succeed' is the way our campaign letter opened."

The consequences of not meeting one's fund raising goal can
be serious for the agency itself, in addition to those consumers

who may be unserved or underserved. "We couldn't come up with the dollars we needed, so had to give up our option on the property we had worked five years to locate. Now I don't know when we'll be able to open up a new center," a trainee admitted in a workshop I conducted. On examination of her fund raising efforts by others in the workshop, it became clear that she and her campaign team had relied too heavily on a single solicitation strategy and had approached only a narrow segment of the public. A wider range of approaches might have been more effective. Moreover, as one participant remarked, "It sometimes helps to test out several different approaches to see which ones work, and then to discard those that don't. You never did a test run, and you put all your eggs into a single basket."

Even the most successful fund raising effort is no guarantee of continued support. Remember that a single gift, like a grant, is rarely a lifetime commitment. What happens when the gift is expended, when the grant period is over? What could happen if a three-year grant is not funded after the second year because of a government cutback or a change in funding priorities? You will need a contingency plan that guarantees continuation. Who should be involved in the design of that plan? Who else cares?

Perhaps it is appropriate that I end this book with a question. That, after all, is the way we started. I will resist the temptation, however. Instead, I will leave you with a thought. Successful agencies generally do pretty well at raising funds and getting grants. Organizations that have been successful in raising funds and getting grants are considered to do pretty well at other things. That may seem redundant. It is not. Samuel Butler phrased it in a more ingenious way: "A hen," he said, "is an egg's way of making another egg."

COMMON AND TECHNICAL TERMS
ASSOCIATED WITH GRANTSMANSHIP AND
FUND RAISING

Accounting: the classifying, summarizing, and recording of financial and related transactions.

Agreements: exchanges between two or more groups or organizations for a variety of commodities and actions. Purchase of Service agreements are essentially contracts for specific services that the contracting agency is mandated to perform but which it finds more effective or efficient to contract out.

Allocation: act of assigning resources to an organization or subunit.

Annual Appropriation: regular allocation of funds for ongoing budget or program, generally from the same source to the same recipient; sometimes modified to reflect inflation, program growth, or program cutback.

Application Kit: information provided by the potential funder about what is desired, the procedures that must be followed, and often including abstracts or summaries of grants given out in previous years.

Appropriation: budget making by a legislature or other public body.

Audit: periodic investigation of financial statements and their relationships to planned or permitted expenditures.

Award: the sum of money given by a contracting or granting agency to cover all or part of the sponsored project's costs.

Budget: a plan for anticipated expenditures, activities, and accomplishments stated primarily in fiscal terms.

Types of budgets:

(1) *Line-item* — budget format organized in tabular and narrative form, in which expenditures are listed as items, each on their own lines, that describe expenditures.

(2) *Performance* — budget format in which costs of performing sets of interrelated activities are aggregated.

(3) *Program* — budget format in which costs are related to outcomes and expectations.

Campaign: organized activity aimed at inducing others to behave in specifically determined manner; as in fund-raising campaign.

Cash Flow: actual movement of money in and out of an organization or subunit; negative cash flow signifies that outflow is greater than income; whereas positive cash flow signifies that income exceeds expenditures.

Constituency: aggregate of individuals and/or organizations that support or can be mobilized for support of an individual or organization, and to which he or she/it/they are in turn responsible.

Contract: an award given for a specific activity in which the funder has specified all the terms (e.g., who can apply, exactly what is to be done, and how, at what cost, and by whom).

Types of Contracts:

(1) *Sole-Source* — where only one party is asked to apply because of the source's specific and unique qualification.

(2) *Open-Bid*: competitive situation where anyone meeting the general qualifications for a particular type of contract can bid for it; RFPs are generally posted and information on them distributed broadly.

(3) *Fixed Price*: contract in which the size of the award is fixed at start. No cost overruns may be allowed.

(4) *Cost Reimbursement*: contract in which the grantee's costs are fully reimbursed; a maximal limit may be set, but this is subject to review in relation to changes in prices, problems in technology, and so on.

(5) *Cost-Sharing*: agreement in which two or more organizations (one of which may be the recipient) share in the cost of the project.

Donors: persons who make cash or material contributions to the organization and its programs.

Fees: money payments made for a service by consumers or a third-party payer such as an insurance company.

Funders: organizations that give grants and award contracts.

Fund Raising: a process of identifying and soliciting potential donors and grantors, and of obtaining money through campaigns, sales, or grantseeking.

Grant: a type of award that is supportive in character, given for a specific purpose, yet permitting the recipient considerable latitude in determining what is to be done, for whom, when, how much, and within limits, at what cost.

Types of Grants:

(1) *Block Grants* — the mechanism by which grants are made to a unit of government (state, regional, or local) for such broad purposes as housing or employment, as authorized by legislation or administrative policy. Recipients have great flexibility in distribution of those funds and may

themselves become grantors or funders within the broad purposes of the grant according to the criteria established by the original grantor.

(2) *Categorical Grants* — funds that are expended for specific purposes, generally by the recipient unless used by the recipient for the purchase of a service that can be provided better or cheaper by a third party.

(3) *Formula Grants* — determination of size of awards to be provided to specified grantees on the basis of a specific formula prescribed in legislation or regulation rather than on the basis of individual project review. Formulas may be set on basis of such factors as population, per capita income, age, and so on. For example, the Administration on Aging may use a formula that includes the proportion of the elderly in the population, the number of those people who fall below the poverty line, the square mileage of the area, and the extent to which it is urban or rural in determining how much money is available to each state, or to subregions within states.

(4) *Discretionary Funds* — awards in which the funding agency or its chief officer has considerable latitude in deciding who can receive funds and for what amount, so long as it falls within the general policies or guidelines governing the funding source.

Grantee: the individual, group, or organization that is the recipient of a contract or grant award.

Grantor or Contractor: the individual or organization making a specific award.

Grantseeking: a process of identifying, soliciting, and proposing activities aimed at getting grant or contract awards.

Guidelines: general information on how to complete a proposal and specification of the issues that must be addressed in a grant application (proposal). Frequently these are found in the application kit. Guidelines must be meticulously followed; improperly submitted or written proposals, especially those that go to government and foundation sources, are likely to be disregarded.

Income: flow of money and in-kind resources to an organization or subunit.

Indirect Costs: a budget item that refers to the costs incurred by the grantee that are difficult or impractical to itemize but that can legitimately be charged to the program.

Marketing: aggregate of activities aimed at the exchange of commodities and services between suppliers, producers and consumers. The marketing of social services includes reaching out to and involving many publics in the exchange of resources and services.

Opportunity Costs: values forfeited by investing time and other resources in certain activities, precluding the possibility of making like investment in other activities.

Price: the cost attached to a service or activity, usually in financial terms, but also in psychological and social terms.

Private Foundations: organizations that have charitable, religious, educational, scientific, or cultural purposes. When identified as philanthropic foundations, they are primarily in the business of funding causes, programs, organizations, and individuals they consider worthwhile.

Types of Foundations:

(1) *Independent* — foundations have their own board of directors and are not affiliated with any other government or private sector organization, or responsible for doing any organization's business other than their own.

(2) *Community Foundations* — often receive some operating funds from local government, and are concerned primarily with local cultural, human service, and economic development needs.

(3) *Family Foundations* — are generally established for charitable or religious purposes and managed by members of the family that endowed the foundation, or their trustees.

(4) *Company Foundations* — are the creatures of business enterprises and are often established to funnel the company's charitable contributions into area that benefit the company, its employees, or the communities in which the company is located.

(5) *Operating Foundations* — solicit funds for their own purposes, allocate them to their own activities, and do not generally fund outside organizations or groups.

Program: a set of interrelated activities aimed at the production of a service or some other outcome.

Project: a program which is time bound and has a relatively clear set of objectives.

Project Officer: official in government or foundation responsible for a particular grant or contract program.

Promotion: activities aimed at advancing an idea, a cause, a program, or an organization; increasing consumer or public receptivity to a product or service; consciousness raising.

Proposal: a plan of action (always in writing when applying for a grant or contract) describing what is to be done, for what purpose, how, by whom, when, and at what cost.

Types of Proposals:

(1) *Solicited Proposal* — one that is requested by a potential funding source (grantor or contractor) that has originated the ideas for the program or project, often through an RFP.

(2) *Unsolicited Proposal* — one in which the idea for the project clearly originated with the proposal writer or submitting agency (potential recipient).

Public: aggregate of persons or organizations that have characteristics in common, or that are perceived by an organization as having a specific and functional relationship to it.

Types of Publics:

(1) *In-put Publics* — provide the organization with the legitimacy of the resources it needs in order to conduct its business.

(2) *Throughput Publics* — turn resources into programs and outputs.

(3) *Output Publics* — are the consumers or recipients of products and services.

Resources: all the means and commodities needed to produce and distribute a product, or achieve an objective.

Revenue: cash income.

RFP: Request For Proposals, generally communicated in writing and sometimes posted in public documents such as the *Commerce Business Daily* or the local press. The term "RFP" was once used exclusively to refer to requests for contract proposals, but it is now increasingly used to refer to grants as well.

Site Visit: visit made by one or more representatives of the grantor to the grantseeking organization in order to get details on applicant's capacity to do work proposed.

Sponsored Project: a specific complex of activities or program financed by funds other than those of the regular budget of the group or organization (sometimes the individual) administering the project. For example, if your agency regularly provides services to the disabled through allocations from the United Fund, but receives a special additional subvention from the United Fund to establish a home-based program, or receives a grant from a government agency to do so, this is considered to be a "sponsored project" because funds outside of the normal allocations of the organization are used for the project and the sponsor (funder) can be readily identified.

Appendix B:
Grantsmanship Information Resources

Look over the suggested information resources in this Appendix, but do not be limited by it. You will find a much wider array of suggestions in the narratives and suggested readings for Chapters 2 through 12. What follows are a number of additional resources that I thought you might find useful. They are divided into four sections: (1) magazines and periodicals, (2) training organizations, (3) search services, and (4) multipurpose fund-raising books and guides.

MAGAZINES AND PERIODICALS

Federal Grants and Contracts Weekly

You already know about the *Commerce Business Daily* and the *Federal Register* (see Chapter 3). The *Weekly* uses those sources to select information nonprofit organizations find useful. It contains information on the latest RFPs (requests for proposals), grants, and contracting opportunities, newly issued federal regulations, and closing dates for grant programs.

It can be ordered from Capitol Publications, 1300 North 17th Street, Arlington, Virginia 22209.

Funding Review

A quarterly review of government, private sector, and foundation funding sources, it features articles on management, book reviews, and selected grant deadlines. Order it from the National Grant Development Institute, 1135 North Garfield, Pocatello, Idaho 83204.

Grants Magazine

Many of its articles focus on the technical aspects of researching government, voluntary, and private sector sources. The magazine, which tends to be of equal interest to funders and grantseekers alike, can be ordered from Plenum Press, 233 Spring Street, New York, New York 10013. It is a quarterly.

Independent Sector

Articles, resource opportunities for both health and welfare are included. A new publication, it focuses on needs of the voluntary and private sectors, but includes descriptions and critiques of government programs. It is available from the Independent Sector, 1828 L Street, NW, Washington, D.C. 20036.

LRC Newsbriefs

Resource materials on program development and government grant programs are made available on a monthly basis from the Lutheran Resources Commission, 1346 Connecticut Avenue, N.W., Washington, D.C. 20036.

The Grantsmanship Center News

A bimonthly publication written in everyday and down-to-earth language, the News is printed in an attractive, easily accessible format. It contains articles on planning and program design, grantseeking and proposal writing, budgeting and fiscal management, fund raising and resource development. It also publishes information on categorical grant programs and deadlines, new directions in foundation grantmaking and other materials of interest.

Currently, between fifty and sixty reprints are available with such titles as:

Anatomy of a Grants Process — Federal Funding for Health
Basic Guide to Salary Management
Contractsmanship
Cost Accounting for Non-Accountants
Exploring Corporate Giving
Funding for Women's Programs
Grantsmanship Resources for Rehabilitation Programs
Guide to Public Relations for Nonprofits
How to Develop a Fund Raising Strategy
How to Use the Catalogue of Federal Domestic Assistance
IRS and Charities
Marketing Nonprofits
Obtaining Funding from Local Government
Researching Foundations
Special Events Fund Raising
The Oil Companies as a Funding Source

For information on subscriptions and a full list of reprints, write to the Grantsmanship Center, 1031 South Grand Avenue, Los Angeles, California 90015.

TRAINING AND TECHNICAL ASSISTANCE ORGANIZATIONS

The Grantsmanship Center (see information on *Grantsmanship Center News*) is a nonprofit organization that conducts five-day workshops in locations throughout the country. At present, three types of workshops are sponsored: Proposal Writing and Program Planning, Fund-Raising Training, and Program Management. Workshop sessions are designed to include mini-lectures, well-designed resource kits, and ample opportunity to engage in a design process with consultation from trainers.

Subscribers to the journals described above, or to search services listed below will receive periodic information on other training opportunities offered under university, foundation, or publisher's auspices. Check also the conferences and continuing education programs of the professional associations to which you belong.

The following organizations also provide some technical asstance and occasional training workshops. Write to those that interest you and find out what services they provide.

Alcoholics Anonymous
P.O. Box 459
Grand Central Station
New York, NY 10017

Alternative Medical Association
7915 S.E. Stark Street
Portland, OR 97215

American Association of Fund-Raising Councils
500 Fifth Ave.
New York, NY 10036

American Council
for the Arts
570 7th Ave.
New York, NY 10018

American Hospital Association
800 North Lake Shore Drive
Chicago, IL 60611

American Nurses Association, Inc.
2420 Pershing Rd.
Kansas City, MO 64108

Association of Volunteer Bureaus
P.O. Box 125
801 North Fairfax Street
Alexandria, VA 22314

Center for Community Economic Development
1320 19th Street, NW
Washington, DC 20036

Child Study Association of America
67 Irving Place
New York, NY 10003

Community Education Skills
Exchange Network (CESEN)
c/o Program for Community
Education Development,
AOB IV
University of California
Davis, CA 95616

Council for Financial Aid to
Education
680 Fifth Ave.
New York, NY 10022

Council of Jewish Federations
575 Lexington Ave.
New York, NY 10022

Family Service Association of
America
44 East 23rd Street
New York, NY 10010

Federation of Protestant
Welfare Agencies
281 Park Ave. South
New York, NY 10010

Gray Panthers
3635 Chestnut Street
Philadelphia, PA 19104

Institute for Responsive
Education
704 Commonwealth Ave.
Boston, MA 02215

Institute for Voluntary
Organizations
175 Jackson Blvd.
Chicago, IL 60604

International City Managers
Association
11200 G Street, NW
Washington, DC 20005

Mental Health Association
1800 N. Kent Street
Rosslyn, VA 22209

National Association of
Accountants for the Public
Interest
45 John Street
New York, NY 10038

National Association of
Community Health Centers,
Inc. (NACHC)
1625 I Street, NW, Suite 420
Washington, DC 20006

National Association for
Retarded Citizens, Inc.
2709 Avenue East
Arlington, TX 76011

National Association of Retired
Persons
1909 K Street, NW
Washington, DC 20049

National Catholic Development
Conference
119 North Park Ave.
Rockville Center, NY 11570

National Center for
Community Action
1328 New York Ave., NW
Washington, DC 20005

National Center for Prevention
and Treatment of Child
Abuse and Neglect
1205 Oneida Street
Denver, CO 80220

National Center for Urban
Ethnic Affairs
Institute for Nonprofit
Management Training
1244 Maryland Ave., NE
Washington, DC 20001

National Center for Voluntary Action
1214 16th Street, NW
Washington, DC 20036

National Council on the Aging
1828 L Street, NW
Washington, DC 20036

National Health Council
20 W. 40th Street
New York, NY 10018

National League of Cities
1301 Pennsylvania Ave., NW
Washington, DC 20004

National Rural Center
1828 L Street, NW, Suite 1000
Washington, DC 20036

National Training and
Information Center
1123 W. Washington Blvd.
Chicago, IL. 60607

National Urban Coalition
1201 Connecticut Ave., NW
Washington, DC 20036

Public Interest Public
Relations, Inc.,
225 West 34th Street
New York, NY 10001

The Alliance for Justice
600 New Jersey Ave., NW
Washington, DC 20001

The Center for Community
Change
1000 Wisconsin Ave., NW
Washington, DC 20001

The Support Center
1709 New Hampshire Ave.,
NW
Washington, DC 20001

The Volunteer Urban
Consulting Group
24 West 40th Street
New York, NY 10018

United Way of America
810 North Fairfax Street
Alexandria, VA 22314

Women's Action Alliance
370 Lexington Ave.
New York, NY 10017

Women's Funding Assistance
Project
Ms Foundation
370 Lexington Ave.
New York, NY 10017

SEARCH AND DETAILED INFORMATION SERVICES

There are a number of search services available that will provide you with information on funding sources that may be tailored to your needs. These can be rather expensive. You might want to consider sharing a subscription with another organization. Do not ignore the additional information sources of the Foundation Center described in Chapter 6.

Aris Funding Messenger

Every six weeks Aris publishes a *Creative Arts and Humanities Report*, and a *Social and Natural Sciences* (including health) *Report*. The latter also includes updates between reports. For more information, write to Aris, 2330 Clay Street, San Francisco, California 94115.

Funding Sources Clearinghouse

A matchmaking service for fund raisers and grantors, FSC sends out a monthly news digest, occasional bulletins, and practical guides on proposal writing. It offers unlimited access to computerized search services and telephone consultation. The service is nonprofit, but not cheap, unless you calculate it in hours saved. Its data bank has over 50,000 corporate, foundation, and government entries. Brochures and costs are available from the Funding Sources Clearinghouse, 2600 Bancroft Way, Berkeley, California 94704.

ORYX Press Grant Information System

Subscribers receive a loose-leaf reference volume, one each year, that includes grant programs listed by deadline and subject matter or interest, grant name, and sponsoring organization. It covers a wide variety of government (federal, state and local), foundation, corporate, and association sources. Quarterly updates and monthly bulletins are issued in six categories: health, humanities, creative and performing arts, life sciences, social sciences, and education. For more information, write to The ORYX Press, 7632 East Edgemont Avenue, Scottsdale, Arizona 85257.

The Taft Information System

The oldest foundation information subscription system, Taft publishes several annual publications including the *Foundation Reporter*, *The Corporate Foundation Directory*, *Trustees of Wealth*, and the *News Monitor of Philanthropy*. The *News* is a monthly publication that includes articles on philanthropy and recent grants, events, or noteworthy gifts. A *News Service Hotline* keeps subscribers up-to-date on funding opportunities in specified areas of interest. For information write to Taft Products, Inc., 100 Vermont Avenue, NW, Washington, D.C. 20005.

Publicly supported search services include the following:

ERIC (Educational Resources Information Center)
National Institute of Education
U.S. Department of Education
Washington, DC 20208

HSIC (Human Service Information Center)
1408 N. Fillmore Street, Suite 7
Arlington, VA 22201

National Center for Education Statistics
Statistical Information Office
Presidential Building, Room 205
400 Maryland Ave., SW
Washington, DC 20202

National Clearinghouse for Alcoholic Information
P.O. Box 2345
Rockville, MD 20852

National Clearinghouse for Drug Abuse Information
P.O. Box 416
Kensington, MD 20795

National Clearinghouse for Mental Health Information
Public Inquiries Section
5600 Fishers Lane
Rockville, MD 20857

NTIS (National Technical Information Service)
U.S. Department of Commerce
5285 Port Royal Road
Springfield, VA 22161

BOOKS AND GUIDES FOR FUND RAISING

The items below tend to cut across government, foundation, and private sector sources; for this reason, they may not have appeared in the suggested reading lists accompanying earlier chapters.

Capitol Publications, Inc. (weekly). *Health Grants and Contracts Weekly.* Washington, DC: Author (Suite G-12, 2430 Pennsylvania Avenue, NW, Washington, DC 20037).
Cohen, Lily, & Oppedisano-Reich, Marie (1979). *Funding sources in aging: Public, private, and voluntary.* New York: Adelphi University Press.
Heywood, Ann M. (1982). *The resources directory for funding and managing nonprofit organizations.* New York: Edna McConnel Clark Foundation.
Marquis Academic Media (1978). *Grantsmanship: Money and how to get it.* Chicago: Author.
National Rural Center (1978). *Private funding for rural programs.* Washington, DC: Author.

President's Task Force on Private Sector Initiatives (1983). *Project bank.* Washington, DC: Author (734 Jackson Place, NW, Washington, DC 20400).

Sweeny, Tim, & Seltzer, Michael (1982). *Fund raising strategies for grass roots organizations.* Washington, DC: Community Careers Resource Center.

Tax economics of charitable giving. (1982). Chicago: Arthur Anderson (revised periodically).

Appendix C:
Sample of a Proposal Narrative

**SYSTEMS BUILDING THROUGH LINKAGE MECHANISMS:
A TRAINING PROJECT OF NATIONAL SIGNIFICANCE
FOCUSING ON SOCIAL SERVICE DELIVERY SYSTEMS**

SECTION 1: INTRODUCTION

OVERVIEW The project will have three main components: (1) the development of training materials; (2) their dissemination; and (3) the training of trainers. These components will be supported by: (a) an intensive assessment procedure; (b) recommendations by a national advisory panel; (c) collaborative testing and evaluation procedures with state and local agencies and training institutions throughout the country.

The project is national in scope. It is scheduled to begin on October 1st, 198 ＿＿ and to conclude on September 30, 198 ＿＿ . It will be directed by ＿＿＿＿＿and codirected by ＿＿＿＿＿of the Continuing Education Program in Human Service at the University of Michigan School of Social Work. It will be lodged administratively within the Program's Child Welfare Learning Laboratory.

OBJECTIVES The project's objectives are to:

(1) design instructional materials and training approaches for use by state and local departments of social services that can be used to overcome problems of practice and management in the child welfare field;

(2) establish a mechanism whereby training needs and interests can be assessed nationally and responded to in a systematic manner (secondary objective).

CONCEPTUAL   Social service agencies interact with many
FRAMEWORK   elements in their environment, elements with
                 which they are interdependent. The agency's
ability to accomplish objectives and to serve its clients properly
depends on its ability to manipulate exchanges with these
elements so as not to be totally dependent on a single supply
of resources, a single source of consumers, or a single source
of legitimacy. Generally, the avenues of exchange include
consumers of the agency's services; resources (such as money,
expertise, manpower, materials, supplies); or particular services
(through purchase, consultation, materials development,
information processing, etc.). The determinants of exchange
include the accessibility of the partners to each other, their
respective needs, the extent to which each expects to gain from
the exchange, and each partner's perception of his or her own
or the other's domain. Consensus over domain—who can service
whom, how, to what purpose—is a requisite for effective
exchange relationships.

A successful exchange also requires that some benefit accrues
to each of the parties involved. Both parties need not gain
equally; it is necessary only that the exchange process have
value for each.

In practice, four operational kinds of exchanges are possible:
(1) programmatic, (2) administrative, (3) facilitative, and (4)
developmental.

The use of exchange as a conceptual framework provides a
focus and gives integrity to this project.

SECTION 2: ASSESSMENT PROCEDURES

Three approaches to assessment will be used: (1) a projective
Delphi survey, (2) a national advisory panel, and (3) feedback
from users in selected test sites.

DELPHI   The Delphi technique is borrowed from the
PROCEDURES   field of technological forecasting. It has been
                    used in the human services only during the
past four or five years for purposes of projection and policy
recommendation. The Continuing Education Program in the
Human Services at the University of Michigan has had
considerable experience with Delphi, having used it in training
projects in the fields of manpower training, mental health, and
aging. Used properly, Delphi has a number of advantages over
other survey techniques.

It can generate multiple assessments of a single issue. For
example, a statement such as

> "Middle-management personnel at the county or district level
> should participate in training activities aimed at improving their
> capability of negotiating exchanges with potential collaborating
> agencies at the local level."

can be rated on a number of dimensions—desirability or importance, feasibility, and cost. Each of these dimensions might
include a five-point rating scale. Space may be left for the
respondent to add comments. Should there be general consensus in terms of desirability, feasibility, and cost, the training
staff's directions are clear. Should there be considerable difference of opinion on desirability or feasibility, then these differences should be probed in order to determine whether or
not to proceed on that topic. Should there be considerable
consensus that the training effort is desirable, but that it is not
feasible, this too should be probed in order to determine whether
or not it is possible to overcome difficulties identified by the
respondents.

Another advantage of the Delphi technique is that it permits
a second or third wave of questionnaires that can be used to
probe into the differences expressed by respondents, or used
to seek responses to items suggested by those respondents. A
third advantage is that respondents can remain anonymous,
permitting them to express their opinions without reservation

and without worrying about how others might react to their opinions.

Should the project be funded, staff members of the Child Welfare Learning Laboratory will design a preliminary version of the Delphi questionnaire prior to the October 1st project start-up date. This will permit immediate dissemination of the questionnaire to state-level training directors. It will reduce the time required for a preliminary assessment of needs and interests. Subsequent Delphi questionnaires will be used throughout the project year should they be found useful. Delphi questionnaires can be designed to be completed quickly by the respondent, coded rapidly by the project team, and fed directly into the planning process.

NATIONAL ADVISORY PANEL   A national advisory panel will be convened within two months of the project start-up time. Results of the first wave of the Delphi survey will be reported to the panel and members will recommend program priorities from among the alternatives suggested.

The advisory panel will be composed of 13 members representing: the Social and Rehabilitation Service; state Departments of Social Service (top management and staff development personnel); and university-based educators. The latter will include directors of continuing education programs that have already proven their excellence and have had considerable experience in training public welfare personnel. Approximately half of the members of the advisory committee will be drawn from agencies and educational institutions that have agreed to participate as collaborators in the testing and evaluation of the project's materials. The advisory panel will meet twice: once in November and once the following September. During the intervening months, members of the advisory panel will be asked to respond to various training materials and approaches developed by the project staff. Items sent to advisory panel members will relate to their particular interests or expertise.

Elements of this proposal were discussed with a number of persons around the country prior to its finalization. These include public welfare officials, trainers, and educators in such states as Massachusetts, Texas, Florida, Colorado, California, Minnesota, and Michigan. Although several have expressed interest in participating on the panel, no determination about the panel's composition will be made without consultation with the SRS Central Office.

FEEDBACK   Five or six collaborating institutions
FROM   (universities or departments of social service)
USERS   will be selected as test sites for the training
               materials to be developed by project staff.
These sites will be selected on the basis of their capacity to utilize training materials effectively and their interest in their particular subject matter or content.

A consultation team will be established within each site. Team members will include representatives of management, training staff, and potential trainees. Teams may be as small as three or as large as ten. Consultation team members will be consulted early in the development of training materials (modules or action guides). Thus they will have input into the assessment process, giving staff a clear picture of what might be needed and useful. The same team members will provide feedback as the materials are developed and tested in their work setting. Details of this process are discussed in the section on evaluation.

MODEL   Together, these three approaches provide an
FOR   assessment of needs and interest model,
ASSESSMENT   which itself will be thoroughly monitored
               and evaluated. Should it prove effective,
recommendations on its standardization will be made to SRS. One of the problems with the assessment approaches used, either nationally or regionally or within a particular state, is that they tend to be ad hoc and nonroutine. Each project develops its own procedure, some of them effective, others

not. Some projects ignore their own procedures. The particular model described herein may not have universal applicability. Nevertheless, it will be designed so that it could be replicated elsewhere. With modifications, it then might be useful to both the federal and state governments in subsequent years.

Should the procedures developed by this project be useful, they will be described in some detail in the project's report to SRS. Moreover, should the project's advisory committee so recommend, they may themselves become the basis of one of the project's training material outputs, a "Guide to Assessing Training Needs and Interests." This product satisfies the project's secondary objective.

SECTION 3: MATERIALS DEVELOPMENT

Two types of training materials will be developed: modular units and action guides. The units will treat a particular content area rather comprehensively. They will include a wide variety of instructional approaches and are intended for use within a work unit. Action guides are more modest booklets, and are intended for use by individuals, although they may serve as resource materials for group training sessions.

EDUCATIONAL A number of principles will inform the design
PRINCIPLES of these materials. One principle has already been expressed: that of responding to assessed interests of needs of potential consumer populations. The second principle calls for a high degree of specificity of learning objectives. These are aimed first, at skill development, and, second, at specifications of tasks that are assumed necessary to acquire those skills. There will be a close integration between the practice problems faced by social service personnel and the instructional activities performed by project staff or addressed to the instructional modules and action guides.

Simultaneously, project staff will attempt to maximize another principle, which at times may seem somewhat contradictory to the above: establishing some rational and ordered sequencing of learning experiences. Efforts will be made to ensure that there will be a cumulative impact for those trainees who participate in the project's test sites, and that can be transferred to those who may use materials at subsequent times. Materials will also be designed so as to assure that training motivation is maintained through interesting, vital, and increasingly complex learning experiences, that opportunities will be structured to provide variations in the plan based on individual backgrounds of the trainees or emerging practice needs.

MODULAR   At least two and possibly three modular
UNITS   training units will be designed. Typically,
               each unit will be composed of the following
components: (1) a guide to the convenor; (2) a self-assessment instrument; (3) modular instructional activities; and (4) a recommended evaluation procedure.

(1) Guide to the Convenor. While each modular unit can be conducted independently of subject matter experts, each will require a convenor. The convenor could be either a training specialist or a supervisor of a particular work unit. The modular units will be designed primarily for use with work units (a supervisor and casework staff, a state-level director of planning and the planning staff, etc.). The convenor may choose to recruit subject matter experts when appropriate. The guide to the convenor will include: (a) description of what is in the unit; (b) how trainees should be motivated and supported through a learning experience; (c) how the modular unit relates to other training materials and experiences; (d) how it might be modified, abbreviated, or expanded upon to articulate with the needs or interests of the training group; (e) how participation in this learning experience might affect trainee performance of practice tasks; (f) what organization or administrative supports might be necessary to ensure changed practice behavior leading to more effective service delivery; and (g) an introduction to the recommended evaluation procedures.

(2) Self-Assessment Instrument. The self-assessment instrument is intended for use by trainees. It will enable them to: (a) assess their learning needs in relationship to the content of the manual and their current practice tasks; (b) help them select components or subunits within the training unit to concentrate on; (c) evaluate changes in their knowledge or skills subsequent to having completed the training activity (by using the assessment instrument as a before-and-after test).

(3) **Instructional Components.** Instructional components or activities may be so designed as to follow each other or to be utilized independently. Some instructional units may be used without reference to the total training unit. Others are best used in conjunction with each other. The subunits might include: (a) a videotaped mini-lecture; (b) frame games; (c) role-play situations; (d) problem-solving exercises; (e) practicum or field experience; (f) manuals and guides.

Mini-lectures and demonstrations on videotape make it possible to utilize scarce human resources more efficiently. While the videotapes provided by project staff can be used as is, it may be possible to substitute or supplement these lectures with live presentations during the training program, or with videotape presentations dealing with specific issues of relevance to a locale or to a state department of social services. Videotapes can be so designed as to permit learners to shut off the monitor while completing an exercise and then turning it on again for new instructions. They can be followed by independent reading, role play, problem-solving exercises, etc.

Frame games are training devices that have been pioneered at the University of Michigan. They usually require between 5 and 20 participants, and often accommodate as many as 60 to 70. The Michigan project will create a frame with the skeleton of the process of problem solving. In fleshing out the skeleton or frame, participants develop new insights, practice skills, and learn to make strategically oriented rules. Other Michigan frame games have been designed under contract with a number of federal agencies, and have been used in the fields of aging, mental health, vocational rehabilitation, and developmental disabilities. Many are currently available commercially and are utilized by human service agencies and universities throughout the country.

Role-play situations permit both the testing out and the modeling of behavior patterns. Problem-solving exercises focus on specific issues of concern to practitioners and administrators. Some will be designed to be done independently, others will require group involvement. In all instances, problem-solving exercises will include evaluative input representing the views of clients, direct service practitioners, supervisors, and administrative personnel.

Modular units may also include some practicum experience, in which learners will utilize a "how-to-do-it" or action guide to direct their behavior in a practice setting, to record that behavior, to evaluate it subsequently, independently or with colleagues. A sample of a modular instructional unit is found in Appendix A [not included here].

Action guides can stand on their own and are less complex than modular training units. Some guides may in fact be used as modular components of one of the more complex units.

Each guide will be designed so as to help the user define a particular problem in operational terms and select from among alternative means of dealing with that problem. In some cases the problem can be dealt with by the direct line worker or his or her supervisor. In other cases, shifts in procedural policy may require changes within the agency. In some of these cases, it will be necessary to affect resources outside of the social service agency.

In the design of a guide for the development of interagency linking mechanisms, for example, they can be used to increase the availability, accessibility, continuity and coherence, efficiency, and responsiveness of service agencies and individual providers. Fiscal linkage mechanisms include the purchase of services, joint budgeting, and joint funding. Providers may also be linked through administrative and supportive facilitating services such as central record keeping; central information processing; publicity and public relations; procedural integration; consultation and the provision of technical assistance; and centralized outreach, intake, diagnostic referral, or follow-up services.

Agencies can also link their services through a variety of exchanges involving personnel. In some cases, these exchanges occur between agencies, at other times within an agency. Such linkages include the use of loaner staff and other staff transfers, outstationing, and the use of liaison teams. Interagency staff collaboration is also increased through joint staff training and development activities, the joint use of volunteers or other "common carriers," grievance procedures, social brokers and ombudsmen, etc.

Such linkages do not come into being without effort and careful planning. The reader will be guided through an examination of the variables that affect and support the establishment of operational linkages. These include the skill and acceptability of the staff involved; money and other resources at their disposal; the extent to which public opinion and environmental conditions support coordination; complimentarity of agency objectives; complimentarity of policies and procedures that govern the functions of those agencies and the workers within them; the existence of a logistical support system; and others.

Other guides might be built around one or more of the topics listed in Appendix B [not included here].

(4) Evaluation Procedures. An evaluation procedure for each guide and modular unit will be designed so as to include input from trainees, their supervisors, relevant department administrators, and central office personnel. These procedures will not only examine the relative utility of each modular unit when utilized under different circumstances, but will also focus on the practice behavior that has been changed or modified on the basis of participation in the learning activity. As such, assessment procedures will address environmental factors within which the trainee practices, and the relationship of those factors to the training experience.

SECTION 4: DISSEMINATION AND TRAINING

The project will conduct two kinds of dissemination and training: distribution of prototype materials and subsequent publication; and the conduct of training conferences in five locations throughout the country.

DISTRIBUTION Prototypes of all published materials will first
AND   be tested in a number of settings throughout
PUBLICATION the country (see Section 2, above). Upon
completion a limited number of copies will be distributed at no charge to all 50 states. Each state department of social services will receive between one and five copies of the modular units (depending upon its size and the structure of its training division) and up to ten copies of the action guides.

Subsequently, arrangements will be made to publish all training materials through a commercial firm. The Continuing Education Program in the Human Services currently has a number of publishing arrangements with commercial firms. These include small publishing houses in the Ann Arbor area as well as two major firms: McGraw-Hill and Sage Publications. Both of these larger firms have targeted human service workers as a new market and perceive partnership arrangements with the University of Michigan's CE Program as a means for hitting the target squarely with the appropriate training materials in the most appropriate format. Both publishers have indicated interest in dissemination of low-cost materials in bulk orders and kit forms. Since funds are not requested for publication (beyond distribution of the prototypes) funds will not be used to subsidize these publishers.

Alternatively, SRS may choose the option of publishing the materials directly through the Government Printing Office. The advantages of publishing through GPO are to be determined by SRS. The advantage of going through commercial firms is that it relieves both the Program and SRS from concern with funding the initial printing cost, distribution, etc. Finally, other arrangements might be made to publish and distribute the materials directly through the Program for Continuing Education. Additional funding would be required. A once-only distribution would be required.

TRAINING   Proposed is a dissemination strategy that
CONFERENCES   utilizes training conferences for key state
                 personnel and follow-up consultation to
assure that the materials and suggested training conferences
are effectively implemented. Conference participants will be
charged with design of implementation strategies at the state,
substate, or territorial levels.

Participants will be introduced to the project's "guides" and
modular units. Project staff will be available for telephone or
mail consultation for a period of six weeks following each
institute.

Training conferences will last about two and one-half days
and are scheduled for different locations. Opportunities for
exchange of information between the states and between state
and federal officials is built in. A library of resource materials
(films, books, pamphlets, etc.) will be available.

Conferences are planned for five locations:

—Boston (Regions I and II)

—Ann Arbor (Regions II and V)

—New Orleans (Regions IV and VI)

—Denver (Regions VII and VIII), and

—San Francisco (Regions IX and X)

Each state will send between two and five participants, depending on population size (the specific number to be determined in advance). At least one person will represent staff
development, and one person will represent services delivery
concerns. Territories may send one representative, if appropriate. One or two central office personnel plus one or two
from each regional office will be invited to attend. Each conference should draw an average of 40–45 participants.

Typically, each conference will be scheduled as shown on
the following chart:

	Wednesday	Thursday	Friday
9:00 am		Exchange session on the utility of action guides.	Using Modular Unit II* and building it into the state training strategy
12:00		Lunch	Lunch
1:30		Using Modular Unit I* and building it into the state training strategy.	Outline of follow-up strategies for each state (Conference ends at 2:30)
4:30	Registration, Logistics, Materials distribution	Library and Consultation Time	
6:00	Dinner with Keynote Address	Dinner—open	
7:30	Orientation to the Conference and to Exchange Concepts	Open	
8:30	First evening ends		

*These two sessions will actually occur simultaneously; half the participants involved in Modular Unit I and half with the second unit at the same time. This will permit smaller groupings.

SECTION 5: TIMING[1]

198X–8X

October	Project begins; staff hired. Delphi first wave goes out; contacts made with potential collaboration sites, advisory panel selected.
November	Sites selected; advisory panel meets; decisions on foci of modular units and action guides made. Design process begun.
December-February	Design process interspersed with some on-site field visits, preliminary testing, plus feedback from advisory panel. Additional Delphi wave if needed.
March-May	Trial runs of all material. Continuation of design and refinement.
June-August	Completion of materials; dissemination strategy and publications arrangement.
August-September	Regional Dissemination Conferences held; final meeting of advisory panel for evaluative purposes; final report submitted to SRS.

SECTION 6:
ABOUT THE CONTINUING EDUCATION PROGRAM
IN THE HUMAN SERVICES

The Michigan School of Social Work's Continuing Education Program is well known to SRS. Under SRS funding, it established the Child Welfare Learning Laboratory in collaboration with the Michigan Department of Social Services. The Lab produced eight training modules that are being used within the state, and that may be duplicated under federal auspice or through one of the Program's contacts with commercial publishers for national distribution. The national EPSDT training project funded to the University of Michigan School of Public

---

1. This schedule is predicated on the need to complete work within one fiscal year. Because production schedules are varied and dependent on inputs from many sources, and because some states may find it difficult to attend conferences in August or September, it may be necessary to request a no-cost extension of two to three months.

Health was conducted in corroboration with the Program. Training guides and pamphlets have been designed and will be distributed nationally. The current grant, funded until Section 426, provides for the design of Staff Development Models to be tested in county and subcounty offices of the Michigan Department of Social Services.

The Program generally conducts four to six training projects per year (budgeted from $400,000 to $600,000) maintains extension courses throughout the state, and sponsors short-term workshops, conferences, and institutes attracting more than 2000 enrollees per year. The Program has an extensive library of training materials—some developed by its own staff, others developed elsewhere. It maintains ongoing contacts with almost 200 other continuing education programs throughout the United States and Canada. Under NIMH auspices, it recently conducted a study of human services continuing education programs, reports of which were published by McGraw-Hill in 1977 and 1978. The Program also has an extensive network of consultants within the University and throughout the country. These consultants participate in Program-sponsored training activities, work on materials design, and consult on substantive and technical issues.

A brief description of some of the more than two dozen training grants conducted by the Program is found in Appendix C [not included here].

SECTION 7: PERSONNEL

The project will be directed by _____and codirected by _____ . _____is a program associate with the University of Michigan Continuing Education Program. He is Associate Director of the Child Welfare Learning Laboratory and serves as its senior trainer on the SRS-funded Staff Development Project. He is coauthor of _____ , a simulation originally used to train area planners in the field of aging, currently being used as a vehicle to introduce local agency people to the advantages of coordination on behalf of the elderly.

Mr. (Associate Director) has also designed a number of other games and social simulations: a public welfare-labor manage-

ment relations game; a juvenile court disposition game; and
an interorganization, client exchange game. He is also expert
in the use of group problem-solving exercises, programmed
instruction, and the use and design of videotapes. He has designed a wide variety of training materials in the fields of aging,
corrections, and child welfare.

Dr. (Program Director) is nationally known in the field of
gaming and simulation design. Four of his games were com-
missioned by federal agencies. These include the _____ ;
_____ ; _____ ; and coauthored _____ .

Professor (Program Director) teaches social planning at The
University of Michigan School of Social Work and is director
of _____ . During the past 8½ years he has directed more
than 10 federally funded projects. He is the author of several
books dealing with management, social planning, community
organizing, and continued education. These include
_____(—1972); _____(GSI—1973), (AoA—1974); and
two new volumes—_____ and _____ .

Other project members will be drawn from the faculty of
the University of Michigan Continuing Education Program and
its consultants. They include Professors _____ , _____ , and
_____ .

The Project director will maintain contacts with the national
advisory panel and the 50 state offices and will have primary
administrative responsibility for the project. He will also assume leadership for the design of one of the action guides or
components of one of the modular units. The Associate Director will direct the bulk of the work done on training materials
and will assume major responsibility for setting up and conducting the regional training workshops.

In addition, there will be two program associates, each working on a full-time basis, whose primary responsibilities will be
to work on the design of training materials. An editor and
technical writer will be assigned to the project half time (although the allocation of time will vary over the 12 months
depending on work put on project needs). An administrative
assistant will manage the technical details relating to confer-

ences and materials production and will maintain the books. A full-time secretary is requested, although the Continuing Education Program will absorb anticipated additional clerical costs beyond that within its regular staff. A dozen staff members will serve on consultant basis, either as subject matter experts or as instructional technologists working with regular project staff on this project.

SECTION 8: BUDGET JUSTIFICATION AND EXPLANATION

What follows is a line-item budget describing project expenditures under each line as summarized on the preceding SRS forms. Consultants and personnel were described in the preceding section. Staff travel flows from an assumption of 30 trips at the average cost of $200. Three staff each for the five regional conferences accounts for 15 trips. Office supplies include telephone, Delphi mailings, etc. A large sum of money, $21,500, is budgeted for materials to be used in the design of training documents, their development in prototype form, and dissemination. Under Equipment, one IBM Executive typewriter, a small room air conditioner that will make possible the use of a room in the Social Work Center Building that is currently nonusable, and two cassette tape recorders are requested. The budget by line item is summarized below.

Personnel:

Project Director	20%		
Project Codirector	50%		
Program Associate A	100%		
Program Associate B	100%		
Editor-Technical Writer	50%		
Administrative Assistant	15%		
Secretary	100%		
Total Salary and Wages		$62,400	
Fringe Benefits (@ 14% University est. rate)		8,736	$ 71, 136

Consultants

Subject matter experts and education technologists-12 x 10 days @ $100/day	$12,000	
Travel and per diem (assuming 30 trips @ $150 each for Ad. Travel, plus 15 trips for experts @ $200)	8,000	$ 20,000

Supplies

Office (disposable) and telephone (includes DELPHI mailings)	$ 1,600	
Materials for design of prototype training materials and their dissemination	21,500	$ 23,100

Equipment

Purchase/rental of typewriter, air conditioner, tape recorders (2)		1,000

Travel

30 trips at $200 plus local travel		6,500

Conference Facility | | 3,000 |

TOTAL DIRECT COSTS	$124,736
Indirect Cost (8% of TDC-University est. rate)	9,979
TOTAL PROJECT COST	$134,715

Based on previous experience, the Program for Continuing Education in the Human Services estimates a cost of roughly $45,000 for the development of a modular instruction unit, as described in this proposal. Functionally, the cost would run as follows: personnel ($30,000); equipment ($800); consumable supplies ($9,000); travel ($600); consultant expenses ($4,600).

The conduct of five conferences in different locations around the country would run approximately $27,000 to $28,000. The cost here would be as follows: personnel ($18,000); travel ($6,000); supplies ($1,000); facilities rental $2–$3,000).

The cost of building a single action guide, testing it, and disseminating a limited number of copies would run between

$5,000–$6,000. Thus the cost of producing two modular units and 8–10 action guides plus conducting five bi-regional training conferences could run at least $160,000. The cost would be considerably higher if a third modular unit were developed, as is a distinct possibility. Under normal circumstances, it would cost the Program for Continuing Education about 10 percent less to conduct a more complex project such as the one described on the preceding pages. In reality, the Program is able to run the project at an added savings of at least $20,000. This is because of the Program's previous experience with the design of training materials and the possibility of modifying some materials used for other projects. The reader is referred particularly to Project TAP, Project CRAFT, and other work of the Child Welfare Learning Laboratory described in Appendix C, [not included here]. Although certainly no precommitments have been made on the specific content of the training materials (this is to be determined subsequent to use of the Delphi and the meeting of the advisory panel), a sufficient range of materials has already been developed by the Program to warrant the expectation of their applicability.

SECTION 9: EVALUATION

The evaluation process will include examination of inputs, efforts, and outputs. Input evaluations are concerned with the methods, resources, and processes used to accomplish the project's objects. For the purpose of this project, for example, input evaluation includes an examination of the assessment procedures (Delphi, inputs from the advisory panel, and from collaborating training institutions). They would also examine the innovativeness of the instructional approaches, the materials used, the facilities used for the regional training conferences, etc.

More important, perhaps, is the evaluation of the project's efforts—its throughput. This refers to the training activity itself: its structure, its content, its focus. Satisfaction measures and voluntary participant responses in each of the five conferences would be used. More important still, however, is the evaluation of the Program's outputs.

Output evaluation places emphasis on results. This means examining the impact or utility of the training materials and approaches developed by the project staff. For purposes of this project, the results would be expressed as impact on the way in which services are delivered in each agency, and how it utilizes the project's materials. On a preliminary basis, these changes can be measured in the five or six locations that will be used to test preliminary versions of the action guides and modular training units. Impact evaluations can be fed into the redesign and modification of these materials. Unfortunately, however, the constraints in time limit the possibility of doing follow-up impact evaluation subsequent to dissemination of training materials to all 50 states (and territories). A twelve-month work period allows sufficient time to test and develop materials. Prototypes will be disseminated at the end of the project. Broader dissemination will not take place until the publisher has printed the final version of these products. This will occur within two to three months of the end of the budget period. A true impact evaluation would have to assess practice prior to use of the training materials, and subsequent to their use. The estimated cost of doing this kind of evaluation in approximately $60,000; in time the cost is approximately six months.

Because this is not feasible, an assessment and evaluation form is included in each piece of training material. This is intended to be useful to the individual user, who may use the form to assess his or her knowledge and skill prior to engaging in training activity and subsequent to it. Moreover, the forms will be designed so as to have some value for the work unit that is undergoing training together. Finally, the completed forms can be used as feedback mechanisms to the training convenor, appropriate staff development person, or social services manager. In this way, the assessment-evaluation forms can be used to suggest modifications in the training program or in agency rules, regulations, and procedures, so as to make the training more useful in the improvement of social service delivery systems.

Evaluation procedures, therefore, are intended to be thoroughly integrated into planning and program development.

About the Author

Armand Lauffer has been editor of the Sage Human Services Guides since they first appeared in 1977. Among his own contributions to the series are the following: *Grantsmanship and Program Design; Understanding Your Social Agency* (with Lawrence Zeff); *Resources for Child Placement; Volunteers* (with Sara Gorodezky); *Getting the Resources You Need;* and *Assessment Tools.* His other recent books include *Community Organizers and Social Planners* (with Joan Levin Ecklein); *Social Planning at the Community Level; Doing Continuing Education and Staff Development; Strategic Marketing;* and *Community Organization for the 1980s* (coedited with Edward Newman).

Professor of Social Work at the University of Michigan, Dr. Lauffer consults frequently with government and voluntary institutions in the United States and abroad. He is currently engaged as a consultant to the Municipality of Jerusalem and to the American Joint Distribution Committee in Israel. He is a frequent lecturer, consultant, and trainer on the subjects of grantsmanship, fund raising, and program design.